The Seventies From Hot Pants to Hot Tubs

Andrew J. Edelstein
and Kevin McDonough

Dutton New York

DUTTON
Published by the Penguin Group
Penguin Books USA Inc., 375 Hudson Street,
New York, New York 10014, U.S.A.
Penguin Books Ltd, 27 Wrights Lane,
London W8 5TZ, England
Penguin Books Australia Ltd, Ringwood,
Victoria, Australia.
Penguin Books Canada Ltd, 2801 John Street,
Markham, Ontario, Canada L3R 1B4
Penguin Books (N.Z.) Ltd, 182-190 Wairau Road,
Auckland 10, New Zealand

Penguin Books Ltd, Registered Offices:
Harmondsworth, Middlesex, England

First published by Dutton, an imprint of Penguin Books USA Inc.

First printing, August, 1990
10   9   8   7   6   5   4   3   2   1

Library of Congress Cataloging-in-Publication Data
Edelstein, Andrew J.
    The seventies: from hot pants to hot tubs/Andrew J. Edelstein and Kevin McDonough.
        p.   cm.
ISBN 0-525-48572-4
    1. United States—Civilization—1970-   2. United States—Social life and customs—1971–
I. McDonough, Kevin. II. Title. E169.12.E34 1990
973.92—dc20   89–26018 CIP

Printed in the United States of America

Designed by Art Lab
Produced by 2M Communications, Ltd

Photo Acknowledgements

AP/Wide World Photos: 68, 79, 82, 87, 124; Jerry Ohlinger: 1, 5, 10, 11, 15, 16, 17, 18, 21, 24, 25, 27, 38, 39, 48, 49, 54, 55, 58, 59, 60, 62, 85, 135, 136, 138, 142, 143, 144, 145, 146, 148, 150, 152, 153, 154, 156, 158, 159, 160, 161, 162, 163, 164, 165, 166, 170, 171, 172, 173, 175, 178, 179, 180, 181, 182, 186, 196, 197; Movie Star News: 36, 56, 168; Courtesy of Simon and Schuster: 104; Courtesy of Fireside Books: 69; National Archives: 75; Carter Presidential Library: 91; Ford Presidential Library: 91; Jeffrey Tamarkin Collection: 137, 139, 140, 141, 147, 149, 157, 169; Pictorial Parade: 74, 77, 81, 86, 89, 92, 93, 94, 97, 98, 99, 100, 101, 112, 116, 120, 121; Russell Reif/Pictorial Parade: 71, 83; Jim Wells/Pictorial Parade: 80; Frank Edwards Fotos Internationl/Pictorial Parade: 66, 73, 118; Popperfoto/Pictorial Parade: 113; AGIP/Pictorial Parade: 103; Central Press/Pictorial Parade: 95

The Seventies

Also by Andrew J. Edelstein
The Pop Sixties: A Personal and Irreverent Guide

To Connie, from the Seventies to today
To Kay

C O N T E N T S

•

•

•

•

INTRODUCTION

his is revisionist history. It's fitting that the Seventies, which gave birth to revisionist histories of everything from John Kennedy to B movies, should deserve its own second look. Ask many people, and they will recall the Seventies as a decade of polyester, disco, pet rocks, and malaise. While this book intends to explore and celebrate many of the decade's more tasteless excesses, it will also portray the period as more fascinating than many have given it credit for. The idea that the Seventies was merely a lull after the frenetic Sixties is simply not true. This often maligned period was the same time in which the women's movement exploded, abortion was legalized, the sexual revolution flowered, the gay movement reached its peak, the Vietnam war "ended," the values and styles of the Sixties counterculture became incorporated into society at large, a multiplicity of life-styles flourished (indeed this was the first decade when the word life-styles gained wide currency), TV became relevant, film became serious (for a brief shining moment), and American culture explored (however superficially) the defeat of its military and the possibility of limits on its economic growth.

It was a long and strange decade that was nothing if not extreme. In ten years, we went from the Days of Rage to business schools, from *Diet for a Small Planet* to Cuisinarts, from Joni Mitchell to Joan Collins, from "The Revolution" to the Reagan revolution. Just how did we get there?

The Seventies has eluded easy labeling. In fact, part of its appeal is that it was a decade that neatly divided itself in half. The first half (1970–1975), whose symbolic end was the mass evacuation of Americans from the rooftop of the American Embassy in Saigon, spread the gospel of the Sixties across the land. It was a head trip: We marched to the wail of a rock-and-roll guitar solo. The second half (1975–1979) was what author Tom Wolfe perceptively dubbed "the Me Decade" and also contained the seeds of the Eighties.

Nostalgia operates in funny ways. We tend to glaze over the painful memories (in much the same way that people who nostalgically salute the Fifties would rather celebrate tail fins and Howdy Doody than Joe McCarthy and the H-bomb). Thus, this encapsulation of the Seventies will concentrate on the fun and outrageous things that were important to the people who came of age during that decade.

Films of the Seventies

eventies' cinema offered up a scene as strange and richly varied as the decade itself. The decade began as the unexpected success of low-budget counterculture flicks stood in stark contrast to the studio's frustrating inability to entertain a nation torn by war and generational strife. Yet as Hollywood served up such pale losers as *The Strawberry Statement* and *Zabriskie Point* (an Antonioni film sponsored by none other than M-G-M), younger filmmakers were turning out some of the most challenging and original American films ever. Jack Nicholson moved from cult favorite to box-office magic. Francis Ford Coppola turned *The Godfather* into a beautifully dark indictment of the American dream, and a strange, bearded loner named Lucas rekindled lost innocence with his low-budget beauty, *American Graffiti*. Ecological and political uncertainties loomed large as disaster and conspiracy films dominated many of the releases between 1970 and '75.

Hollywood's yearning for a more predictable audience became apparent with such retread releases as *That's Entertainment* and as Mel Brooks turned his zany talents toward a string of genre parodies. But it was the kids, young directors like George Lucas and Steven Spielberg, who re-created box-office magic in the late Seventies. Reweaving the cliff-hanger plots of the timeless B serials with high-technology effects, *Jaws*, *Star Wars*, *Close Encounters of the Third Kind*, as well as *Superman*, served up an endless frappé of painless escapism for an audience seemingly exausted by real-life traumas. The decade concluded with Hollywood filmmakers very much in the dough once again, but far less willing to experiment or take chances with the kind of dark, quirky films that the Seventies will be best remembered for.

Bruce Davison gets carried away in The Strawberry Statement.

JANUARY 1970

2: J. Edgar Hoover blasts Black Panthers for deaths of at least seven policemen.

3: The Beatles record last song together, "I, Me Mine."

5: United Mine Worker's of America reformer Joseph Yablonski murdered with wife and daughter.

18: Buckminster Fuller receives American Institute of Architects Award for Geodesic domes.

8: Mormons renew ban on black priests

15: End of Nigeria's Biafran Civil War

CAMPUS REVOLUTION

From the Andy Hardy movies of the Thirties, juvenile delinquent movies of the Fifties, and beach-party films of the Sixties, Hollywood was never shy about trying to cash in on the latest youth trend. The success of *Easy Rider* (1969) convinced the film biz that there were plenty of bucks to be made by chronicling the counterculture. For a brief time in 1970, student revolutionaries were the hottest items on the big screen. Alas, the only thing that was revolting were the movies themselves:

☮ *The Strawberry Statement* (1970): An M-G-M flack unintentionally said it all about this misguided effort: "It's a gutsy film that tells what it's like to be part of the Now Generation, the Wow Generation."

Oh, wow.

Actually, what *The Strawberry Statement* did was take James Simon Kunen's diary of the 1968 Columbia riots and turn it into something much less compelling. (Even the movie's locale was shifted from New York to San Francisco's fictitious Pacific Northwest University after Columbia University and New York Mayor John Lindsay refused to give permission to film in New York.)

Bruce Davison stars as a jocky crew member who joins a campus sit-in, primarily as a way to meet coeds (and he does, it's his co-star Kim Darby). The movie ends with the students huddling in the gymnasium singing "Give Peace a Chance" as they try to avoid a bloody police riot.

Europeans, who seem to love distorted views of America, dug this movie. Before it was released in the States, it won a Jury Prize at Cannes. American critics weren't as sanguine. In fact, Judith Crist said it "reduces young people to groin-dominated bumblers motivated by sexual drives rather than intellect."

☮ *The Magic Garden of Stanley Sweetheart* (1970): Don Johnson, then nineteen years old, made his movie debut as Stanley, a sixteen-year-old Columbia junior, most pleasurably corrupted by off-campus drugs and sex. Among his pastimes: a menage à trois with two lesbians in a Lower East Side apartment.

The future star of *Miami Vice* did not bowl over critics with his performance. "Johnson's a hopeless case of non-talent," said one. Nonetheless, he

Bruce Davison, Kim Darby and James Coco in more radical days.

The late, great Mark Frechette
in Zabriskie Point

behaved on the set as if he already was a star. The movie's costume designer complained: "I've worked with all the big names—McQueen, Brando, you name it—and the bigger they are, the littler they act. This kid has only been here a week and he already thinks he's John Wayne. Forget it, kid, you'll never make it." The wardrobe man, however, had a more encouraging opinion: "He's got a marvelous ass. That's where his talent is."

RPM (1970): Writer Erich Segal (*Love Story*) and director Stanley Kramer (*Guess Who's Coming to Dinner?*) teamed up for this effort, which no doubt was well intentioned, but it ended up being nothing short of comical. Anthony Quinn stars as F.W.J. "Paco" Perez, a liberal sociology professor of Hispanic descent, who is named president of a troubled college to deal with radicals. Since Perez rides a motorcycle and wears turtlenecks, the trustees think he will be able to communuicate with the troublemakers. The good professor finds his liberal beliefs tested as the militants (led by Paul Winfield and Gary "*2001*" Lockwood) keep increasing their demands.

While he's trying to quell the demonstrators, Paco is also bedding Ann-Margret, playing a graduate student who writes papers with such titles as "Technological Pressures in Personality Development." The studio claimed that former sex kitten Ann-Margret had "deglamorized" herself for the role. "She wears little makeup, a pony tail, inexpensive shirts and blouses and a Navy pea jacket," a publicity release claimed. "Her total wardrobe cost $49.78." The money saved could have been used to purchase a more plausible plot.

Getting Straight (1970): This picture had the bad timing to be released theatrically only ten days after four students were killed by National Guardsmen at Kent State. Timing aside, this was no classic; *Newsweek* called it a "contemptible piece of apocalypse peddling, a swinish attempt to please the youth market."

Elliott Gould—in all his Fu Manchu'd, bushy-sideburned glory—stars as a Vietnam vet who returns to college to go to graduate school. At twenty-eight, he's ambivalent about whether he should pursue academia or join his younger colleagues in protesting. He opts for the latter, prodded by his student-girlfriend (Candice Bergen). He tells her he thinks campus demonstrations are "sexy," adding that "I bet you that every girl who goes out there will be screwing tonight."

FEBRUARY 1970

2: Bertrand Russell dies.

17: Chicago Seven found guilty of conspiracy to riot.

25: California Governor Reagan accuses radical lawyer William Kunstler of inciting a riot.

16: Joe Frazier wins heavyweight title.

19: Detroit Tiger ace Denny McLain suspended three months for gambling connections.

☮ *Zabriskie Point* (1970): M-G-M hired arty Italian director Michelangelo Antonioni (*Blow-Up*) to reach the youth market with this visually stunning film with an extremely confusing plot that had something to do with the director's skewed vision of Pig Amerika. Male lead Mark Frechette would later die in a freak accident: crushed to death when the weights he was lifting fell on his chest.

BLAXPLOITATION

So long Sidney Poitier. See ya, Stepin Fetchit. Say hello to John Shaft, Sweet Sweetback, and Superfly. By 1970, blacks were finally being recognized as a heavy movie-going audience, and Hollywood was ready to cash in.

Melvin Van Peebles's X-rated *Sweet Sweetback's Baadasssss Song* (1970) (which he wrote, financed, and directed himself) kicked off the cycle, followed in 1971 by the enormously successful *Shaft*, the story of a swinging black private eye.

With the success of these two films, dozens of black-themed films were rushed into production, although the studios were not motivated by visions of brotherhood. "White filmmakers aren't really seeing black," said an astute black film producer named Jack Jordan. "They're seeing black and green." The films themselves were never meant to be high art. Most resorted to a successful, crowd-pleasing formula: action, blood, tough talk, hot women, and a soul-drenched soundtrack. And most of the time, Whitey got his.

The so-called blaxploitation films also generated plenty of controversy, especially within the black community. The Beverly Hills–Hollywood chapter of the NAACP passed out leaflets asking the producers of *Superfly* (1972) to reshoot the

John Shaft: The baddest black private dick of them all.

#1 Singles:
Shocking Blue—"Venus"
Sly and the Family Stone—"Thank You"
Simon and Garfunkel—"Bridge over Troubled Water"

MARCH 1970

3: In Lamar, South Carolina, two hundred whites attack and mob school buses carrying black students.

26: The Beatles release *Hey Jude* album.

Selected Gold Record Albums:
Simon and Garfunkel—*Bridge over Troubled Water*
Bobby Sherman—*Bobby Sherman*
Doors—*Morrison Hotel*

5: *Airport* released.

6: Charles Manson releases album, *Lie.*

ending so that its cocaine-dealing hero would die. "We must insist that our children are not constantly exposed to a steady diet of so-called black films that glorify black males as pimps, pushers, gangsters and super males with vast physical prowess, but no cognitive skills," the leaflet said. CORE president Roy Innis demanded a black film review board to prescreen all black films. And by September 1972, even *The New York Times* was editorializing on the controversy: "It may be personally ego-gratifying for blacks to see one of their own stick it to The Man, but what these films have failed to do is go beyond their limited medium of expression and provide something new, something more imaginative than enticement purely on a black vs. white society."

By 1974, much of the controversy had quieted as Hollywood turned its interests elsewhere and the blaxploitation cycle neared its end. But during those four years, several memorable films were released. Here's a look at the baddest.

*Even guest appearances by Tony Curtis couldn't save the **Shaft** TV show, a pale imitation of the film.*

● ***Shaft*** (1971): John Shaft (played by Richard Roundtree)—a character created by white writer Ernest Tidyman—is a "black James Bond," a swinging, turtlenecked dude with a pearl-handled revolver. He joins forces with black militants to liberate a black hoodlum's daughter who has been kidnaped by white hoodlums. Directed by the gifted photographer Gordon Parks, the film grossed $17 million and spawned two popular sequels (*Shaft's Big Score* and *Shaft in Africa*) and a lame TV version. Isaac Hayes's menacing theme song ("Who's the black private dick who's a sex machine to all the chicks?") became a classic.

● ***Superfly*** (1972): The most controversial of the genre, this film seemingly glorifies a black cocaine dealer named Priest (played by Ron O'Neal) who wants to make one last million-dollar score before getting out of the business. Wearing a fur coat, wide-brimmed hat and a gold cross around his neck (from which he sniffs his own coke), O'Neal became an unusual role model. "He makes Shaft look like Little Jack Horner," enthused one young female fan.

O'Neal, a light-skinned black (whose skin color worked against him when he auditioned for the role of Shaft), found himself forced to defend the nature of his character. "The story is opposed to the whole drug scene. If we had made a film about a cat's rise to the top of the coke scene, that would

6: Three die as Weather Underground bomb factory explodes in New York's Greenwich Village.

7: U.S. and North Vietnamese troops battle near Cambodian border.

#1 Singles:
Simon and Garfunkel—"Bridge over Troubled Water"

6: Death of Motown soloist Tammi Terrell.

20: Marriage of David Bowie and Angela Barnett.

31: Seattle Pilots sold to Milwaukee concern.

Selected Gold Record Albums:
The Beatles—*Hey Jude*
Steppenwolf—*Monster*
Crosby, Stills, Nash and Young—*Deja Vu*

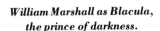

William Marshall as Blacula, the prince of darkness.

have been different. But our story is about a guy who is already there and is dying to get out."

And he went on to offer a rationale that seems positively quaint from today's crack-ravaged perspective: "Our movie is not about heroin," he stressed. "The heroin pusher is the scourge of the black community. But we're talking about coke, which is basically a white drug. Since coke is not physically addictive, people do not steal and rob to get it. There are no coke junkies."

● **Cleopatra Jones** (1973): Women's liberation meets blaxploitation in this movie about a karate-chopping, Stingray-driving federal agent played by six-foot-two-inch former model Tamara Dobson. She battles drug pushers, whose leader is "Mommy," a bull-dyke mobster played ultra-campy by Shelley Winters.

● **Coffy** (1973): Another mean mama, this one played by Pam Grier. Coffy is a nurse who goes after the pushers who turned her sister into a junkie. Among her weapons: razor blades, which she keeps hidden in her Afro, to cut opponents to shreds when they tangle with her. Grier would go on to star in three more thrillers: *Sheba Baby, Foxy Brown* and *Friday Foster*.

● **Black Caesar** (1973): Many blaxploitation films stole shamelessly from established films. This one was the black *Godfather*, tracing the rise of a mob mogul from his days as a Harlem shoeshine boy. There's no horse's head in a movie producer's bed; but there is a scene in which a severed human ear turns up in a plate of spaghetti. Ex-pro football star Fred "The Hammer" Williamson, who had a long and honorable career in blaxploitation films, played the baddie.

● **Trouble Man** (1972): This film is notable more for its sleek Marvin Gaye score than for its plot, which features distinguished actor Robert Hooks as a swinging private eye named Mr. T., a West Coast version of Shaft. It's also one of the most violent of the genre.

● **Blacula** (1972): Blaxploitation-horror films were a fascinating subgenre, created by those masters of the grade-Z cheapie, American International. Here, Shakespearean actor William Marshall played a 19th-century African prince who was bitten by the original Count Dracula and goes on a biting spree when he is revived in modern-day Los Angeles. Blac came

APRIL 1970

1: Vietnamese Communists launch major offensive.

8: Nixon's Supreme Court nominee Harrold Carswell rejected.

11-13: Damaged Apollo 13 craft returns to earth after spectacula near disaster 205,000 miles from earth.

7: X-rated *Midnight Cowboy* wins Oscar for Best Picture.

17: Paul McCartney releases solo album, *McCartney*.

back in the sequel *Scream Blacula Scream.* American International was also responsible for the forgettable *Blackenstein* (1974), which featured a black medic named Dr. Stein (that's right), who grafted zebra legs on to female victims; and *Abby* (1974), a black version of *The Exorcist,* featuring ex-Blacula William Marshall as the exorcist who must purge the demons from a minister's wife (one dreadful side effect of the possession: Her eyes turned blue!).

PATTON AND M*A*S*H

Patton and *M*A*S*H* emerged as the two blockbuster films of 1970. While both are technically "war" movies, the similarities end there. Their differences point to the huge chasm in public opinon in the year of Kent State, the Cambodian "incursion," and the continuing trials of Lt. William Calley.

Patton is a classic film, the very last of its breed—the epic war picture premised on the undiluted faith in the American war effort. No movie since could have gotten away with it's unforgettable scene of Patton exorting his troops to victory before an enormous American flag. Yet far from being a bit of jingoistic propaganda, *Patton* is a huge celebration of a maniac. Patton is not merely a good general, he is in love with war; he communes with the spirits of bygone chieftans and centurians. When he wins one battle, he is on to the next. Having won the war, he is hot to trot to bash the Russian bastards before it's too late. In the face of our miserable quagmire of Vietnam, *Patton* provided a rallying cry similar to that of General Douglas Mac-Arthur's during the Korean stalemate. After all, if American wasn't winning "the first televised war," at least you could go to the movies and watch George C. Scott kick some butt.

In many ways, Scott as *Patton* was remarkably similar in his ranting and raving to Scott as General Buck Turgeson in Stanley Kubrick's *Dr. Strangelove.* But this was not a black-humor movie. Such humor was more suited to *M*A*S*H,* a stunning big budget debut for Robert Altman, whose earlier work was limited to television. Set in a Korean War field hospital, the *M*A*S*H* surgeons (Donald Sutherland and Elliott Gould) serve up body parts and wisecracks with equal abandon. This irreverent send-up of army buddy films mocked God and country and anyone not hip enough to think it

22: Millions commemorate "Earth Day."

30: Nixon sends 30,000 U.S. troops into sanctuaries in Cambodia.

23: James Dickey's *Deliverance* published.

24: Grace Slick and Abbie Hoffman turned away from White House reception hosted by Tricia Nixon.

was funny to do so. This very smug, antiestablishment attitude is what has dated the film. Too much of its humor depends on one's absolute allegiance to the boyish shenanigans of the "Pros from Dover," and too many of their high jinks cross the line between comedy and cruelty. Yet this was not just a *McHale's Navy* episode; *M*A*S*H* presented a desperate battle between the hip and the "war machine." Gould and Sutherland presided over the movie like cinematic equivalents of those anti-war media mavens Jerry Rubin and Abbie Hoffman.

Much of Gould's screen prescence in this and other films of the era, including *Bob and Carol and Ted and Alice* (1969) and *Getting Straight* (1970), depend on a similarly smug, smart-assed allure that did not translate well as the passions of the Sixties cooled. Gould did everything he could to speed along his demise, including getting thrown off the set of *A Glimpse of the Tiger*. To add insult to injury, the film was remade as *What's Up Doc?* (1972), starring Gould's ex-wife, Barbra Streisand.

Saccharine escapism for troubled times.
Ryan O'Neal and Ali MacGraw in Love Story.

LOVE STORY

While colleges burned and generations battled, *Love Story* packed them in in 1970 with a Hollywood formula love story about a preppie millionaire WASP who challenged his dad, caste, and inheritance by marrying beautiful Italian, harpsichord-playing, foul-mouthed ball-buster Jenny Cavilleri. Half of the campus buildings are named after the immediate family of smug Oliver Barrett (Ryan O'Neal). Jenny's (Ali MacGraw) loving Italian Catholic dad runs a pastry shop. After three years of law school, music teaching, and an endless honeymoon of constantly cute undergraduate repartee, Jenny succumbs to a rare and unexplained disease in one of Hollywood's least realistic death scenes: "Dying is like falling off a cliff. You've never fallen off a cliff, have you, Ollie?"— "Yes I did. When I met you."

Segal's dialogue is delivered with wooden understatement by MacGraw and O'Neal, who are at the very outer limits of their range here. *Love Story* is one of those period pieces that did not age well or at all. A half-baked sequel, *Oliver's Story* (1978), bombed as O'Neal's career continued its downward trend toward *So Fine*. Ali MacGraw's ultra-long straight, parted-in-the-middle hair beneath tight-fitting knit cap, and a miniskirt

beneath a longish coat virtually defined a certain early Seventies style.

Despite its incredibly cornball moments (who can forget the repeated scenes of Oliver and Jenny falling backward into the snow?), *Love Story* provided 1970 viewers a perfect haven from the superheated atmosphere of Kent State, domestic terrorism, and a film and televison industry obsessed with "relevance." Oliver may have worried about law school and his uptight dad, but not a word is uttered about his draft status. *Love Story* also continued a spate of lawyer-obsessed movies and shows (*The Young Lawyers*, *The Paper Chase*) that gave the profession just the right blend of earnestness and upward mobility. Little wonder more latter-day boomers made law one of the most oversubscribed professions of the Seventies and early Eighties.

Even Nixon liked *Love Story*: "I recommend it though I'm mildly upset at the film's profanity. I know they [the kids] use them. I know it's the 'in' thing to do."

A CLOCKWORK ORANGE AND THE POLITICS OF ULTRAVIOLENCE

In 1971, just before glitter and years before punk, *A Clockwork Orange*'s Alex burst on the scene as the weirdest bad boy the movies had ever created. Stanley Kubrick's icy re-creation of Anthony Burgess's tale of chaos and social conditioning in a not-to-distant future remains one of the most brilliant and devisive films of the decade.

Malcolm McDowell plays Alex with such twisted abandon that many critics considered his portrayal a celebration of violence. By allowing the audience to experience gang fights, gang bangs, murder, robbery, and surrealistic pillaging through Alex's eyes, Kubrick pushed most of his audience to the outer limits of tolerance. Yet this was exactly his intention. He wanted them to see violence, "not with the disapproving eye of the moralist, but subjectively, as Alex experienced it." Kubrick set out to portray a future society where "citizens live in a vandalized pop art culture, gaudy, icy and filthy." His depiction of Alex and his droogs as postindustrial punks, and of England as a postmodern slum, has proved just a bit too prophetic for some.

The film earned an initial X rating in the United States, just as many

12: Newark, N.J. voters elect Kenneth Gibson first black mayor of a large eastern city.

16: *M*A*S*H* wins top honors at Cannes Film Festival.

Selected Gold Record Albums:
Soundtrack—*Midnight Cowboy*
Beatles—*Let It Be*
Soundtrack—*Woodstock*

#1 Singles:
Jackson Five—"ABC"
Guess Who—"American Woman"
Ray Stevens—"Everything Is Beautiful"

JUNE 1970

1: The Pentagon accuses Soviet navy of cruising within fifty miles of Louisiana.

10

*Alex (Malcolm McDowell) and his droogs
enjoy a spot of synthmesc
at the Moloko milk bar.*

newspapers had decided not to carry advertising for such films. For all of the film's glorious use of "good old Ludwig Van," and much original electronic music by Walter Carlos, the score is best remembered for Alex's perverse rendition of "Singin' in the Rain" while he rapes and cripples a scholar and his wife.

Kubrick's film touched off a controversy among liberal film critics and filmgoers who were shocked by the not-so-subtle messages in the violent films of the early Seventies. Many of the films of this psycho-obsessed period depict a manmade hell. Sam Peckinpah, the godfather of gratuitous violence, brutalized the audience of *Strawdogs* (1971) with a tale of a gentle liberal mathematician driven to medieval vigilantism when a drooling goon squad hangs his cat, rapes his wife, and finally lays siege to his hearth and home. Films like *Billy Jack* (1971), *Deathwish* (1974), and *Walking Tall* (1973) picked up on this theme and made millions.

For all of its on-screen violence, including a balletic gang rape set to Rossini, *A Clockwork Orange* never descends to such cheap exploitative conclusions. By forcing the viewer to experience Alex's exploits as well as his "cure" (by the "Lodovico" technique), Kubrick forces his audience to see the futility of taking away an individual's ability to choose between good and evil. In Kubrick's words: "man is an ignoble savage, irrational, brutal, weak. . . . You identify with Alex becasue you recognize yourself. It's for this reason that some people become uncomfortable." Kubrick saw Alex as an ultimate evil hero, who like Richard III seduced his audiences with his wicked sense of freedom. Yet making Alex a symbol of freedom was precisely what most liberals saw as Kubrick's most unforgivable act. One critic said that the film was filled with "the deeply anti-liberal totalitarian nihilism emanating beneath the surface of the counterculture."

Yet for all of Alex's detractors, he certainly had company. The cinema of the early to mid-Seventies is a virtual rogues' gallery of screen dementos.

21: Penn Central Company bankruptcy approved.

26: Britain elects Conservative Prime Minister Edward Heath.

3: Ray Davies flies six thousand miles to re-record change in "Lola" lyrics from "Coca Cola" to "Cherry Cola" to allow BBC airplay.

9: Princeton University awards Bob Dylan an honorary degree.

SEVENTIES SCREEN WACKOS

Late Sixties moviegoers were shocked to see the celebration of the "antihero" in such successful films as *Bonnie and Clyde* (1967) and *The Graduate* (1967). Adored by the counterculture, these crooks and losers as heroes absolutely baffled an older generation of audiences used to good guys and bad guys. President Johnson was personally repulsed by Dustin Hoffman's *Graduate* character and couldn't understand how anyone found him appealing.

By the early Seventies, as the counterculture became the dominant entertainment culture, the screen was filled with crazed and criminal protagonists. Almost all of the best roles of the early Seventies were written for wackos. We characterized them in three categories: Highbrow, Middlebrow and Lowbrow.

I. Highbrow Nutballs—nuts and rebels whose aberrant or criminal behavior is either caused by or in rebellion against a "sick society."

Lenny Bruce in *Lenny* (1974): Lenny is the St. Francis of Assisi of the Seventies' wacko screen set. Dustin Hoffman plays the acerbic and brilliant comic who drives the audience and his beautiful wife (Valerie Perrine) insane with his search to prove his First Amendment rights to say all the nasty things on his mind.

Randell P. McMurphy in *One Flew Over the Cuckoo's Nest* (1975): This film depicts the psycho (Jack Nicholson) as sane man in a psycho ward as a metaphor for a world gone mad.

Howard Beale in *Network* (1976): On the verge of getting pink-slipped, a talking-head newscaster lets loose with an on-air nervous breakdown, and the ratings go wild. The cloud-bursting "I'm mad as hell and I'm not going to take it anymore" rant by Beale (played by Peter Finch) remains one of the great anticorporate outbursts of the Seventies.

Travis Bickle in *Taxi Driver* (1976): This is another descent into madness in a view of New York as a hellhole sewer in need of a righteous avenger. Robert De Niro is eerily convincing as the ultimate outsider who innocently takes his beautiful date to a porno show and wonders why she is

outraged. His "Are you talking to me?" mirror speech ranks as one of the paramount moments of Seventies' wackodom.

II. Middlebrow Nutballs —guys on the right side of the law who let it all hang out in their pursuit of justice and the American way.

Patton in *Patton* (1970): George C. Scott plays a coward-slapping, commie-hating, fighting machine who communed with the spirits of dead Roman and Carthaginian generals before going into battle. Nixon reportedly watched the film over and over before invading Cambodia.

Joe in *Joe* (1970): Before director John G. Avildsen created *Rocky*, he served up *Joe* (Peter Boyle), a working-class, wish-fulfillment fantasy of quite a different stripe. Joe delivers some of the great lines of the early Seventies, including: "Forty-two percent of all liberals are queer. The Wallace people took a poll."

Harry Callahan in *Dirty Harry* (1971), *Magnum Force* (1973) and *The Enforcer* (1976): Years before Son of Sam, Harry Callahan made the .44 Magnum the psycho's gun of choice. Whether storming Alcatraz or blowing away creeps with a bazooka, Clint Eastwood's Harry dispatched bad guys with a chilling existential aplomb that drove critics crazy and audiences wild.

III. Lowbrow Nutballs —basically Middlebrow nutballs in blatantly exploitative movies.

Paul Kersey in *Death Wish* (1974): Charles Bronson's Paul Kersey, a contemplative liberal architect, is driven to righteous fury when his wife is murdered and daughter driven mad by rampaging delinquents (led by a young Jeff Goldblum in a jughead cap). Bronson picks up a pistol in Arizona and decides to bring justice to New York's Wild West anarchy.

Billy Jack in *Billy Jack* (1971): This most quintissentially Seventies Vietnam vet/Native American mystic wacko uses his violent powers only to protect a biracial Montessori school from rampaging racist locals who hassle the students and kill wild horses for fun. Described as "a hippie superman,' and "the Jack Webb of the left," Billy Jack (played by Tom Laughlin) learns his super kung-fuesque skills by becoming "one with a snake." *Billy Jack*'s meticulously politically correct premise did little to hide the fact that this was a film about "going berserk" and beating up bad guys.

1: New York State enacts nation's most liberal abortion law.

4: Bob Hope and Billy Graham host "Stand Up for America" rally in Washington, D.C.

13: FBI names Black Panthers as "most dangerous and extremist prone" group of the year.

5-25: Race riots flare in Asbury Park, N.J., Michigan City, IN, New Bedford, MA., New Brunswick, N.J. and Lawrence, KS.

29: Cesar Chavez calls off nationwide grape boycott.

20: Federal Trade Commission busts McDonald's for contest fraud

29: *Future Shock* published.

EARLY WOODY

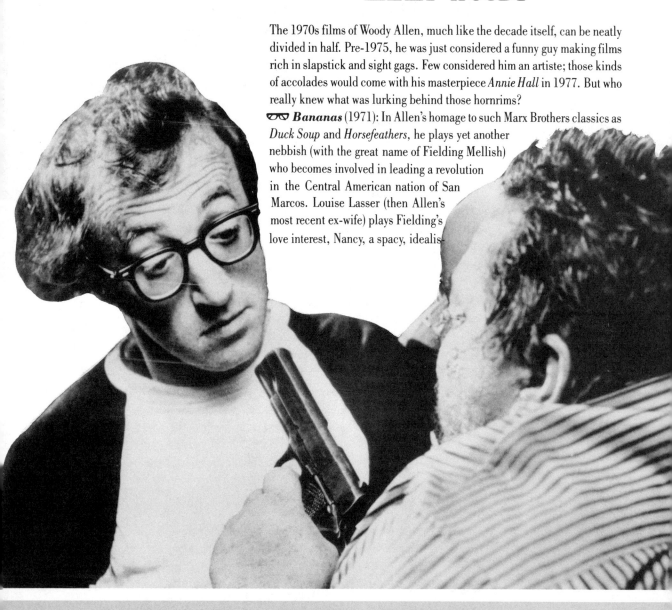

The 1970s films of Woody Allen, much like the decade itself, can be neatly divided in half. Pre-1975, he was just considered a funny guy making films rich in slapstick and sight gags. Few considered him an artiste; those kinds of accolades would come with his masterpiece *Annie Hall* in 1977. But who really knew what was lurking behind those hornrims?

👓 *Bananas* (1971): In Allen's homage to such Marx Brothers classics as *Duck Soup* and *Horsefeathers*, he plays yet another nebbish (with the great name of Fielding Mellish) who becomes involved in leading a revolution in the Central American nation of San Marcos. Louise Lasser (then Allen's most recent ex-wife) plays Fielding's love interest, Nancy, a spacy, idealis-

30: Thirty thousand attend cancelled Powder Ridge Rock Festival only to hear Melanie in lieu of Led Zeppelin, Janis Joplin, Chuck Berry, and Sly and the Family Stone.

31: Chet Huntley retires from *Huntley-Brinkley Report*.

14

tic college student, in what seems like a dress rehearsal for her TV series *Mary Hartman, Mary Hartman*. In one of the movie's funniest scenes, Howard Cosell (then at the height of his *Monday Night Football* popularity) narrates the blow-by-blow description of Fielding and Nancy's wedding night. And speaking of cameos, be on the lookout for Sylvester Stallone in one of his earliest film appearances as a subway mugger.

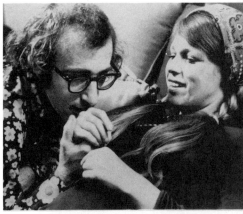

Neurotics in love: Fielding Mellish (Woody Allen) finds his soul mate (Louise Lasser) in **Bananas.**

👓 *Play It Again Sam* (1972): Allen successfully adapted his late-Sixties Broadway play into a hit movie (even though he changed the locale from New York to San Francisco). Woody plays Allan Felix, a Bogart-obsessed writer whose wife (Susan Anspach) dumps him. To help him cope and improve his relationships with women, he calls on the ghost of Bogart (Jerry Lacy) as well as the advice of his friends, Dick and Linda Christie (played, in their first Allen-movie roles, by Tony Roberts and Diane Keaton). The movie contains several wonderful *Casablanca* references as well as scenes of Woody at his ultra-nebbishest, especially as he prepares for a blind date.

👓 *Everything You Always Wanted to Know About Sex (But Were Afraid to Ask)* (1972): Allen based this film loosely—very loosely—on Dr. David Reuben's best-selling sex manual. The film consists of several vignettes dramatizing questions from the book. In one of the funniest, Allen plays a spermatazoon inside a penis about to be "launched." Some of the vignettes are tasteless, especially one in which Gene Wilder plays a man in love with his sheep who guests on a quiz show called "Name My Perversion." He shoulda waited for the Eighties so he could appear on Oprah instead.

👓 *Sleeper* (1973): Allen took his boldest step yet in the film that would mark his transition to influential filmmaker. In this futuristic fantasy, he

plays Miles Monroe, a health food store owner from Greenwich Village who enters the hospital for a routine operation in 1973 and wakes up two-hundred years later after being inadvertently cryogenically frozen. The society of the future is a dictatorial state and only Miles is undocumented, so he becomes a hero of the revolution. The Orb, the orgasmatron, giant fruits, and a Dixleland score made for one hilarious picture.

JACK NICHOLSON

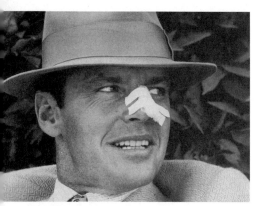

In **Chinatown** *Nicholson gets his nosey comeuppance as J. J. Gittes, the Seventies' most celebrated snoop.*

Jack Nicholson rode into the early Seventies on the surprise success of *Easy Rider* (1969), a film he stole from its two bigger stars, Dennis Hopper and Peter Fonda. Fonda and Hopper would quickly lose themselves to drugs and B movies, as Jack Nicholson went on to dominate Hollywood during the fertile first half of the Seventies. Nicholson has settled so securely into stardom and occasional self-parody that it is sometimes difficult to imagine or remember just how refreshing he was in his early roles. During a period when many actors were playing the role of "existential heroes" and campus "revolutionaries," Nicholson filled the screen with a knowing intensity that spoke to an entire generation raised on a steady diet of the Beats, Keroac, Vietnam, and drugs. Easily the most sardonic hero since Bogart, Nicholson had all the world-weary wisdom of a baby-boomer Bogie marinated in marijuana and acid.

Nicholson was perfectly suited to the low-budget, personal films of the period. He had paid his dues for eleven years with one B film after another, beginning with parts in Roger Corman's *Cry Baby Killer* in '58 and followed soon by the classic $25,000 cheapie, *The Little Shop of Horrors* (1960). In the Sixties, he wrote the screenplays for such midnight classics as the drug-drenched *The Trip* (1967) and the Monkees's notorious *Head* (1968), directed by Bob Rafelson.

In 1970 Bob Rafelson cast Nicholson as Bobby Duprea in *Five Easy Pieces*. In perhaps the most intense and strangely sympathetic of Nicholson's rebel characters of the early Seventies, Bobby Duprea is a man adrift, running from his roots and from anything that ties him down: his smothering intellectual/musical family, his simple, loving white-trash mistress Rayette Dipesto (Karen Black).

The strength of Nicholson's performance is the utter believability he lends to the preposterousness of Bobby Duprea, a man equally estranged from highbrow and white-trash culture, as not at home with Mozart as he is with Tammy Wynette. The film has a great soundtrack and a wonderful cast, and an on-the-road script that

10: U.S. Army buries nerve gas cannisters in Atlantic ocean.

11: Radical priest Daniel Berrigan arrested for destroying draft documents.

24: University of Wisconsin math center bombed by radicals, scientist killed.

3: NFL players end three-day strike.

8: Janis Joplin buys and dedicates headstone for Bessie Smith's unmarked grave.

22: Elvis Presley announces first tour sin 1958.

lends itself to one riveting performance after another. Bobby's exasperating struggle to get toast out of a rule-bound waitress remains one of the most memorable of Nicholson's career. The most painful and poignant moment of the film is not when Nicholson attempts communication with his mute, stricken father, but when Rayette barges onto his family's musical compound, confronting Bobby with both sides of his divided nature.

Carnal Knowledge (1971) cast Jack opposite Candace Bergen at her best. Sixties' icons Art Garfunkel and Ann-Margret also turned in superb performances. In his least sympathetic role, Nicholson brilliantly brings life to what might have been a stereotypical male heel in constant heat. In fact, Nicholson was so good at portraying director Mike Nichols' misogynist cad that he got a reputation as an "antifeminist." Nicholson would later explain that he saw his portrayal as a "legitimate representation of male attitudes of our time. . . . I didn't pander, didn't try to make the audience feel one way or the other."

In *The Last Detail* (1973), Nicholson portrayed "Badass" Buddusky, an unlikely existential hero with the unpleasant task of escorting the hapless Meadows (Randy Quaid) to the brig to begin an eight-year sentence for an absurdly minor infraction. Playing on this quintessentially countercultural theme of a corrupt and arbitrary system, the film allows Nicholson to transcend the self-centeredness of his earlier roles and play Buddusky as a tough son of a bitch who is sentimental and hard-assed at the same time.

Hard-boiled, cynical, horny, and passionate at the same time, J. J. Gittes of *Chinatown* is Jack at his Bogart best. By the film's release in 1974, Nicholson had passed from cult status to one of the hottest draws in Hollywood. Robert Towne's complex tale of conspiracies within conspiracies remains one of the best films of the Watergate era. For all of the plot's convolutions, the screen is dominated by the palpable heat between the doomed romantic Gittes and the disturbed eroticism of Faye Dunaway's Evelyn Mulray. Like the Bogart heroes of old, Gittes, for all of his indifference, is after both the truth and the girl. But in this Seventies' classic both are found and lost in the murky moral no-man's land of Chinatown, where naked power rules and it's best not to get too close.

Nicholson finally won an Oscar when *One Flew Over the Cuckoo's Nest* swept the Academy Awards for 1975. Nicholson's R. P. McMurphy is per-

Nicholson as McMurphy in One Flew Over the Cuckoo's Nest: *Always the joker.*

#1 Singles:
Carpenters—"Close to You"
Bread—"Make It With You"
Edwin Starr—"War"

SEPTEMBER 1970

4: Marxist Salvador Allende Gossens elected President of Chile.

10: Spiro Agnew blasts liberal Democrats as "troglodyte leftists," and accuses them of "pusillanimous pussyfooting."

5: Two hundred and fifty thousand attend e of Wight Pop festival, Jimi Hendrix's st live performance.

Selected Gold Record Albums:
Mountain—*Climbing*
The Who—*Live at Leeds*
Joe Cocker—*Mad Dogs and Englishmen*
Grand Funk Railroad—*Closer to Home*

3: Vince Lombardi dies

3: Canned Heat's Al Wilson dies of barbituate overdose.

Five Easy Pieces: *Chicken salad would never be the same.*

haps just a bit too pat as the criminal hero locked in a madhouse. Nevertheless, the film is elevated by an inspired ensemble cast of lunatics and the cinematography of Haskell Wexler. McMurphy's sexual frankness and zany anarchism are doomed to fail before the sadistic power of nurse Ratched, and McMurphy can escape only via spiritual transcendence provided by the silent Indian's murderous pillow.

The huge success of author Ken Kesey's *Cuckoo's Nest* best reflects Hollywood's acceptance and mainstreaming of both Nicholson and countercultural themes. The rest of the decade saw Nicholson in a string of largely disappointing films with bloated budgets and mediocre performances. He ended the Seventies on a losing streak, which would last until his Oscar-winning performance in *Terms of Endearment* (1983).

THE GODFATHER

The Godfather and *The Godfather Part II* are not only the best films of the decade, they are arguably two of the best films ever—combining both high art and popular entertainment in ways few films have even tried before or since.

After the success of Mario Puzo's pulp best-seller, everyone wondered what Hollywood would do with it. Tinseltown's history of turning potboilers into great films is at best spotty, as anyone who has ever seen *Valley of the Dolls* would attest. Yet speculation surrounding *The Godfather* set the rumor mills abuzz as no film-to-book project had since *Gone With the Wind*.

Filmed in as much secrecy as you can get when shooting on location in New York City, *The Godfather* (1972) was constantly in the news. Paramount was under constant pressure to avoid making a film that could be perceived as an ethnic slur. Yet at the same time, millions of Americans, Italians and non-Italians were convinced that Puzo had perfectly captured the mythology of postwar America with his epic saga of the Corleone family.

The Godfather was shot in 120 New York City locations in all five boroughs. Cooperation with local labor and neighborhood groups was not forthcoming as long as locals felt Paramount was making an insulting film. Singer Vic Damone gave up the role as the Sinatra-like Johnny Fontaine when he felt that he was involved in an anti-Italian project.

27: Egyptian President Gamal Abdel Nasser negotiates cease-fire in Jordanian civil war.

28: Egyptian President Nasser dies of heart attack.

12: *Josie and the Pussycats* debuts on CBS-TV.

15: Spiro Agnew blasts music and media for promoting drug culture.

18: Jimi Hendrix dies. Coronor rules: "inhalation of vomit due to barbituate intoxication."

20: Jim Morrison found guilty of indecent exposure and profanity.

Producer Albert Ruddy shocked everyone when he made a public deal with the Italian-American Civil Rights League in New York. Headed by the son of reputed mob boss Joe Columbo, the league demanded that the film forgo any use of the words, Mafia or Cosa Nostra. In return, Columbo's group provided access to New York locations and "character faces" as extras. Paramount found that many locals became much more cooperative after the agreement. On the other hand, Paramount's parent company, Gulf + Western, was less than pleased with this apparent deal with the mob.

Ruddy and director Francis Ford Coppola used this local access to the hilt. James Caan practiced for his role as the hotheaded Sonny Santino by hanging out with real live "button men." He was seen so often in the company of Carmine "The Snake" Persico that the local FBI had begun to tail him as an up-and-coming hit man. Luckily, the film finished shooting before real shooting broke out again in New York's Mafia wars. Not long after *The Godfather*'s New York wrap, Joe Columbo was assassinated at a Columbus Circle rally on June 28, 1971.

Marlon Brando's role as Vito Corleone has become so legendary that it is hard to believe that he was not always the first choice for the role. Paramount had originally wanted Laurence Olivier. Despite his method mastery and legendary status, Brando was considered box-office poison and had a reputation for being difficult. However, it took only one unsolicited screen test to convince Ruddy that no other actor but Brando could possibly play the Don.

Believe it or not, the studio's first choice for the part of the brooding Michael was Warren Beatty! Except for a few Broadway successes and an outstanding performance in *Panic in Needle Park* (1971), Al Pacino was a Hollywood nobody. He got a flat $35,000 for his performance.

For all its production woes, *The Godfather* was made for less than $6 million dollars. It was an instant classic, grossing a million a day after its opening. It quickly became clear that this sumptuously violent ode to organized crime would quickly pass *The Sound of Music* and *Gone With the Wind* as the biggest grossing film of all time. It's important to remember how *The Godfather* shook Hollywood out of its post-Sixties' malaise. It was the first film to prove to the studios that they still knew how to make blockbusters.

The mob meets the method:
Marlon Brando as the Don.

#1 Singles:
Edwin Starr—"War"
Diana Ross—"Aint No Mountain High Enough"

OCTOBER 1970

2: Federal court okays eighteen-year-old voting age.

29: Congress creates the Public Broadcasting System.

#1 Albums:
Creedence Clearwater Revival—*Cosmos Factory*.

3: Janis Joplin dies of apparent heroin overdose.

Variety hailed it as "a great boost to a nervous, if not dying industry."

The Godfather could have been made only in the Seventies. In a decade obsessed with ethnicity and roots, it provided an intricate pulp mythology of postwar American ethnic warfare. It glorified Italian culture while at the same time indulging in the most blatant ethnic stereotypes and elevating them to almost godlike figures. Though murderous and scheming, Vito Corleone is portrayed first and foremost as a loving father and benefactor to all of his flock. At very worst, he is a man driven to violent means because he and his people are excluded from justice in the "real America" by the domineering WASPs and Irish.

Vito and his boys represent the high tide of Hollywood's obsession with the antihero that dominated Vietnam-era films. For all of their murderous doings, Vito, Michael, and Sonny became the biggest pin-up stars of the early Seventies as the oversized poster of Connie's wedding adorned untold millions of bedroom walls.

In its cynical and sinister take on American society and political morality *The Godfather* perfectly reflected the spirit of the early Seventies. Tired of assassinated heroes and unfulfilled utopias, Americans took to the Cor-

Pacino, Brando, Caan, and Cazale as the Corleones at Connie's wedding.

7: Anwar al-Sadat succeeds Nasser as Egypt's president.

13: FBI apprehends Angela Davis, wanted in murder of California judge.

8: Alexandr I. Solzhenitsyn awarded Nobel prize for literature.

12: Release of album *Jesus Christ Superstar.*

13: Publication of *The Greening of America.*

leones as a kind of bleak inversion of the Kennedys. The brutal realpolitik of Michael Corleone's deals and executions and his philosophy of "keep your friends close, but your enemies closer" made perfect sense to movie audiences watching the cold warrior Nixon flying to China and making deals with Brezhnev while still bombing Hanoi. For many, the rhetoric of détente was about as sincere and lasting as the Corleones' deals with "the five families" and Hymen Roth.

For many, including Brando, the Corleones represented a perfect symbol of corporate capitalism gone berserk. He told *Newsweek* magazine that "the mafia is the best example of capitalists we have. . . . I don't think the tactics the Don used are all that different than GM. . . . The American government does the same thing [murder people] for reasons that are not all that different than the mafia."

Yet for most, *The Godfather* remained good old-fashioned entertainment, complete with love, betrayal, and revenge. Coppola denied that the film was made with any overarching political or sociological message. It offered, he suggested, "a whopping sundae of suspense, melodrama and American mythology, topped by a matchless performance by an American master."

Though his on-screen time in this masterpiece is relatively short, Brando still turns in the performance of a lifetime. Perfectly capturing the nuances and actions of a sixty-five-year-old Italian patriarch, Brando created a role that to this day can be parodied but not equaled. As the apostle of method acting, Brando was surrounded by a brilliant cast of acolytes—Robert Duvall, John Cazale, and Pacino. James Caan is so natural as the explosive Sonny that you almost overlook just how great he can be. His violent intensity is so often funny, it provides a welcome relief from the grim proceedings. His almost sacramental slaughter on the causeway is easily the most gut-wrenching moment of the film.

Almost three hours long, *The Godfather* moves more quickly and bears rewatching more than films half its length. Coppola's brilliant direction and the beautiful camera work of Gordon Willis make it easy to forget that you are witnessing high art disguised as pop entertainment. But *The Godfather* was not without its detractors. Many felt that its very beauty merely glorified violence. Others felt that it made every Italian out to be a criminal. It is a film that Mario Cuomo, governor of New York, finds personally offensive.

Al Pacino as the brooding, brainy Michael Corleone.

Fredo returns to the family in **The Godfather, Part II.**

Perhaps most shocking of all was Coppola's use of Catholic ritual as a narrative device. In his two *Godfather* films, practically all of the sacraments of the church are used as key points in the story. The first film opens with a wedding and closes with a symbolic blood-drenched baptism. The second film opens with a first communion and concludes just after Fredo is bumped off while saying the Hail Mary. In the pre-Madonna Seventies this perversion of the sacraments proved a scandal.

After making the most popular and lucrative film of all time, Coppola went on to top himself with *The Godfather, Part II* (1974). In this sequel, arguably the only decent sequel ever made, Coppola continues the Corleone saga (with the family under Michael's lead) and at the same time shows a parallel tale of young Vito growing from a sickly mute Sicilian youth to the undisputed and benevolent boss of his Lower East Side neighbohood. With dialogue spoken almost exclusively in Sicilian, Coppola succeeds in creating a "foreign film" within a popular American movie. The second film benefits from the dueling method brilliance of Lee Strasberg as the aging Jewish gangster Hymen Roth and Robert De Niro as the young Don. Pacino continues the role of a lifetime as Michael as he sinks further and further into the pure evil born from his unstoppable quest for power and control.

If the first film quietly reflected the evils of American capitalism, the second leaves no room for subtle hints. Michael is seen hobnobbing in pre-Castro Cuba with the heads of American corporations while he and Roth plot to create a Mafia power base just ninety miles offshore where they can launch a bid to run their own candidate for president. The Kennedy assassination is openly alluded to when Michael paraphrases John Kennedy in saying that "if history has taught us anything, it's that you can kill anybody." Roth is gunned down at the airport by a Jack Ruby look-alike who is quickly shot down himself.

Unsurpassed as both entertainment and pop mythology, *The Godfather* films have gained respect and historical resonance with the passing years. They remain the masterpieces of our generation.

DEEP THROAT

Deep Throat was *the* movie that made pornography acceptable to the

21: Fifty Green Berets attempt daring raid on N. Vietnamese POW camp.

25: Japanese writer Yukio Mishima commits ritual hara-kiri.

#1 Singles:
Jackson 5—"I'll Be There"
The Partridge Family—"I Think I Love You"

11: John Lennon and Yoko Ono release two *Plastic Ono Band* albums with identical front covers.

27: George Harrison releases *All Things Must Pass.*

Selected Gold Record Albums:
Led Zeppelin—*Led Zeppelin III*
Santana—*Abraxas*

22

average citizen. A sixty-two-minute ode to one young woman's fellating talents eventually grossed more than $30 million and became the target of a landmark court case.

Unlike most other stroke films, *Deep Throat* had a coherent plot as well as a sense of humor. Its protagonist, played by Linda Lovelace, confided a deep secret in her doctor: She felt "no tingle" in her sex life—even orgies couldn't turn her on. But leave it up to kindly Dr. Young (Harry Reems), who discovered that Linda's clitoris had been misplaced in her throat and only fellatio could satisfy her. Once she learned this, there was no stopping Linda, and boy, did she have one powerful throat.

The film opened in 1972 at Manhattan's World Theatre and almost immediately received favorable publicity—at least from that esteemed journal *Screw* magazine, which deemed *Deep Throat* "The very best porn film ever made." That review also piqued the interest of the New York cops, causing an unintended side effect. "Business had already peaked and would have died in a few weeks had not the police decided to try and close us down," said theater operator Bob Sumner. "Attendance was average until the police handed us all that publicity. The legal reaction is what made 'Deep Throat' take off the way it did."

And take off it did. Suddenly a better class of citizen began showing up at the seedy theater, including several *New York Times* editors who wandered over on their lunch hour (they were not allowed to put the $5 charge on their expense accounts). It was reported that such celebrities as Johnny Carson, Mike Nichols, Ben Gazzara, Jack Nicholson, and Truman Capote dropped by to satisfy their curiosity. It was not uncommon for unescorted women—unthinkable just a year earlier—to catch a matinee.

Meanwhile, the film found another unwitting press agent: New York City Judge Joel Tyler, who had ruled that the film was obscene and banned it from the five boroughs. The New York trial had moments of comic relief. One film critic testified that the film had value because it showed that there was more to sex than just the missionary position. "What's the missionary position?" asked Judge Tyler, the last innocent. The banning of *Deep Throat* in New York City caused "art" theaters in other communities to book the film. Oddly enough, a judge in staid Binghamton, New York, ruled that *Deep Throat* was acceptable for local residents.

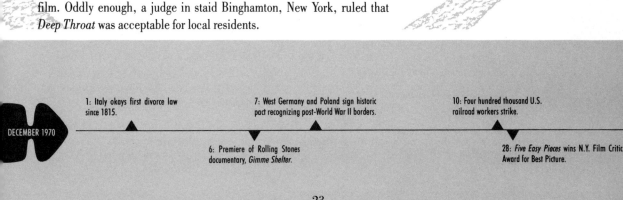

DECEMBER 1970

1: Italy okays first divorce law since 1815.

6: Premiere of Rolling Stones documentary, *Gimme Shelter*.

7: West Germany and Poland sign historic pact recognizing post-World War II borders.

10: Four hundred thousand U.S. railroad workers strike.

28: *Five Easy Pieces* wins N.Y. Film Critic Award for Best Picture.

*Smokey redux: Bandit and
the Frog on the road again.*

After Tyler's verdict, the counterrevolution was swift. In June 1973 the U.S. Supreme Court ruled that "community standards" should determine what was pornographic, replacing the old standard of redeeming social value. Three years later an ambitious Memphis prosecutor put several *Deep Throat*-connected personnel, including director Gerard Damianio and star Harry Reems, on trial for obscenity. Reems's cause became a rallying point for First Amendment advocates, and eventually obscenity charges against him were dropped.

Nonetheless, the popularity of *Deep Throat* spurred the success of other hardcore porno films, most notably *Behind the Green Door*, which starred the lusty Marilyn Chambers. It was soon revealed that Chambers was the same model who had posed scrubbed faced on a box of Ivory Snow. An embarrassed Procter & Gamble pulled the offending boxes off the shelves.

As for Linda Lovelace (née Boreman), she became an overnight instant celebrity and was even photographed hobnobbing with filmdom's elite at the Cannes Film Festival. In reality, her circumstances weren't so happy. In the late Eighties she revealed that during the *Deep Throat* era, she was a virtual prisoner of her sadistic husband-manager Chuck Traynor. She tried making R-rated movies, but she was typecast as a porn queen. Today, after surviving a liver transplant and double mastectomy, she lectures on the effect of pornography on women and lives an otherwise quiet life as Long Island housewife Linda Marchiano.

Today the term Deep Throat probably recalls the mysterious Watergate source and not the movie. In fact, you no longer have to sit in a sleazy movie theater to watch *Deep Throat*. It's readily available for rental at your neighborhood video store, and when you check it out, odds are no one will blink.

BURT MANIA

For a man who would reign as Middle America's heartthrob for much of the decade, Burt Reynolds started the Seventies on a losing streak. Perceived as a washed-up TV star after the failure of his *Dan August* series, Reynolds even appeared as a bachelor on *The Dating Game*, and wasn't chosen. He nearly beat up the winning bachelor after he called Burt "a Nazi." To top off this indignation, Burt was in the throes of a Hollywood love affair with *The*

13-20: Polish regime toppled by food riots.

#1 Singles:
The Partridge Family—"I Think I Love You"
Smokey Robinson—"Tears of a Clown"
George Harrison—"My Sweet Lord"

JANUARY 1971

18: George McGovern opens presidential race.

31: Paul McCartney files suit to break up Beatles.

4: Premiere of *Performance*, starring Mick Jagger.

5: Sonny Liston found dead in Las Vegas.

19: *No, No, Nanette* opens Broadway.

Farmer's Daughter star Inger Stevens when the moody Swede went and killed herself.

To console himself, Burt threw himself into the talk-show circuit and carried on a well-publicized affair with Dinah Shore, the crooning cooking-show host who looked old enough to be his mother. The Oedipal kinkiness of the Burt-Dinah combo underscored the sexual weirdness that has always surrounded Reynolds—a man who looks so macho, almost too macho.

Appearing on eleven straight Merv Griffin shows provided Burt a perfect forum for his down-home, good-ol'-boy self-deprecation. On *The Tonight Show*, Johnny Carson let him guest host for a while. There Burt had a spontaneous reconciliation with his ex, Judy ("Sock it to me"/*Love on a Rooftop*) Carne.

Director John Boorman saw Reynolds do this show and decided he had to cast Reynolds for his epic film *De-*

Burt Reynolds at his Good Ol' Boy best.

25: Charles Manson convicted of Tate-LaBianca killings.

25: Grace Slick and Paul Kanter announce birth of daughter, China.

31: Launch of Apollo 14 lunar mission.

FEBRUARY 1971

4: Rolls Royce declares bankruptcy.

liverance (1972). Reynolds was perfect in this beautiful and savage film. Playing a philosophical good ol' boy who takes his suburban buddies out for a doomed weekend in the wild, Reynolds projects just the right combination of bullshit and bravado. Reynolds saw *Deliverance* as his ticket out of B movies and bad TV shows. Unfortunately, his decision to pose naked for a *Cosmopolitan* centerfold overshadowed his performance and gave him an unshakeable reputation as a publicity hog and one-dimensional stud. Over two and half million copies were sold, not counting the hundreds of thousands of bootleg Burts that came out of the woodwork. His stud reputation was humorously reinforced with his cameo in Woody Allen's *Everything You Wanted to Know About Sex* . . . as a technician in "Sperm Control."

With his hunk status firmly established, Burt churned out a series of sucessful action adventure films, including *White Lightning* (1973), the first of his "Gator McClusky" films in which he avenges his brother's death at the hands of an evil city official. Checkout counter tabloids tracked new Burt romances with every passing feature. *Shamus* (1973) was made amid rumors of trysts with Dyan Cannon. During *The Man Who Loved Cat Dancing* (1973) Burt was implicated in a torrid romance with Sarah Miles. He had to appear at an official inquest after one of her assistants killed himself. The Gila Bend, Arizona, inquest revealed that Burt and Sarah spent a lot of time together in terry-cloth robes giving each other rubdowns. During *The Longest Yard* (1974), he was linked with Bernadette Peters, and *Semi-Tough* (1977) was not completed without rumors of a Burt romance with Jill (*An Unmarried Woman*) Clayburgh. Nobody accused Burt of landing Catherine Deneuve in the sack during *Hustle* (1975), but it was during this film that he and the long-suffering Dinah finally called it quits. She went on to date Mac ("Don't Get Hooked on Me") Davis, while Burt made *Lucky Lady* (1975), *Gator* (1976), and *Nickelodeon* (1976).

With *Gator* and *Smokey and the Bandit* (1977), Reynolds hit upon a tear-'em-up, bustin'-loose, good-ol'-boys with Trans Ams formula that reaped hundreds of millions of dollars. In 1977 *Smokey* raked in more than a hundred million and was second only to *Star Wars* for top-grossing film. Burt's *Gator* character was light-years removed from the brooding stars of Hollywood's screen wackos. Burt described them as "swamp smart . . . guys who fight the system with dignity and a sense of humor. Men want to be like him.

13: Spiro Agnew hits three bystanders with golf balls at Bob Hope Classic.

16: Hot Pants show at New York City's Alexander's draws throngs.

17: James Taylor appears on Johnny Cash TV show.

#1 Singles:
George Harrison—"My Sweet Lord"

Selected Gold Record Albums:
Elton John—*Elton John*
Soundtrack—*Love Story*
Janis Joplin—*Pearl*
Chicago—*Chicago III*

MARCH 1971

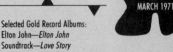

The women want to be with him." *Smokey* revived the career of Sally (*Gidget/The Flying Nun*) Field as they became romantically linked in the tabloids. Faced with rumors of simultaneous Reynolds/Clayburgh and Reynolds/Chris Evert affairs, Field (a.k.a. "The Frog") seemed to take Burt's sexual reputation with a modicum of good humor: "I'd hate to hear what they'd say if he ever made a film with Lassie." For all of the profits of both *Smokey* films and the critical success of the genuinely funny *Semi-Tough*, Burt ended the decade on a downward spiral that would follow him well into the 1980s. Suffering a collapse from a chronic case of hypoglycemia, Burt lost most of his "the stunt man" luster. The sad fact was that as age caught up with him, his good ol' boy was becoming a frumpy middle-aged man. He ended the 1970s with *The End* (1978), a comedy about middle age and suicide that pits him not against some sexy thing but with that ubiquitous fatso Dom De Luise. *The End* grossed over forty million, but left most of Burt's fans with the feeling that the master had lost his touch.

BURT FACTS, FIASCOS, AND MIGHT-HAVE-BEENS

Hot bod' in a wet suit.

- On why he dated Dinah instead of younger women: "What can you do with a great pair of breasts after three or four hours?"
- Hollywood's Lion Country Safari named Burt "Sensuous Man of the Year" in '72.
- Burt wanted to be in *Semi-Tough* very badly. Unfortunately, the rights to the book were originally bought by David Merrick who wanted to make a Broadway musical! Undaunted, Burt threw himself into vocal training to prepare for his musical debut. He hired Bobby ("Honey") Goldsboro to produce an album for him. The resulting atrocity, the "Ask Me What I Am" album, was released by Mercury and quickly consigned to the cutout bins.
- When production costs threatened to doom the Georgia location shooting of *The Longest Yard* (1974), Burt personally asked Governor Jimmy Carter to help. Carter provided free locations and prison labor to help shore up what would become a major redneck film industry.
- Only a bout with hypoglycemia after *Cat Dancing* kept Burt from playing the Sean Connery role in John Boorman's bizarre *Zardoz* (1974).

: Bomb rocks Senate wing
f Capitol building.

21: Two U.S. platoons refuse order to advance in Vietnam.

23: Senate defies Nixon and ends funding
of U.S. SST development.

29: Ford recalls all Pintos for
engine defects.

4: Canadian Prime Minister Trudeau, 51,
marries Margaret Sinclair, 22.

8: Smokin' Joe Frazier defeats
Muhammad Ali in 15-round decision.

13: The Allman Brothers record
Live at the Fillmore East.

● Sally Field was so consumed in nursing Burt back from his post-*Smokey* collapse that she turned down the "Lois Lane" role in *Superman*.

BARBRA STREISAND

Of all of the female stars of the Seventies, Barbra Streisand is the only one to have dominated the box office while avoiding the bizarre, degrading sicko roles that Hollywood was doling out. An entertainer in her own right, Streisand continued to sell millions of records without doing rock and roll, (although her version of Bowie's "Life on Mars" is something else indeed!)

After the 1968 success of *Funny Girl*, Streisand participated in *Hello, Dolly* (1969), a titanic flop that is often blamed for single-handedly destroying the Hollywood studios. Her early Seventies comedies, *The Owl and the Pussycat* (1970), *Up the Sand Box* (1972), and *What's Up Doc?* (1972), are characteristically lightweight and zany. Like Woody Allen, Streisand's intensely New York, Jewish humor had huge appeal during this period when ethnicity dominated the screen, both big and small.

While the title song of *The Way We Were* (1972) haunted the airwaves for much of '73 and 74, it was a dismal film, sunk by a shallow plot about a stereotypical WASP (Robert Redford) married to a leftist firebrand (Babs, of course) set against a dizzying array of red-baiting periods. The film switches from the Spanish Civil War to the McCarthy era to the ban-the-bomb movement with only a sappy Marvin Hamlisch score to hold it together. *The Way We Were* proved that it was impossible to watch a Barbra Streisand picture without constantly being reminded that you were watching Barbra Streisand trying to act like somebody else. Yet this was precisely why her millions of fans went to her films.

Funny Lady (1975) reprised her Fanny Brice triumph with a two-dimensional script that hardly mattered to those who wanted to hear Barbra sing. In retrospect, the film's greatest sin is that it became one more trite vehicle for James Caan, whose career was already on a downward spiral.

Partially written by Joan Didion and John Gregory Dunne, and largely rewritten by Babs and her lover-hairdresser Jon Peters, *A Star Is Born* (1976) marks a clear demarcation in Streisand's evolution from kooky inge-

29: Manson sentenced to gas chamber.

31: Lt. William L. Calley, Jr. sentenced to life for My Lai massacre.

#1 Singles:
The Osmonds—"One Bad Apple"
Janis Joplin—"Me and Bobby McGee"

APRIL 1971

26: Spencer Haywood jumps to American Basketball Association.

27: WNBC Radio in New York bans airplay of Brewer and Shipley's "One Toke over the Line" for alleged drug lyrics.

Selected Gold Record Albums:
Elton John—*Tumbleweed Connection*
The Partridge Family—*Up to Date*
Merle Haggard—*The Fighting Side of Me*

nue to self-obsessed megalomaniac. Her attempt to portray a rock star is ludicrous to all but herself and her fans (who feel she could portray anything). Even the usually upbeat *Time* magazine complained that "hearing Streisand sing rock is like hearing Al Jolson sing Leadbelly." Kris Kristofferson's role as a declining star was perhaps too close to the truth for his career. After this, could *Convoy* and *Rollover* be that far behind?

Barbra capped off the decade with a pathetic Rocky ripoff *The Main Event*, a raunchy locker-room farce that has her trying to goad has-been boxer (and actor) Ryan O'Neal back into championship form. (O'Neal could have had it worse. His fellow washed-up Seventies superstar Elliott Gould ended the decade boxing a kangaroo!) For critics, O'Neal offered what would be a prophetic assessment of Streisand's career: "If audiences are tired of seeing Barbra Streisand playing Barbra Streisand, wait till they see her as Yentl, the Yeshiva girl. They'll want her to go back to being Barbra Streisand."

Boxing Babs (with Ryan O'Neal) in The Main Event.

: Nixon frees Lt. William Calley pending review of conviction.

6: Death of composer Igor Stravinsky.

15: *Patton* wins seven Oscars.

19: U.S. Ping-Pong team visits China; first official contact since revolution.

4: *Follies* opens on Broadway.

13: Rolling Stones release "Brown Sugar."

29

UNHINGED WOMEN: FEMALE ROLES IN THE EARLY SEVENTIES

With most male roles written for deranged characters (see Screen Wacko section), it's little wonder why the Seventies proved to be a low point in heterosexual relations both on and off the screen. Movies reflected a society where men and woman could no longer communicate in a common language of romance and respect.

The sexual revolution and the advent of unabashed nudity and unsubtle sex scenes took some of the magic out of the screen's age-old image of romantic starlets. In fact, by the beginning of the Seventies, many of the best female roles were women who were both sexually confused and emotionally unhinged. The battle of the sexes had definitely entered a new phase of viciousness, and no one was taking any prisoners.

Evelyn Draper in *Play Misty for Me* (1971): Jessica Walter's Evelyn Draper is every guy's nightmare as the one-night stand who wouldn't go away. Clint Eastwood's jazzy, poetry-reading DJ Dave Garland gets more than he bargains for when he spends the night with this obsessive fan. Evelyn demolishes his apartment and his career before Clint throws this heartsick psychopath out the window. While certainly short of Hitchcock standards, Eastwood's directorial debut showed what he could do with a thriller before getting into a decadelong rut with *Dirty Harry*.

Jacy Farrow in *The Last Picture Show* (1971): The best role of Cybill Shephard's first superstar period as the ultimate rich bitch in a dusty one-plex town who turns her defloration into a theatrical event, who sets best friends against each other, and who denies the pathetic Ruth Popper (Cloris Leachman) the only good sex she's ever had.

Bree Daniels in *Klute* (1971): Jane Fonda turns in a stellar role as streetwalker whose psychoanalysis helps her discover that her profession is nothing but another form of "acting."

Sally Bowles in *Cabaret* (1972): Liza Minnelli's brilliant Sally Bowles literally set the stage for the glam- and glitter-drenched early-Seventies ob-

Sissy Spacek in Carrie, *a prom date to die for.*

18: *Summer of '42* released.

25: Antiwar demonstrators close New Jersey Turnpike.

25: Bangladesh declares independence from Pakistan.

Selected Gold Record Albums:
Elton John—*Friends*
Barbra Striesand—*Stoney End*
Grand Funk Railroad—*Survival*
James Taylor—*Mud Slide Slim*
Crosby, Stills, Nash and Young—*Four Way Street*

#1 Singles:
The Temptations—"Just My Imagination"
Three Dog Night—"Joy to the World"

session with Weimar decadence. Only an early-Seventies movie could end Sally's romance with bisexual Michael York with an abortion followed by a rip-roaring musical finale. *Cabaret* made it all too clear that it's hard to believe in love when you don't know who you are and the world is going straight to hell.

Evelyn Mulray in *Chinatown* (1974): Faye Dunaway's role as Daddy's little girl is the sexual/psychotic attraction that gives Jack Nicholson's J. J. Gittes some motivation for getting into the whole sordid mess of water rights and nose-ripping conspiracies. *Chinatown* marked a new phase in Faye's career when she passed from merely beautiful to the campy intense eroticism that would continue in *Three Days of the Condor* (1975) and reach its peak in *Network* (1976) and *Mommie Dearest* (1981).

Barbara Jean in *Nashville* (1975): "Don't go nutsy on me now, Barbara Jean." The mentally broken country-western star (played by Ronee Blakley) at the center of this brilliant pastiche is Hollywood's most original and moving portrayal of a performer whose stardom has clearly outlived her ability to function as a coherent human being. Her climactic assasination remains Robert Altman's most shocking directorial touch as well as a disturbingly casual echo of the Sixties and a haunting precursor of the Eighties when perfomers replaced politicians as the targets with the most potent emotional force.

Nurse Ratched in *One Flew Over the Cuckoo's Nest* (1975): The most clearly defined—if one dimensional—bitch of the decade. In this role Louise Fletcher is the drug-dispensing symbol of the inhuman rules, regulations, and order that keep the mad mad and oppose McMurphy's humanistic therapy of freewheeling anarchy. She's so bad, she punishes poor Billy Bibbit just for having sex. When this drives the poor vulnerable kid to suicide, she engages McMurphy in a battle to the death—and wins.

Carrie in *Carrie* (1976): If Nurse Ratched personifies evil incarnate, *Carrie* sure shows a side of feminine revenge never attempted on the silver screen before. In a film that begins with menstruation and ends with the heroine dowsed in a bucket of pig blood, *Carrie* presents one of the strangest tales

Faye Dunaway

3: Ten thousand arrested during D.C. May Day demonstrations.

7: Indira Gandhi wins Gallup poll as world's most admired person.

3: New York critics boycott Grand Funk Railroad press conference.

12: Mick Jagger married to Bianca Perez Morena in St. Tropez.

24: Bob Dylan's thirtieth birthday lampooned in *Peanuts*.

of the blossoming power of female sexuality. Beset by the repression of her holy roller/nut mom and the unrelenting cruelty of her classmates, Carrie, played by Sissy Spacek, develops and uses her telekinetic powers to bring the house down.

AMERICAN GRAFFITI

American Graffiti (1973), George Lucas's funny and endearing look at teenage social mores in the waning days of doo-wop innocence arrived like a needed tonic during the dismal days of Watergate hearings and gasoline rationing. This paean to the gas-guzzling life-style of teenage cruising opened in the summer of '73, the last summer before OPEC extortionists put an end to America's love affair with cheap gas and mindless joy riding.

For all of the institutionalized "oldies" nostalgia that has washed over us since the early Seventies, *Graffiti* remains a true original. It's interesting (if not frightening) to note that while only eleven years elapsed between *Graffiti*'s fabled summer of '62 and the film's production, at the time of its release critics acted as if Lucas had uncovered a Stone Age cult. To viewers still numb from the onslaught of the Sixties and overwhelmed by the tawdry drama of Nixon's undoing, *Graffiti* provided an exotic and romanticized look back at teen life before events in Danang and Dealy Plaza rendered such innocent high jinks irrelevant. It is perhaps most interesting to note that *Graffiti* can be seen as one transitional period commenting on another. The film marked a true turning point in American pop culture—the institutionalization of a past-centered entertainment, a culture of nostalgia that has marked American pop culture ever since.

Yet *Graffiti*'s success was hardly preordained by media hype. Every major studio turned Lucas down before Universal agreed to back him. A former member of Coppola's famed Zoetrope studios, Lucas's only other commercial film had been the less-than profitable *THX-1138* (1971), an icy sci-fi film that he described as "allegory with a touch of cubism." Hardly words to warm a marketing man's heart. Based on this track record, Universal insisted Lucas get a bankable quantity to shore up the film. Lucas brought Coppola on as producer. This proved critical since no studio could stand up to the man who had just made a fortune with *The Godfather*.

Pre-Nazi naughtiness: Liza as Sally Bowles in Cabaret.

Lucas insists that *Graffiti* is a composite of his own life experiences. In high school He was Terry "the Toad," the awkward scooter-driving girl chaser. After graduation he became the daredevil dragster Milner till a near-fatal crash, and then became Kurt the writer, wise-cracking, introspective and just a little bit removed from the Steves of the world who go from class big shots to Modesto insurance salesman without ever broadening their horizons.

No movie costing less than a million dollars has ever made more. Few movies have spawned more imitators or launched as many careers. Lucas went from unbankable weirdo to major mogul overnight. Richard Dreyfuss and Ron Howard went on to dominate film and television for the rest of the decade. Some of the film's lesser lights—MacKenzie Phillips, Suzanne Somers, Paul LeMat, and Harrison Ford—all went on to varying degrees of stardom.

Shot in only twenty-eight nights for just over $700,000, *Graffiti* has a dark and almost murky look. Cinematographer Haskell Wexler and Lucas chose this otherworldly jukeboxlike lighting to provide a stunning contrast with the oldies' soundtrack and teen shenanigans on-screen. Universal was so opposed that they tried to hold up distribution, until Coppola tried to buy the film. Their decision to relent was rewarded with over one hundred million dollars in grosses. Yet even with this success Universal did not pick up a $50,000 option on Lucas's next script, a film he described as "a real gee-whiz movie" he called *The Star Wars*.

THE DEVIL MADE ME DO IT

Paralleling the rise of cults and Jesus freaks, popular interest in the occult and witchcraft exploded in the early Seventies. Even with the mega success of *Jaws* and *Star Wars*, *The Exorcist* (1973) remains the most hysterically received picture of the decade. *Exorcist* mania reached almost religious proportions as the screen's sinister doings drove legions of theatergoers to nightmares, fainting spells, and vomiting.

Like *The Godfather*, director William Friedkin's film uses the more exotic and sinister subtext of Catholic ritual as a backdrop to shocking violence. Both films reawakened latent fears of lapsed Catholics and assimilated eth-

Linda Blair rises to the occasion in **The Exorcist.**

14: Attorney General Mitchell demands *The New York Times* cease publication of "Pentagon Papers".

15: Federal Judge orders halt to "Pentagon Papers" publication.

26: Arrest issued for Daniel Ellsberg for theft of "Pentagon Papers".

27: Five thousand march for gay rights in New York's Central Park.

6: John Lennon and Yoko Ono jam with Frank Zappa at Fillmore East.

10: Police tear-gas crowd at Denver Jethro Tull concert.

12: Tricia Nixon marries Edward Cox.

nics. Priests complained that many Catholics were being scared to death by the reawakened fears of hell drummed into them in Catholic school and catechism. In early '74, some priests reported a rash of calls from people convinced that they or someone they knew were possessed. At the same time most serious theologians dismissed the film as the *Going My Way* of the Seventies, Pauline Kael called the film "a recruiting poster for Catholicism."

Friedkin added a real horror-show veneer to Blatty's pulpy plot. Mrs. MacNeil (Ellen Burstyn) knows something strange is up with little Regan (Linda Blair) when she keeps talking to a Captain Howdie and urinates on the rug in front of guests. After all the tests modern science can provide prove futile, she turns reluctantly to the bosom of the Catholic Church. Father Karras (Jason Miller), a bit shaky in the faith himself, is shocked to find that cute little Regan has been turned into a crucifix-masturbating little demon. He brings on that old devil beater Father Marrin (Max von Sydow), who gets more than he bargains for when Regan does a 360-degree head turn and sprays him with a face full of otherworldly guacamole. The devil gets the better of both priests during the exorcisms when he drives Marrin to a fatal heart attack and then leaves Regan's soul to possess Karras only moments before the tortured priest hurls himself to his death.

Doing *The Exorcist* one better, *The Omen* (1976) presents the tale of an ordinary little boy sired by Satan destined to rule the world from a position of political power. Katherine and Robert Thorn (Lee Remick and Gregory Peck, a distinguished actor whose sagging career was salvaged by this less than dignified shocker) hardly know what they have on their hands when they adopt little Damian in a Rome hospital. Yet after Damien's nanny is hanged, Thorn is told the bad news that his little boy is a chip off old Satan's block and that he can be killed only by a secret ritual. Damien gets a devilishly devoted new nanny, and Father Brennan meets a gruesome end (death by falling church steeple) before Thorn starts to

Gregory Peck in The Omen.

take action. Thorn has a battle to the death with the nasty nanny and is on the verge of slaying his son in the old-fashioned ritual when he is shot by a policeman. The mild mannered orphan Damian is then adopted by Thorn's rich and powerful brother, spawning a spree of sequels from which we may never escape.

Gregory Peck and Lee Remick (with Harvey Stephens) in The Omen: *Satan's surrogate parents.*

Combining both the devil-obsessed occultism of *The Exorcist* and a dash of the apocalyptic prophesy popularized in Hal Lindsay's *The Late Great Planet Earth*, *The Omen* serves up an entertaining blend of Seventies shocker and conspiracy. Set against the political, social, and economic upheaval and ecological paranoia of the times, *The Omen*'s apocalyptic plot panders to the most pervasive fear that something evil and chaotic has been let loose in the world. In the Seventies, Satan takes the place of the invaders from space that dominated the B movies of the Fifties. While most of these earlier monsters and pod people were thinly disguised metaphors for the Communist menace of the cold war years, the satanic obsession of the Seventies reflects a fundamental fear of decay from within. In the words of Pogo: "We have met the enemy and they is us."

Yet for many, the fear and obsession of Satan and the coming of the "final days" went far beyond the merely metaphoric. The fact that *The Late Great Planet Earth* was the best-selling nonfiction book of the decade indicates a fascination with, if not a belief in, a coming apocalypse. While most of the media focused on the more exotic Eastern cults and human potential fads, a huge groundswell of old time religion was occurring that would go largely unnoticed until called into action in 1980 by such conservatives as Jerry Falwell and Ronald Reagan.

CONSPIRACY-O-RAMA

First the President gets his head blown off, then the country descends into a long, bloody, divisive, and unwinnable war, and no sooner does *that* end when another presidency unravels in a sticky thicket of payoffs, sleaze, and petty burglaries while foreign sheiks pull the plug on the nation's energy supply.

A bad movie? No, real life circa 1963 to 1974. Set against this back-

15: Nixon announces 1972 trip to China.

26: Suicide death of photographer Diane Arbus.

#1 Singles:
Carole King—"It's Too Late"
Raiders—"Indian Reservation"

3: John Newcombe and Evonne Goolagong top Wimbledon.

6: Death of Louis Armstrong.

20: *Billy Jack* released for the first time.

24: T. Rex's "Get it On" goes gold in UK, beginning glitter rock phenomenon.

Selected Gold Record Albums:
Jethro Tull—*Aqualung*
Doors—*L.A. Woman*

Hoffman and Redford on Nixon's case
in **All the President's Men.**

ground of malaise-inducing historical downers, Hollywood churned out its share of dark conspiracy classics, films in which "they" were out to control America, and somebody had to find out and make a stand.

Conspiracy flicks were hardly invented in the Seventies. *The Manchurian Candidate*, perhaps the best of the genre, was released in 1962, just before JFK's assassination, and dozens of anti-Nazi and anti-Commie propaganda films were made in the Forties and Fifties. Seventies' conspiracy films grafted Hollywood's traditional Capraesque anti-big business sentiment to a vaguely New Left notion that Mafia-dominated corporations secretly controlled America.

Playing on the fears and doubts generated by the huge holes in the report of the Warren Commission on President Kennedy's assassination, Alan Pakula's *The Parallax View* (1974), has gallant reporter Warren Beatty unraveling the mystery surrounding a liberal senator's assassination and its murderous coverup. It seems a secret conspiracy of brainwashed psychos are being used by a murky Parallax Corporation to rub out everyone in their

way. The psycho-political, light-show brainwashing scene is the best period piece of this predictable thriller once dismissed by the *New York Daily News* as "The Manchurian Candidate in hot pants."

Produced between *Godfathers* (hardly slouches in the conspiracy department), *The Conversation* (1974) is a wonderful small film about the obsession of an unhinged wiretapper (Harry Caul, played by Gene Hackman) with a single conversation. His misinterpretation of a single line of dialogue is the entire trick of the movie. While he fears that the bugged couple are going to be rubbed out by "The Director," quite the opposite occurs.

Released during the climax of the Watergate fiasco, this wiretapping drama was conceived years before. Nevertheless, it captures the creepy paranoia of the era and concludes with a perfectly Nixonian scene of the wiretapper destroying his apartment to discover who is eavesdropping on him. This tale of a bugger bugged is arguably Coppola's finest film. Its plot is more like a perfect short story than the sprawling pulp novels of *The Godfather* films. Inspired by a lecture on surveillance techniques, Coppola made the film "to liberate sound from the tyranny of image." It is, ultimately, a movie to be listened to as much as seen. Although it won a Palme d'Or at Cannes '74, *The Conversation* was poorly distributed and rarely

Mad as hell: Peter Finch in **Network.**

AUGUST 1971

2: CIA admits existence of thirty-thousand-man "secret" army in Laos.

5: George Wallace launches 1972 presidential bid.

20: Lt. Calley's sentence reduced to twenty years.

1: Concert for Bangladesh refugees at New York's Madison Square Garden. Performances by George Harrison, Eric Clapton, Bob Dylan, and more.

3: The group Wings is formed by Paul and Linda McCartney.

13: Soul saxophonist King Curtis murdered.

seen, considering it was by the most successful director of his time. A conspiracy of silence perhaps?

Taking cues right from the headlines, Robert Redford appeared in two conspiracy thrillers, *Three Days of the Condor* (1975) and *All the President's Men* (1976). Both films become backdrops for Redford's hunky earnestness and paled beside the real life events unfolding on the news. Director Pakula reduced much of *All the President's Men* to a standard newsroom thriller, while *Condor* started out with a slam bang only to bog down with a meaningless tryst between Redford and Faye Dunaway.

For the decade's wackiest conspiracy, none surpasses *Network* (1976). Written as a satire by the always overwrought Paddy Chayefsky and packaged by M-G-M as "a perfectly outrageous film," *Network* was swallowed hook, line, and sinker by millions of viewers who echoed Howard Beale's anguished cry, "I'm mad as hell and I'm not going to take it anymore."

Beale's madness is packaged and exploited by the heartless programmer Diana Christianson (Faye Dunaway) who sets him up as a reactionary lightning rod years before controversial talk-show host Morton Downey: "The people want someone to articulate their rage for them." She also packages a revolutionary group (modeled after the Symbionese Liberation Army) as the "Chairman Mao Hour"—a touch that already seemed wildly ananachronistic when the film was released.

It is only when Beale challenges the network's purchase by rich oilmen do we hear the ultimate Seventies' conspiracy oration. Summoned to Mr. Big's office, Beale is given the unvarnished truth about how things "really" work:

"You have meddled with the primal forces of nature Mr. Beale. There is no America. . . . There is only IBM, ITT and AT&T and Dupont, Dow, Union Carbide, and Exxon. . . ."

You know that after getting this lowdown, Beale is not long for this world. Even after toadying to the corporate line, he is rubbed out in an on-air climax that sends the ratings to the top.

Although many later Seventies films incorporate conspiracy themes (the biggest bad guy in *King Kong* [1976] is the Petrox oil company, *Silent Movie* [1976] has its "Engulf and Devour" Corporation, and mutterings about "them Rockefellers" are heard on the rigs of *Convoy* [1978]), few films

Warren Beatty** gets brainwashed by a lightshow in **The Parallax View.

25: Nixon announces end of gold standard; "floats" dollar against other currencies; invokes wage-price contols; blasted by labor and conservatives.

26: New York Giants football team announces move to New Jersey.

#1 Singles:
The Bee Gees—"How Can You Mend a Broken Heart"

Selected Gold Record Albums:
Emerson, Lake and Palmer—*Emerson, Lake and Palmer*
Derek and the Dominoes—*Layla*
Roberta Flack—*Chapter Two*

SEPTEMBER 1971

7: BBC bans *Sesame Street;* cites "authoritarian aims."

9: Prisoners at New York's Attica prison riot, take hostages.

37

dwelled on evil cabals. For most, giant sharks and Darth Vaders took their place as the ultimate bad guys.

DISASTER MOVIES

Disaster films were the perfect recession-era entertainment for audiences frightened to death about Watergate, energy shortages, and inflation; with money tight, it made more sense to spend time in a movie theater rather than a resort. Filled with casts of aging stars, middle-age *Hollywood Squares* panelists, and young never-will-bes, these movies were designed to elicit two responses from audiences. The first was to scare them out of their minds, and the second was to have them say "Isn't that so and so?" as often as possible.

Critics were split about the genre. Rex Reed opined that the reason they are called disaster films was because "they really were disasters." But Vincent Canby of *The New York Times* took a more pragmatic view: "We don't want to be emotionally shattered by disaster movies," he said. "We want to be invigorated as much by the excitement as by the fact that the victims on the screen suffer instead of us."

Heartening words, no doubt, to Irwin Allen, the ex-literary agent turned TV producer (*Time Tunnel, Voyage to the Bottom of the Sea*) who became known as the "master of disaster"—or, when the hyperbole worked overtime, as the "caliph of catastrophe, the count of calamity, and the duke of destruction."

Allen had his own theories about the popularity of his pictures: "I take ordinary people—your butcher, your baker, your fireman and put them in extraordinary circumstances that require superhuman effort to overcome," he explained. "The moviegoer sees it happen on the screen, and when he exits, he believes he could have done it, too. I don't make films about astronauts or brain surgeons because there aren't enough of them to fill a theater. But there are 26 million fireman in the country, and they have wives and friends, and they all come to see my picture."

And come they did. Here's a rundown on some of that mind-boggling movie mayhem:

🔥 The *Airport* series: Based on Arthur Hailey's best-seller, the original

Voyage of the damp:
Shelley Winters in The Poseidon Adventure.

11: Ousted Soviet leader Khrushchev dies in obscurity.

12: Ex-Mao aide Lin Piao killed in mysterious plane accident.

13: Police storm Attica prison, killing twenty-eight prisoners and nine hostages.

16: *Look* magazine ceases publication.

#1 Singles:
Paul and Linda McCartney—"Uncle Albert/Admiral Halsey"
Donny Osmond—"Go Away Little Girl"

Selected Gold Record Albums:
Jefferson Airplane—*Bark*
The Partridge Family—*Sound Machine*
Who—*Who's Next*
John Denver—*Poems, Prayers and Promises*
Osmond Brothers—*Osmonds*

Airport (1970) was an old-fashioned movie in an era of increasingly sophisticated fare. It was also the most successful and accomplished (to use that term loosely) of the lot. The plot revolves around what happens when a blizzard closes a midwestern airport (and a mad bomber threatens passengers on board another plane). The cast includes Burt Lancaster, Dean Martin, Jean Seberg, and George Kennedy, but it is Helen Hayes, as a stowaway, who steals the show and won an Oscar.

Airport 1975 (1974) is the campiest and most reviled of the series. "Inspired" by the original film, this sequel was described by Jay Cocks of *Time* magazine as being "American film making at its shabbiest, most unimaginative and most exploitative."

Come on, Jay, was it that bad? Just because the plot deals with a private plane that crashes into a 747, killing the crew and forcing the stewardess (Karen Black) to attempt to fly the thing until Charlton Heston (who, conveniently, is also her lover) successfully attempts a midair transfer from a helicopter? Just because the passengers include Linda Blair as a girl who needs a kidney transplant, Helen Reddy as a singing nun, Gloria Swanson playing herself, and Myrna Loy as a fading lush belting down boilermakers? This makes it bad?

Robert Vaughn and Paul Newman in **The Towering Inferno.**

Oh, yeah, the movie also features some choice Nixon-era remarks. As when George Kennedy (now the president of the airline) responded to reporters' insistent questions about the accident by saying "The public's right to know gives me a huge pain in the ass." And before the crash, two copilots are checking out the stewardesses and then change their minds. "It would be wrong," he says, and knowing audiences howled.

The third film, *Airport '77*, (1977) spends more time underwater than in the air; James Stewart plays a millionaire whose luxury 747 filled with wealthy patrons is hijacked and crashes into the Bermuda triangle. The oldies but goodies on board this time include Joseph Cotten and Olivia de Havilland.

And as for the fourth and final (we think) installment, *Airport '79: The Concorde* (1979), the less said the better, except to note that Charo is in the cast.

Karen Black flies the unfriendly skies in **Airport 1975.**

🌿 **The Poseidon Adventure** (1972): This enormously successful opus really kicked off the cycle of Seventies disas-

OCTOBER 1971

14: Shah of Iran throws three-day, $100-million party.

16: Black militant H. "Rap" Brown wounded in shoot-out with police.

18: NFL player Charles Hughes dies during game.

12: Gene Vincent dies of bleeding ulcer.

15: Rick Nelson booed at Madison Square Garden oldies show, inspiring "Garden Party."

Dean Martin seeks a stewardess's solace in **Airport.**

William Holden on the horn for help *in* **The Towering Inferno.**

ter films. Like many, the plot is triggered by greedy executives who put profits above people. In this case, the nogoodnik is the ship's owner who orders the captain of the SS *Poseidon* to steer the aging ship beyond its capacities. Unfortunately, an undersea earthquake produces a mammoth tidal wave that turns the ship upside down, upsetting the cruisers' New Year's Eve revelry and causing us to gasp at the sight of a bloated Shelley Winters attempting to survive.

You might also be interested to know that the film's public relations man advertised for survivors of shipwrecks and then flew them to New York for a symposium on survival at sea. The symposium, not coincidentally, took place on the same day as the premiere of *The Poseidon Adventure*.

The Towering Inferno (1974): "One tiny spark becomes a night of blazing suspense!" blared the ads for Irwin Allen's $14 million epic about a fire that breaks out on the dedication night of a 135-story skyscraper, the result of shoddy construction and contracting. This movie was financed by two major studios because both bought rights to similar books (*The Tower* and *The Glass Inferno*). Instead of making competing films, they decided to combine forces. For a while (until *Jaws* was released the following summer), *The Towering Inferno* was the top grossing film of all time.

Allen managed to get two idols, Paul Newman and Steve McQueen, to head the cast, although McQueen demanded and got top billing. The film had an unexpected consequence for Newman: He formerly went to a dentist on the fourteenth floor of an office building. But after filming this movie, he decided to switch to one whose offices were on the third floor.

Earthquake (1974): Charlton Heston starred in this epic, which showed us what would happen when an earthquake "more devastating than Hiroshima and Nagasaki A-bombs combined" hit Los Angeles. But the real attraction wasn't Heston, it was the gimmick used to simulate the quake: Sensurround. The movie's hypers claimed Sensurround would "thrust each moviegoer into the epicenter of the cataclysmic earthquake," but most customers likened it to those Magic Fingers machines found in motel rooms or to standing on a New York City subway platform as a train approached the station. That's not the response theater owners expected when they shelled out $500 a week for the privilege of using the system. There were other unexpected consequences as well. One gift shop owner in Reno, Nevada,

complained to the cops that every time the theater next door used Sensurround, shelves in his store would fall off the wall and cause the burglar
alarm to go off. The effect was caused, by the way, by a bank of speakers
placed near the screen and at the back of theaters that emitted a low-
pitched rumbling sound whenever tremors were heard on screen.

BIG-BUDGET ESCAPISM

The history of Seventies' cinema neatly divides in two, with the summer '75
release of *Jaws* as the pivotal event. Pre-*Jaws*, Hollywood produced some of
the most creatively subversive films of all time. Filled with gangsters, demons, disasters, and psychopaths, they explored the inner soul of a nation
undergoing a nervous breakdown. After *Jaws*, the huge-grossing escapist
blockbuster dominated the box office as no films ever have. The irony is that
while in the early Seventies, when Hollywood believed it had lost its touch,
it turned out compelling features. Once it found it could make a quarter of
billion dollars with a single release, many of the studios began to concentrate on films that had nothing to say.

Jaws: *taking a bite out of the box office.*

Released just months after defeat in Vietnam, during the deepest recession since the depression, *Jaws*
became a national craze. Hyped to the max by every
major magazine (*Time* devoted more than twenty
pages to the film a week before its release), *Jaws* shattered every box office record and made a young genius
of thirty-year-old Steven Spielberg. Its very basic plot
pitted the good guys—an idealist ichthyologist, a
sherriff and an old salt—against both the forces of
greed and the mysterious monster of the deep. The
John Williams score (dunh, dunh, dunh, dunh, etc.)
set audiences tingling every time with almost Pavlov-
ian regularity.

For all of its hype and success, *Jaws* almost floun-
dered in red ink. Both the ocean and the cranky (and
often larcenous) residents of Martha's Vinyard proved

uncooperative. Spielberg called the ocean "a real pain in the ass." His three mechanical sharks (each "Bruce" costing $150,000) often floundered in the rough Atlantic. Richard Dreyfus whined on every talk show about the island location. (He compared it to the desert island setting of *Papillon*.)Robert Shaw hated the story: "a novel written by committee, a real piece of shit." Nevertheless, *Jaws* created a film and licensing craze that changed the face of movies forever.

JAWS FACT BITES

• *Jaws* was screen-tested in landlocked Dallas to be as far as possible from beachgoers. They were petrified nontheless.

• According to *Boxoffice Showmandiser*, over 2 million *Jaws* tumblers, half-a-million *Jaws* T-shirts, and 200,000 soundtrack albums were sold within three months of the film's release.

• In addition to gimmicky toys, shark's teeth made a brief appearance as a luxury jewelry item in fall '75.

• Peter Benchley wrote the best-selling novel soon after being fired as a Nixon speechwriter. Movie rights sold before the book was even in galleys.

• The television debut of *Jaws* in November '79 grabbed a huge 57 percent share of the market and kept many people from seeing Teddy Kennedy's infamous interview with Roger Mudd in which he could not explain why he was running for President.

STAR WARS

Long ago and far away science fiction was considered box-office death and Hollywood believed that all major money-makers had to based on a best-selling book. George Lucas's high-tech fairy tale *Star Wars* (1977) changed all that by eventually earning a quarter of a billion dollars. Since *Star Wars*, the comic book has replaced the novel as the literary source for most summer blockbusters, and merchandising tie-ins have become essential parts of their profit picture. Plot, dialogue, and characterization have taken a backseat to laser lights and animated mattes as escapist movies have become a cross between the roller coaster and arcade games.

To give Lucas his due, *Star Wars* brilliantly brought out the twelve-year-old boy in everyone as a steady stream of minicliff-hangers and shoot-'em-up resolutions combined with the hokeyest dialogue since the original *Hardy Boy* movies. The plot runs every Hollywood western, sci-fi novel,

18: Nixon announces 8.5 percent devaluation of dollar.

23: Nixon commutes sentence of Teamster boss Jimmy Hoffa for "humanitarian reasons."

26: Protesting Vietnam veterans barricade themselves inside Statue of Liberty.

26-7: Pentagon announces heaviest bombing of N. Vietnam since 1968.

#1 Singles:
Sly and Family Stone—"Family Affair
Melanie—"Brand New Key"

28: *A Clockwork Orange* wins New York Film Critics Award for Best Picture.

42

and fairy tale through a cinematic Cuisinart to achieve a movie that appeals to an unbeatable (and highly repeatable) audience of stoned teenagers, sci-fi freaks, and Hobbit Heads, as well as the Disney family audience. Although set in space, it is not the icy, alienated space of Kubrick's *2001*, Bowie's "Space Oddity," or even Elton John's "Rocket Man." Harking back to the well-worn clichés of Westerns and Buck Rogers B serials, Lucas served up a gee-shucks black versus white, good versus bad struggle with robots and a few cute furry creatures thrown in for local color. Clearly the biggest Seventies' influence was "the force." Call it Zen, call it est, call it faith, "the force" summed up all of comic-book mysticism of the emerging "new age."

For all its success, *Star Wars* was never a sure thing. Only Twentieth Century-Fox and producer Allan Ladd's personal faith in Lucas kept the project alive. Experts were dubious that Seventies' audiences would fall for furry creatures. Market research proved that women would not go to see a film with "war" in the title. What Twentieth Century did like was Lucas' modest salary demands. Figuring the film was marginal at best, they gave him final editing privileges and 40 percent of profits.

Lucas knew something big was up when six thousand production stills were stolen and became big collectors' items two months before release. Two months after release, R2D2, Darth Vader, and C-3PO were already putting their feet in cement at Mann's Chinese theater.

STAR WARS FACTS:

- Lucas on the film's success: "It just has to do with people liking dumb movies."
- Over $2.6 billion sold in *Star Wars* merchandising from 1977–1987.
- During Christmas '77 Kenner had to give away *Star Wars* certificates for merchandise they couldn't supply in time.
- The name R2D2 comes from editor's slang for "Reel 2, Dialog 2."
- Han Solo was originally to be Nick Nolte, not Harrison Ford. Princess Leia was to be Amy Irving, not Carrie Fisher.

As part of the **Star Wars** *craze, Chewbacca got his own Christmas special in 1977.*

JANUARY 1972

3: Columnist Jack Anderson leaks documents showing U.S. "tilt" towards Pakistan in border war with India.

16: U.S. religious leaders call for immediate end to Vietnam war.

25: Nixon offers complete U.S. Vietnam pull-out in exchange for cease-fire and POW exchange.

16: *Chipmunks* creator Ross Bagdasarian dies at 52.

21: Evonne Goolagong named A.P. Female Athelete of the Year.

43

NASHVILLE

After a preview screening of *Nashville* (1975) in Boston, one obviously distressed young woman spied director Robert Altman in the lobby and buttonholed him with a provocative question.

"Are you making films for crazy people?" she protested. Nonplussed, Altman replied with characteristic cheekiness. "Well, you're here, aren't you?"

Take that, infidel.

Later that evening, Altman modified his remarks: ""What would be wrong with making films for crazy people?"

Nothing. But you don't have to be crazy to like *Nashville*. You just needed more concentration to pay attention to Altman's sprawling, twenty-four-character, multiplot movie than to that summer's other smash, *Jaws*, or to most other contemporary Hollywood movies. You also needed an ability to pontificate, since the deeper meanings of *Nashville* fueled hours of conversations, columns, and commentary during those pre-bicentennial months.

Tom Wicker, the *New York Times* columnist, took a break from his usual political punditry to ponder the meaning of *Nashville*, and his musing was a doozy: "A two-and-a-half-hour cascade of minutely detailed vulgarity. greed, deceit, cruelty, barely contained hysteria and the frantic lack of root and grace into which American life has been driven by its own heedless vitality."

It was that and more. It was Altman's assessment of where America was as it headed into its 200th year. He chose the metaphor of Nashville, the capital of country music, to draw the connections between show business and politics. "I think country music stars and politicians are alike in this country," Altman said. "Basically, they're just involved in popularity contests." In the mid-1970s, the post-Kennedy, pre-Reagan era, this was still a fresh, exciting notion to explore.

The plot, if one can say such a conceit exists in the film, concerns the efforts of operatives for an unseen third-party presidential candidate named Hal Phillip Walker to enlist several popular country music stars to perform on his behalf. Throughout the film, a sound truck bearing the slogan of Walker's Replacement Party ("New Roots for America") cruises the streets of Nashville, its PA system blaring the candidate's homilies. Walker is a prescient creation: His folksy reassuring voice anticipated Ronald Reagan's soothing delivery, while his vague populist platitudes would soon be echoed by a Southern politician who was just beginning to receive some publicity in his presidential campaign. One wonders if Jimmy Carter had sat in a darkened theater, soaking up Altman's message.

The heart of the film is its cross-section of characters. Altman's casting was offbeat and brilliant, among them: *Laugh-In*'s Henry Gibson as a tyrannical Roy Acuff-like country music patriarch who sings paeans to the bicentennial; Lily Tomlin as a housewife and mother of two deaf children, who also sings in an all-black choir; and Geraldine Chaplin as a BBC reporter who babbles pseudoprofundities into her ever-present tape recorder.

Playing an important role in the film was the music. Altman encouraged the cast to write their own material, and they created songs that reflected traditional country music concerns such as patriotism, family, divorce, and unrequited love. One song, Keith Carradine's "I'm Easy," would go on to become a top-ten hit and win an Oscar as Best Song. (*Nashville* would be nominated for Best Picture, but would lose out to *One Flew Over the Cuckoo's Nest*). Nonetheless, the film's musical director Richard Baskin, took great pains to make it clear that *Nashville* was no mere "country-and-Western musical."

If there is one scene that hammered home that notion, it is the film's controversial finale. In a scene that recalls too many acts of senseless violence during the previous decade, a Loretta Lynn-like icon named Barbara Jean (Ronee Blakley) is assassinated during a Walker rally at Nashville's Parthenon. Without missing a beat, Barbara Jean's microphone is turned over to a stunned aspiring singer (Barbara Harris), who soothes the crowd with a version of the old spiritual "It Don't Worry Me."

Altman told an interviewer that the scene was deliberately ambiguous: "It can be taken as two sides of a coin, one saying 'look at these people—after a tragedy, they have decided to go on'; and the other saying, 'with something as terrible as this, they've forgotten it already.'"

Audiences didn't forget the scene, and it remains etched in memory a decade and a half later. The real-life assassination of John Lennon in 1980 only enhanced its chilling credibility.

FEBRUARY 1972

15: Attorney General John Mitchell resigns to run Nixon's campaign.

24: Activist Father Daniel Berrigan freed from jail to attend his brother Philip's trial for plotting to kidnap Henry Kissinger.

14: John Lennon and Yoko Ono host *Mike Douglas Show*.

14: *Grease* opens off-Broadway.

16: Wilt Chamberlain scores thirty-thousandth point.

And while the lessons of *Nashville* are still fresh, a movie like this probably wouldn't be made today. Studios wouldn't take the risk, and audiences would find it too challenging. In retrospect, it's clear that *Nashville* is a dinosaur—the last large-scale thinking-person's movie before an ever bottom-line conscious Hollywood chose the blockbuster route.

VIETNAM ON FILM

The last beleaguered helicopters had just escaped Saigon when Hollywood began its desperate and often acrimonious effort to make the ultimate "statement" about Vietnam.

While accepting his Oscar for the anti-war documentary *Hearts and Minds* (1974), producer Burt Schneider offered "greetings from the Provisional Revolutionary Government of Vietnam" on their "liberation" of South Vietnam. For a major Hollywood figure to effectively celebrate the defeat and disgrace of the U.S. military was not entirely radical in Hollywood circa 1975. He received hesitant applause for his remarks. Backstage, presenters Frank Sinatra and Bob Hope were fuming. Old Blue Eyes later seized the stage to read an hasty statement disassociating the Motion Picture Academy from any political stance. He was booed. Sinatra was apparently so steamed by the unpatriotic goings-on that he later had to be dragged bodily back on stage by Sammy Davis, Jr., to complete his musical number with Shirley MacLaine.

Seen with fifteen years of hindsight, *Hearts and Minds* is a remarkable document of American self-loathing. Vietnamese are portrayed exclusively as victims and Americans as innately violent, racist, and insensitive. Scenes of football games are portrayed as warfare rituals leading directly from the huddle to future My Lai massacres. The film's most celebrated moment juxtaposes General Westmoreland's remarks about Orientals' lack of reverence for life with a scene of an hysterical South Vietnamese widow at her husband's funeral. For all of its excesses, *Hearts and Minds* accurately portrayed the open wounds Vietnam had seared in the nation's conscience. It was perhaps the last Vietnam film to focus on the Vietnamese themselves.

By 1978, a film like **Coming Home** could be considered the ultimate

Martin Sheen is up to his neck in trouble in Apocalypse Now.

#1 Singles:
Al Green—"Let's Stay Together"
Nilsson—"Without You"

2: Pioneer 10 begins 620-million-mile trip beyond Jupiter.

7: Senator Muskie win New Hampshire pri mary.

21-29: Nixon makes eight-day trip to China, breaking twenty-three-year freeze in relations.

Selected Gold Record Albums:
Traffic—*Low Spark of High Heel Boys*
Neil Young—*Harvest*
Elton John—*Madman Across the Water*

MARCH 1972

6: New York immigration servic cancels John Lennon's visa.

46

Vietnam war film, although it didn't show any Vietnamese. *Coming Home* is first and foremost about what the war has done to Americans. Sally Hyde (Jane Fonda) is transformed from the straight-laced wife of Captain Bob Hyde (Bruce Dern) to a liberated woman having an affair with a paraplegic Vietnam-Veteran-Against-the-War, Luke Martin (Jon Voight). For all of the film's earnest attempts at emotional intensity, much of Jane Fonda's transformations are stylistic at best as she metamorphizes from a white lipsticked prude to a sexually uninhibited, frizzy-haired lady right before our very eyes. The film anticipates the *Big Chill* phenomenon of the early Eighties by leaning heavily on a period soundtrack. One crazed vet o.d.'s to Hendrix's "Manic Depression"; Fonda reaches her first satisfying orgasm (Bruce Dern was a boring missionary man) with Luke to the strains of "Strawberry Fields." Although showered with praise, including Best Acting Oscars for both Voight and Fonda, *Coming Home* has aged rather poorly. For all of its Vietnam era trappings, it remains, as critic Stanley Kaufman described it, "a wobbly, sentimental triangle drama that could have been about the War of 1812."

Released only months after *Coming Home*, **The Deer Hunter** (1978) blew away audiences and critics alike, and fundamentally changed the way many people looked at and talked about the war. With its beautiful cinematography, and excellent ensemble cast, *The Deer Hunter* remains the most intense and cathartic Vietnam film experience. Its strange, almost mythic, portrayal of working-class Pennsylvania provides a startling backdrop for the violence that would unfold. It proceeds in quirky fits and starts from a seemingly pointless hunting trip to an interminable wedding followed by a sudden plunge into the horrors of Nam.

Critics on the left were shocked by its depiction of the Vietnamese, who seemed as vile as the Americans were romantic. The film's central element, the North Vietnamese insistence that their prisoners play Russian roulette, has no historical basis, but became a powerful metaphor for the war's cruelty and destructive pointlessness. Director Michael Cimino got the idea from the classic '68 photograph of a Vietcong soldier having his brains blown out. Both the film and the metaphor become a little hard to take as Christopher Walken's deranged addiction to the game keeps him in a doomed Saigon. Robert De Niro's Rambo-like rescue attempt during the

Jon Voight is a vet on the rebound in Coming Home.

14: George Wallace wins big in Florida primary.

22: Presidential commission urges decriminalization of marijuana.

22: Senate backs Women's Rights Amendment 84-0.

30: N. Vietnamese forces begin largest offensive since 1968.

13: Clifford Irving admits $750-thousand Howard Hughes biography fraud.

15: *The Godfather* and *The Sorrow and the Pity* released.

27: Elvis Presley records "Burnin' Love."

collapse of South Vietnam takes the film from the sublime to the absurd. The peculiar last scene of the survivors putting down their Rolling Rock beers to sing "God Bless America" moved many, disturbed some, and left many completely puzzled. No one left *The Deer Hunter* unmoved or unchallenged. The American soldiers depicted by De Niro, John Savage, and Walken were neither heroes nor war criminals, but next-door neighbors plunged into hell.

The film's critical and popular success saved Cimino's young career after his autocratic ways had sent the budget to over $15 million. His insistence that the film remain over three hours long got him fired, but the studio relented after he kidnapped the original print.

Many years in the making, ***Apocalypse Now*** (1979) remains the big enchilada of Vietnam films. A script was originally kicked around by directors John Milius and George Lucas before it became a Coppola obsession. More than five years in production, *Apocalypse Now* became the most anticipated film of the Seventies. As early as '75, Coppola was reported in Cuba with Bert Schneider and Candace Bergen scouting locations for the film. In January '76, Steve McQueen was to play the Willard role, but he backed out rather than spend six months in the jungle. By March it was to be Harvey Keitel. Martin Sheen was finally chosen for the part, but he suffered a heart attack in the midst of shooting, and much of the film had to be shot around him. Millions of dollars worth of sets were destroyed in a typhoon, and rumors spread that Coppola was being engulfed in a quagmire costing more than $50 million. When the film was finally cut, Michael Herr (author of *Dispatches*) was called in to write a dubbed voice-over to give it a coherent narration. As late as the Cannes Film Festival, Coppola was still playing with two different endings.

For all of its birth pains, *Apocalypse Now* remains one of the most visually spectacular films of all time. At a time when other "big" movies used special effects for fluffer-nutter escapism, Coppola blew his budget re-creating Vietnam. Vittorio Storaro's photography gave it the unforgettable texture of a stoned mission in a lost war. The

Dennis Hopper made his film comeback as the crazed photojournalist in Apocalypse Now.

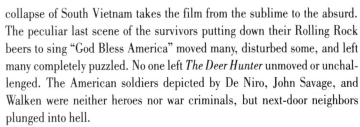

#1 Singles:
Neil Young—"Heart of Gold"
America—"Horse with No Name"

4: McGovern takes Wisconsin primary, Muskie sinks to fourth place.

4: Soviets deny visa to Nobel winner Alexandr Solzhenitsyn.

8: Mafia assassination of Joseph "Crazy Joe" Gallo in New York's Little Italy.

APRIL 1972

Selected Gold Record Albums:
Paul Simon—*Paul Simon*
Yes—*Fragile*
America—*America*
Nilsson—*Nilsson Smilsson*

11: *The Last Whole Earth Catalog* wins National Book Award.

plot, a wobbly bit of Joseph Conrad at best, loses all meaning when Willard finally arrived at Jonestown-on-the-Mekong. But who better to welcome us than Dennis Hopper as the zonked out photojournalist? Marlon Brando's Kurtz is an anticlimax at best. After his *Godfather* part, the master settled down to million-dollar cameos. Maybe he was really practicing for his part as Superman's dad, Jor-El. Indifferently received in 1979, *Apocolypse Now* has remained the most beautiful and enigmatic Vietnam film to date, proving that some things were worth waiting for.

ROCKY

America was desperately in need of heroes in 1976, and one was supplied in the most unlikeliest form: a stumblebum, blue-collar boxer portrayed by a journeyman character actor. But Sylvester Stallone's *Rocky* was able to tap into some communal emotion that had escaped other Hollywood filmmakers. Sensing that American filmgoers were tired of psychos, vigilantes, and neurotics on-screen, and Vietnam, Watergate, and energy shortages off-screen, Stallone gambled they would fall once more for a fairy tale in which a far-from-perfect hero defies the odds.

Fueled by caffeine pills, in eighty-six hours Stallone, then thirty, banged out a script that centered on Rocky Balboa, a South Philly club boxer who works as a loan shark's enforcer. He's going nowhere, gets no respect, and his life seems to be heading down the toilet quickly. But his life suddenly takes on meaning when Apollo Creed, an Ali-like heavyweight champ, cooks up a bicentennial publicity stunt in which he gives Rocky the chance of a lifetime: a shot at the heavyweight title. Rocky trains vigorously for the bout, and although he loses (but he does go the distance), he has won something more important: self-esteem, as well as the love of the shy wallflower (Talia Shire) he has been courting.

Besides its extremely Capra-esque plot (in fact, Frank Capra himself called it "a picture I wish I had made"), *Rocky* defied several other contemporary Hollywood conventions. It had no big-name stars (Stallone insisted on starring, even though the producer had wanted someone like James Caan or Warren Beatty), no random violence, no nudity, no on-screen sex, and a relatively small budget (about $1.1 million).

Sylvester Stallone pumped up for **Rocky II**

Stallone's instincts, of course, were on the mark. The movie was a smash that cut across all audiences. It received ten Oscar nominations and won Best Picture (beating out such films as *Network* and *All the President's Men*). Stallone was nominated for Best Actor (losing to Peter Finch of *Network*) and best screenwriter, a distinction he shared with Orson Welles and Charlie Chaplin. The film made a *People* magazine regular of Stallone and spawned three sequels, the quality of each declining in direct proportion to the expansion of Stallone's ego.

Some nuggets about *Rocky*:

- Stallone's inspiration for *Rocky* was real-life boxer Chuck "The Bayonne Bleeder" Wepner, an aging, little-known heavyweight who was given the chance to fight heavyweight champ Muhammad Ali in March 1975. Wepner lost, but he nearly went the distance and even managed to knock down the champ. Stallone had first thought about writ-

Rocky and Adriene uncorrupted by fame, fortune, and sequels.

#1 Singles:
Roberta Flack—"The First Time Ever I Saw Your Face"

Selected Gold Record Albums:
Allman Brothers—*Eat a Peach*
ELP—*Pictures at an Exhibition*
Cher—*Cher*
Aretha Franklin—*Young, Gifted and Black*

MAY 1972

1: N. Vietnamese troops overrun Provincial capital of Quang Tri.

1: *The Tonight Show* moves permanently to Los Angeles.

2: FBI Director J. Edgar Hoover dies.

4: Wallace captures 70 percent o Tennessee primary vote.

4: *Play it Again, Sam* released.

ing a script about a Philadelphia cabbie who became mayor. When he decided to write a boxing story, the original ending had Rocky throwing the fight.

● Stallone had been kicking around Hollywood for a long time before *Rocky*. His work included roles in porn films, bit parts as muggers in *Bananas* and *The Prisoner of Second Avenue* and supporting roles in *Death Race 2000*, *Farewell My Lovely*, and *Al Capone*. He had auditioned for and lost roles in *Dog Day Afternoon*, *Serpico*, *The Godfather*, and *Stay Hungry* (losing out in the latter to Arnold Schwarzenegger angered Stallone, who had considered himself as the only bodybuilder in Hollywood who had movie aspirations). He had received some notice for his role as a gang member in *The Lords of Flatbush* (1974), but it had not provided the career boost he had expected. At the time he sold the *Rocky* screenplay, Stallone claimed he had only $106 in the bank.

● After speed-writing the *Rocky* script, Stallone showed early traces of his giant ego as he pondered why other writers should take so long: "I'm astounded by people who take eighteen years to write something. That's how long it took that guy to write *Madam Bovary*, and was that ever on the bestseller list? No, it was a lousy book and it made a lousy movie."

● *Rocky* tapped into the new feel-good spirit of America that was evidenced by the bicentennial and Jimmy Carter's election as President. In fact, Stallone drew parallels between the Philadelphia pug and the toothy Georgian: "A peanut farmer has just become President of the United States. that's the greatest inspiration story of all time. He didn't come from wealth. he made his wealth. He went to his mother with dirt on his overalls and said I'm going to be President. He's a common man and that's why he won. I always say, if you lead with your heart, it will carry you much further than your brains will."

● Stallone trained for the big bout scene for five months, even though the fight scenes were elaborately choreographed, by watching every boxing film ever made and by studying tapes of the Rocky Marciano–Ezzard Charles fight. "I had to teach myself to be a flatfooted steam engine who took ten pounds to give one."

● Stallone made *Rocky* a family affair. He cast his father as a boxing timekeeper, his younger brother Frank as a streetcorner singer, and even his bull mastiff, Butkus, got a credited role.

8: Nixon orders mining of N. Vietnamese ports.

15: Wallace shot by Arthur Bremer.

22-29: Nixon becomes first President to visit Moscow; signs landmark nuclear arms treaty as U.S. bombs N. Vietnam ports.

30: Japanese terrorists kill twenty-eight; wound seventy-six at Tel Aviv's Lod airport.

#1 Singles:
Roberta Flack—"The First Time Ever I Saw Your Face"
Chi-lites—"Oh Girl"

13: Dan Blocker (a.k.a Hoss Cartwright) dies.

29: Paul McCartney releases single: "Mary Had a Little Lamb."

Selected Gold Record Albums:
The Partridge Family—*Partridge Family Shopping Bag*
Jethro Tull—*Thick as a Brick*
Stephen Stills—*Manassas*
Rolling Stones—*Exile on Main Street*

ROCK MOVIES
OF THE SEVENTIES

Some time between *A Hard Day's Night* (1964) and MTV, they made rock and roll movies to show stoned kids at midnight screenings or on the late, late show. High rents and VCRs have put an end to most midnight showings. Here's a random sampling of midnight masterpieces and just plain atrocities:

Gimme Shelter (1970): You have to give Mick and the boys some avant-garde credit for putting their concert film in the hands of directors (David and Albert Maysles) who turned a promotional film into a dismally revealing look at rock's ugly underside. Of course, the murder at Altamont has become a metaphor for this very phenomenon. For all of this malaise, the film captures the group during their *Let it Bleed* period, clearly one of their creative peaks.

Let It Be (1970): With the exception of the climactic rooftop rendition of "Get Back," this film is an eighty-one-minute drag. There are some nice, un-Spectorized numbers by the boys, but for the most part it's all too reflective of the last bitter days of the Beatles. Everyone bickers with Paul while Yoko casts an enigmatic pall over the whole affair.

Celebration at Big Sur (1971): This documentary of the '69 Big Sur Folk Festival presents an overload of post–Woodstock hippie naïveté. It boasts the largest collection of fringed vests ever assembled. Performances by Joni Mitchell, Crosby, Stills, Nash and Young, John Sebastian, and Joan Baez make you realize how *white* the whole scene was. Watch out for Stephen Stills's temper tantrum as he beats up a heckler in the crowd.

Concert for Bangladesh (1972): The orange-boxed *Concert for Bangladesh* triple album contains more recorded applause than any other album of all time. It also features ten minutes of sitar tuning by Ravi Shankar. The documentary film turns this not-bad-but-for-a-good-cause concert into an exercise in claustrophobia with its static camera work. At times it looks as if the whole thing's been shot from one angle. Audiences used to MTV's frenetic editing pace will find this unwatchable. Even Woodstock's primitive split screens provides some relief. Best moment: when Ringo forgets the words to his own song, "It Don't Come Easy."

JUNE 1972

6: McGovern sweeps four major primaries; clinches nomination.

17: Four men, including former CIA agents, arrested while breaking into Democratic Headquarters in Washington's Watergate hotel.

3: Rolling Stones begin North American tour.

7: *Grease* opens on Broadway.

9: Columbia record V.P./talent scout signs unknown Bruce Springsteen.

14: "Together Again for McGovern" rally features reunion of Nichols and May, Simon and Garfunkel, Peter, Paul and Mary, and The Mamas and the Papas.

52

The Harder They Come (1973): This gritty low-budget Jamaican classic remains a cult favorite. The knockout soundtrack features a great introduction to reggae with songs by star Jimmy Cliff ("The Harder They Come," "Sitting in Limbo," "You Can Get It If You Really Want"), the Maytalls ("Sweet and Dandy" and "Pressure Drop"), Desmond Deckker ("Shanty Town"), and The Slickers ("Johnny Too Bad"). The film practically created a reggae market in the United States and paved the way for Bob Marley's greater success. The story is an unbeatable combination of rock and roll and revolution with down-and-out Cliff sneaking a chartbuster past the system while becoming the island's most wanted outlaw. Set against the stylized rock and roll of the early Seventies, *The Harder They Come* presents an arresting blend of graphic sex and violence. Choir girls sing themselves into orgasmic frenzy; Cliff urinates after being publicly flogged; and a lovemaking couple are savagely machine-gunned. This movie doesn't kid around. Still, it's the best rock and roll movie of the decade.

Jesus Christ Superstar (1973): Considering the popular and critical success of the stage show and double album, and the highly charged Jesus-freak atmosphere of the early Seventies, this film should have walked on water to box-office success. Instead, this 108-minute bore is interesting only for its tastelessness. Don't miss Herod pelting Jesus with bagels, or those Israeli tanks and jets during Jesus' last roundup. Yvonne Elliman wins the Miss Versatile Award of the Seventies for her role of Mary Magdalene in this turkey and her hit "If I Can't Have You (I Don't Want Nobody Baby)" in *Saturday Night Fever.*

Phantom of the Paradise (1974): This garish, overblown cult favorite gave the diminutive talk show perennial Paul Williams the greatest role of his career as Swan, the Faustian head of Death Records. Though it never caught on quite as well as *Rocky Horror Picture Show,* this film has diehard fans who feel that it remains Brian DePalma's best picture to date. For all the excess of its production and the wild twists and turns of its *Phantom of the Opera*-like plot, this glitter rock nugget lacks any memorable musical numbers to merit classic status.

Lisztomania (1975): Garish, surreal, ridiculous. Of course, it's a Ken Russell movie. Filmed in Excess-orama with the Who's Roger Daltrey as Liszt and the ever pretentious Rick Wakeman at the sound machine, this

George Burns and the Bee Gees in the Stigwood stinker **Sgt. Pepper's Lonely Hearts Club Band.**

Their faces say it all.
The Fab Four go through the motions
in the dismal Let it Be.

film represents the high tide of the early Seventies' music phenomenon of ripping off classical riffs for a largely ignorant and gullible audience of middle-class culture seekers. Back then, "classic rock" meant something else entirely—mooging it up with a little Chopin to enhance your smoke machine and overall showmanship. Only drugs can explain how any audience could endure this piano-man farce, which succeeded only in making Liberace look good.

Rocky Horror Picture Show (1975): Featuring Tim Curry, Susan Sarandon, Barry Bostwick, and Meatloaf, *RHPS* makes you wonder what Susan Sarandon *hasn't* been in. Adapted from the London stage, this kinky classic presents an outrageous spoof on those two most anarchic strains of pop culture: rock and roll and monster movies. Curry's performance as a transvestite Transylvanian continues to overshadow his career, and "Timewarp" remains the most campy and frenetic musical number of all time. What the makers of *RHPS* never had in mind was that this film would touch a transvestite nerve in middle-class mall America. In midnight theaters across the nation, kids continue to ape, mimic, and anticipate every motion, reaction, and line of dialogue.

All This and World War II (1976): Imagine the following performances:

The Bee Gees: "Carry That Weight," "Golden Slumbers," "Sun King"
Bryan Ferry: "She's Leaving Home"
4 Seasons: "We Can Work It Out"
Elton John: "Lucy In the Sky"
Leo Sayer: "Let It Be," "Long and Winding Road"
Peter Gabriel: "Strawberry Fields Forever"

and you begin to get the drift of possibly the most perplexing and tasteless film idea of the decade. Stop waiting for the "next Beatles" to show up. Just have a lot of big stars record covers to Fab Four tunes and have these songs provide background music for news footage of World War II! After all, if you can't stomach Leo Sayer's desecration of "The Long and Winding Road," at least you can concentrate on the Hitler footage. Yet even this was topped in the Beatle exploitation department by the excremental *Sgt. Pepper's Lonely Hearts Club Band.*

Sgt. Pepper's Lonely Hearts Club Band (1978): Aerosmith, the Bee

10-14: Democrats nominate McGovern and Eagleton at Miami convention.

14: Former Treasury Secretary John Connally organizes Democrats for Nixon.

25: V.P. candidate Engleton admits history of shock treatment.

28: Jane Fonda returns from trip to Hanoi. "Vietnamese are not my enemy."

29: McGovern backs Eagleton "1,000 percent."

31: McGovern announces Ec ton's withdrawal.

8-9: Democratic Party holds telethon on ABC to cut Party debt.

13: Owners of L.A. Rams and Baltimore Colts swap teams.

30: *Deliverance* released.

Gees, Earth, Wind & Fire, Billy Preston, Alice Cooper, and Peter Frampton all appear in this astoundingly stupid morality play about the good guys of Heartland battling the forces of evil (Aerosmith mostly). Coming on the heels of *Saturday Night Fever*'s unprecedented success, this Robert Stigwood/Bee Gees collaboration sank like a stone. The film packaged every awful cliché from the history of rock-and-roll movies, including musical numbers totally unsuited to the Beatles' music and a cartoonlike plot that relied on George Burns to provide the sophisticated wit. Its dismal failure sent both Stigwood and the Bee Gees into well-deserved declines.

Renaldo and Clara (1979): Tops many people's list as the all-time most unendurable film of the seventies. Bob Dylan's version of *The Sorrow and The Pity* weighs in at close to four hours of obscure self-absorption and self-promotion. Not even Dylan's fans of several decades could sit through this nonsense in which Dylan and Joan Baez sometimes play themselves and sometimes appear as white-face clowns. Look out for appearance by pre-hunk, pre-genius Sam Sheperd.

The Last Waltz (1978): Martin Scorsese made a thinking man's rock documentary with great cinematography, editing, and series of Q & A sessions with The Band that were so impressive (and occasionally pretentious) that they were themselves brilliantly parodied in Rob Reiner's *Spinal Tap* (1984) and SCTV's *The Last Polka* (1984). Great performances by a veritable who's who of folk, rock, blues, and honky tonk (Bob Dylan, The Band, Dr. John, Eric Clapton, Van Morrison, Muddy Waters, Ringo Starr, and Neil Young) make this film an elegy for the Sixties sound. Neil Diamond's surprising appearance is a rude reminder of his roots and how appallingly far he has strayed.

Thank God It's Friday (1978): This film is the best time capsule of the disco inferno era. Unlike *Saturday Night Fever*, this is a pure disco experience unencumbered by a plot of any consequence. It's always good to see Lionel Richie sporting a freak flag Afro as he and the Commodores make a cameo appearance. Donna Summer sings "Last Dance," a pre-AIDs anthem to unabashed horniness that almost makes you nostalgic for Qiana.

Rock 'n' Roll High School (1979): Witless high school rebellion film climaxes with the performance of the Ramones. It's worth watching only for the great loboto-rock music of the boys from Queens at their peak.

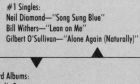

#1 Singles:
Neil Diamond—"Song Sung Blue"
Bill Withers—"Lean on Me"
Gilbert O'Sullivan—"Alone Again (Naturally)"

AUGUST 1972

2: Egypt and Libya announce "merger."

3: Senate ratifies SALT treaty with Soviets.

4: Wallace assailant Bremer sentenced to sixty-three years.

Selected Gold Record Albums:
Alice Cooper—*School's Out*
Eric Clapton—*History of Eric Clapton*
Cheech and Chong—*Cheech and Chong*

2: Former Association member Brian Cole dies of heroin overdose.

4: *Superfly* released.

JOHN TRAVOLTA

The other Italian Stallion of the Seventies was a tenth-grade dropout son of an Englewood, New Jersey, drama coach. John Travolta, he of the most dazzling set of baby blues since Paul Newman, had already become a teen and preteen idol because of his television role as lovable hood Vinnie Barbarino, one of the *Welcome Back, Kotter* sweathogs. But it was *Saturday Night Fever* (1977) that turned him into a superstar.

"At once mean-looking and pretty, he conveys the kind of threatening sexuality that floors an audience," wrote *Time* magazine's Frank Rich of Travolta's performance in *Saturday Night Fever*. And indeed, an otherwise melodramatic, cliché-ridden film was supercharged by the erotic presence of Travolta as a working-class stiff from Bay Ridge, Brooklyn, whose world only comes alive on Saturday night at the local disco.

Travolta's transition from TV star to screen idol began in late 1976 when he signed a $1 million three-film contract with producer Robert Stigwood, the Australian impresario responsible for the Bee Gees, Peter Frampton, and the film version of *Sgt. Pepper's Lonely Hearts Band*.

Saturday Night Fever, based on a *New York* magazine article about blue-collar kids whose attitudes had more in common with the 1950s than the 1960s, became the first project and one that was tailored for Travolta. "Tony is almost like what Vinnie Barbarino would be like if he grew up," explained Travolta. "It's a next step, definitely an expansion of that character." In fact, one of the reasons Stigwood fired original director John Avildsen (*Rocky*) was because of differences over how Travolta should play Tony. (Avildsen was replaced by John Badham, who hewed closer to the Tony-as-latter-day-Vinnie line).

For the role of "head face" Tony Manero, Travolta underwent a rigorous training routine that included two hours daily of running and physical conditioning with Jimmy Gambino, the trainer Sylvester Stallone had used for the fight scene in *Rocky*, and three hours daily of dancing under the tutelage of Denny Terrio, the future host of *Dance Fever*. After five months, Travolta had lost twenty pounds and told a reporter he "had a whole new body."

He also hung out at several Brooklyn discos ("But one time they recognized me, so I ended up being a judge at a dance contest"). He studied the

8: R. Sargent Shriver becomes Democrat V.P. candidate.

11: Last U.S. ground combat unit withdrawn from Vietnam.

21-23: Nixon and Agnew renominated at Miami Republican convention.

#1 Singles:
Looking Glass—"Brandy (You're a Fine Girl)"

10: Swedish police arrest Paul and Linda McCartney for pot possession.

11: City of San Antonio declares "Cheech and Chong Day."

28: David Bowie and The Spiders from Mars play New York's Carnegie Hall.

Selected Gold Record Albums:
Neil Diamond—*Moods*
Andy Williams—*Love Theme from The Godfath*

real-life model, a delivery boy named Eugene "Tony" Robinson (who would later sue Stigwood and Travolta for not getting his fair share). And he was dressed in a size-38 long, white three-piece suit purchased at Brooklyn's very own the Leading Man.

Fueled by a calculated marketing campaign, *Saturday Night Fever* became a box-office smash, grossing more than $21 million in eighteen days, and eventually grossing more than $100 million. Most critics didn't like the movie's hackneyed plot, some of which seemed lifted from *West Side Story* and *Rebel Without a Cause*, but they raved over Travolta.

Said *Newsweek*'s David Ansen: "In a less engaging actor's hands, Tony could have been insufferably arrogant and dense. But Travolta's big slab of a face is surprisingly expressive, revealing a little boy's embarrassment and hurt as well as a stud's posturing. Travolta understands Tony with his whole body—needless to say, he can dance up a storm—and you can't keep your eyes off him. It's a fresh, funny, downright friendly performance." He received an Academy Award nomination and also received the Best Actor of the Year award from the National Film Board.

By the time *Fever* was released, Travolta had completed filming *Grease*, the movie version of the 1950s musical that was still running strong on Broadway (in 1972, as an eighteen-year-old, Travolta appeared in the roadshow version of the play). This second of the Stigwood deal films became the hot movie of 1978, and as yet another warmhearted, lunkish hood, this one named Danny Zuko, Travolta again won critics' hearts, though not as favorably as his portrayal of Tony Manero.

And then Travolta's career plateaued. The third film, *Moment by Moment*, in which he played a man in love with an older woman (played by Lily Tomlin) was a certified bomb. ("The number of people who like it could convene in a Pinto," sniffed one critic). His career in the Eighties—including a sequel to *Fever* called *Staying Alive*—has been uneven, and as of this writing, he's still looking for the right script that will help him regain the glory of more than a decade ago.

John Travolta is the ultimate working-class hero in Saturday Night Fever.

SEPTEMBER 1972

1: American Bobby Fischer wins chess world championship.

4: Mark Spitz wins record seven Olympic gold medals.

5-6: At Munich games, eight Palestinian terrorists kill two Israeli atheletes and kidnap nine others. Five terrorists, all hostages and one German policeman die in shoot-out.

8: McGovern charges corruption in Nixon's Soviet wheat deal.

10: Soviets top Olympics with ninety-nine medals to United States's ninety-four.

ANIMAL HOUSE

Bluto cheers up Flounder (Stephen Furst) in a peerless moment of screen empathy.

As noted earlier, at the start of the Seventies, Hollywood mistakenly thought it could make a bundle with movies about revolutionary college students. But it wouldn't be until the decade was nearly over that Hollywood finally would have its successful campus movie about revolting students. (We're using the word here in its adjectival form, not its verbal.) Because by 1978, contemporary collegians were about as radical as members of the Kiwanis Club. So for campus kicks, Hollywood had to look back some sixteen years earlier when life was more innocent: when students could get drunk, dance lasciviously wearing bedsheets, and have food fights. This set-in-'62 epic, *National Lampoon's Animal House*, wouldn't contain the bittersweet recollections of *American Graffiti*. It would be more like "going down memory lane with a blowtorch," according to its twenty-seven-year-old director John Landis.

The film's title was not misleading. Its heroes, the boys of the Delta House at Faber College, were gross fuckoffs who were despised by nearly everyone on campus and in the neighboring town. If the Deltas weren't being hassled by the clean-cut Omegas, then oily Dean Wormer was putting them on "double secret probation" and threatening to expel them and notify their draft boards. Their collective grade-point average was the lowest in Faber College history.

Rarely are box-office smashes made of such heroic figures. But to the surprise of nearly everyone connected with the film, *Animal House* began packing in the audiences in the summer of '78, and they continued to file in through the fall. What the audiences saw went beyond escapism. They saw a wildly, obscenely funny film, whose comedic anarchy has never been duplicated by its legion of imitators. Much of its success was due to its fortunate confluence of some of the most creative forces that shaped Seventies' humor. Co-writers Harold Ramis, *National Lampoon* founder Doug Kenney, and *Lampoon* contributor Chris Miller fused the take-no-prisoners approach of that humor magazine with the brilliant comic timing of *Saturday Night Live*'s John Belushi. Chevy Chase was originally considered to be the big name for the cast, but when he declined, Landis and the writers looked instead to the beefy Belushi, who was eager to break out beyond *SNL*. He

11: Democratic party sues Nixon reelection committee over Watergate break-in.

16: TV premiere of *Bridget Loves Bernie*.

#1 Singles:
Three Dog Night—"Black and White"
Mac Davis—"Baby Don't Get Hooked on Me"

Selected Gold Record Albums:
Curtis Mayfield—*Superfly*
Leon Russell—*Carney*
Humble Pie—*Smokin'*

OCTOBER 1972

58

was cast as Bluto Blutarsky, the mangiest animal of them all, a food-fight-starting, "Louie-Louie"-singing Neanderthal. In a stroke of genius, Landis opted to delete from the script most of Bluto's dialogue and forced Belushi to rely on his amazingly expressive face. Landis's hunch was justified by those wonderful scenes in which Bluto crushes a beer can against his forehead or when he watches a group of coeds undressing as he totters on a ladder propped up against their second-story dorm window. Belushi was so impressive that *Time* magazine's critic Frank Rich called him "the funniest fat comic since Jackie Gleason."

The movie made a superstar out of Belushi, who died in 1982, before an *Animal House* sequel could be contemplated. Most of the other cast members—Tim Matheson, Stephen Furst, Bruce McGill, Peter Riegert—have gone on to passable Hollywood careers.

The boys of Delta House in informal repose.

: *Washington Post* reports Watergate ·eak-in part of bigger GOP conspiracy.

15: Fellini's *Roma* released.

12: Study finds 45 percent of all New York City high-school students use "some psychoactive drug."

16: Creedence Clearwater Revival breaks up.

24: Standard Oil changes name to Exxon.

26: Henry Kissinger declares "peace is at hand" in Vietnam.

30: Elton John gives command performance for Queen Elizabeth.

59

Clash of the titans: Neidermeyer (Mark Metcalf) vs. Blutarsky (John Belushi).

In addition to its surprise box-office success, *Animal House* had some unexpected fallout:

● It created a national mania for toga parties. As one Brooklyn College student noted, they served as the perfect escape valve for Carter-era collegians. "People don't want to think," this student observed. "They want to do what feels good." On one weekend in October 1978, *Newsweek* reported more than one hundred campuses were planning to have these gatherings where students donned bedsheets and laurel wreaths and drank themselves blind. At the University of Wisconsin, 10,000 students attended one such

all-night bash in which they attempted to enter the *Guinness Book of World Records* by creating the world's largest mixed drink—a vat filled with every liquid each partier brought along.

Other college students imitated another memorable scene from the movie. Students at Ohio State designed a "deathmobile," like the one that disrupted the homecoming parade during the movie's climactic scene. Meanwhile, University of Colorado students organized a John Belushi look-alike contest.

● Robert Ketter, president of SUNY-Buffalo, said that 1,483 incidents of damage were reported at the school in 1979, compared to 948 the previous year. "I hate to say this," the educator moaned, "but in every city where *Animal House* was shown, instances of vandalism grew by leaps and bounds."

● Principal John Hagman of Sibley High School in West St. Paul, Minnesota, became alarmed about the increase in food fights in his institution's cafeteria. "A food fight is like a hand grenade being thrown into the midst of 500 people. The food is thrown. It explodes. Then the kids are gone and the whole place is a mess." There's no record of whether the offending students were placed on double secret probation.

● The ultimate tribute to *Animal House*'s popularity, however, was the fact that three imitation sitcoms were created in 1979. The most faithful was ABC's *Delta House*, which featured Josh Mostel (son of Zero) as Blotto Blutarsky, Bluto's younger brother, as well as several of the movie's stars, including Stephen "Flounder" Furst, Bruce "D-Day" McGill, James "Hoover" Widdoes and John "Dean Wormer" Vernon. But without the film's sex and raunch, the show failed. The other two series, *Co-ed Fever* (which was so bad it aired only once) and *Brothers and Sisters* (which starred Jack Lemmon's son and Bing Crosby's daughter) were eminently forgettable.

Delta House: *TV's lame* Animal House *rip-off.*

WOODY GETS SERIOUS

Coming on the heels of his early slapstick period, which culminated with the hilarious *Sleeper* (1973), Woody Allen entered the late Seventies with movies where he took himself and his audiences much more seriously. While his early films joined the physical comedy of Buster Keaton and

14: Dow Jones tops 1,000 mark for first time.

16: Pepsico announces soda deal with Soviets.

#1 Singles:
Johnny Nash—"I Can See Clearly Now"

1: Allman Brothers' Berry Oakley dies in motercycle accident.

24: TV premiere of Don Kirshner's *In Concert.*

Selected Gold Record Albums:
The Band—*Rock of Ages*
Deep Purple—*Machine Head*
Alice Cooper—*Love It to Death*
Bread—*Guitar Man*

61

Charlie Chaplin with his own idiosyncratic standup schtick, in *Love and Death* (1975) Woody insisted on running through Lit 101 to make jokes about Tolstoy, Dostoyevski, and even T. S. Eliot. This almost undergraduate tendency to show off is a trait that continues to plague much of his work.

Annie Hall (1977) returned Allen to his classic form. A perfect movie that gets better with time, *Annie* is Woody Allen at a peak. It is the last film in which he appears as a comedian and the last role that allows him to be funny at all times. With a style that owes more to the whimsy of Fellini than to the ponderous Bergman, *Annie Hall* allows Allen to drag Marshall McLuhan on-screen to put down a pretentious filmgoer and shows Alvy's six-year-old grade-school compatriots giving us an update on their dismal lives.

Annie Hall also established what would become the predictable Woody Allen plot—neurotic boy meets wonderful girl; boy "educates" girl; boy gets dumped by newly sophisticated girl.

As much as *Annie Hall* owes to Allen, it is unquestionably Diane Keaton's movie. In a decade when women were asking where all the great roles had gone, Annie Hall burst on the scene like a dizzy, pot-smoking Katharine Hepburn. Neither a flower child nor a feminist, vulnerable but not weak, Annie's endearing shyness was perfectly accompanied by her huge baggy pants, men's vests, oversized shirts and signature bowler and glasses—a style that became the most copied look of the year. In retrospect, it is amazing that this small neurotic comedy with its modest gross became the most talked about movie during the *Star Wars* summer of '77.

Interiors, Woody's 1978 stab at Bergman-esque misery among the rich, famous and emotionally constipated is a kind of *Cries and Whispers* goes to the Hamptons that bears watching only for its camp value. This tale includes a poet, a near suicide, an emotionally illiterate interior decorator, and a frantic scene before an altar that earned this movie a place high on John Waters's list of all-time favorites.

If nobody appreciated *Interiors*, *Manhattan* (1978), Woody's black-and-white valentine to the fabled borough, was met with a chorus of fawning praise. Hailed as a masterpiece by just about everyone, *Manhattan* has hardly lived up to its early billings. In re-creating a talky clique of earnestly intellectual New Yorkers, Woody presents a pack of vain, shallow, and emotionally immature adults who sit around arguing about whether Vivaldi is

Annie Hall: *Love means always having to call your shrink.*

DECEMBER 1972

7: Launch of last moon mission, Apollo 17.

11: George Bush named Republican Party Chairman.

11: James Brown arrested for disorderly conduct in Knoxville, TN.

12: *Posiedon Adventure* released.

18: Citing stalled peace talks, Nixon launches massive B-52 raids on Hanoi and Haiphong; twenty-seven planes lost (including fifteen B-52s).

21: *Cries and Whispers* released.

overrated when they're not trying to sleep with their best friend's last mistress. Into this Elaine's-based fray comes fresh-faced Tracy (Mariel Hemingway), a seventeen-year-old Dalton (where else?) student whom Isaac (Woody Allen) seduces with his urbane wit and bedtime lectures on De Sica films. All of the coupling and decoupling in *Manhattan* remain secondary to the lush black-and-white cinematography by Gordon Willis and the rousing Gershwin score. The entire film suffers from a case of New York infatuation. One wit called the film "I Love New York (But I hate myself)." Yet Woody's New York includes only the toniest spots on Manhattan's Upper East Side (Dalton's, Sutton Place, Elaine's). One of the film's climactic scenes reveals Woody at his most middlebrow and and didactic as he recites a list of what makes life worth living. Although Tracy (and her cheekbones) rate high on this list, it also includes Mozart's fortieth as well as most of Western culture's greatest hits. If *Annie Hall* is Woody at his peak, *Manhattan* is the beginning of the decadelong trend of Woody as neo-conservative, cranky fart who never misses a chance to put down rock and roll while praising Bobby Short to the skies. Bring back *Bananas*.

Annie (Diane Keaton) and Alvie (Woody Allen) pursue a meaningful dialogue in Annie Hall.

Politics and Culture in the Seventies

any still consider the Seventies a time when "nothing happened," a cooling-off period after the seething Sixties. Yet consider the following.

A bitter war ended in stalemate and delayed defeat; a series of scandals climaxed in the President's resignation and disgrace; an unelected President was defeated by a virtual unknown from Baptist Georgia; the country was ravaged by inflation, recession, and the energy crisis; fundamental changes occurred in the attitudes and living patterns of millions of Americans as women took to the workplace, young people abandoned religion, took drugs, and postponed marriage, children, and careers in unprecedented numbers. The fact is, so much dramatic change occurred in the Seventies that we are only now able to digest the results.

More than sweeping political and demographic changes, the Seventies were a time of bizarre and uncanny individuals. Originals like Spiro Agnew, Martha Mitchell, Billy Carter, Earl Butz, Elizabeth Ray, Margaret Trudeau, Jerry Brown, and Sun Myung Moon paraded across the political horizon. Like much of Seventies' fashion design, most of its main political characters were extreme exaggerations of the wants and needs of the people at a very particular "point in time." While many of the most outlandish characters of the decade are as outmoded as leisure suits, most of the political and social concerns, including consumerism, energy conservation, women's rights, economic opportunities, and a concern for the environment, have moved to the forefront of national concern, pushing many of the pre-Seventies concerns (East versus West, unions versus management, and the dominaton of political parties) out of the spotlight. While some pine for the days of "revolution" during the Sixties, many are just starting to realize that

JANUARY 1973

11: B-52 pilot refuses mission over N. Vietnam.

11: Watergate burglar E. Howard Hunt, Jr., pleads guilty.

18: Juan Corona found guilty of killing twenty-five migrant farm workers.

22: Supreme Court's *Roe* vs. *Wade* decision legalizes abortion.

23: Former President Lyndon Johnson dies.

11: Baseball's American League announces designated hitter "experiment."

20: Tom Hayden marries Jane Fonda.

22: George Foreman over Joe Frazier in TKO.

64

it was the Seventies that revolutionized everyday life.

BACK TO NATURE

Although environmental concern was not entirely new to the Seventies, it got a huge public relations boost on "Earth Day," April 22, 1970. Based on a casual suggestion by Senator Gaylord Nelson, Earth Day spontaneously blossomed into a nationwide Woodstock of recycling, trash collection, and consciousness raising at over 1,500 college campuses and 10,000 high schools. The industrious, well-behaved students were a remarkable contrast from the angry rabble of many antiwar protests. This led many observers to believe that "the kids had cooled it." Such prophesies proved premature when campuses (including Kent State) exploded two weeks later with Nixon's announcement of the Cambodian "incursion."

On Earth Day, the greatest violence was committed against cars. Untold dozens of gas burners were ceremonially buried across the nation.

Earth Day's unexpectedly wide following resulted in largely bipartisan support for environmental legislation, including the Clean Air Act and the creation of the Environmental Protection Agency. The government's quick response surprised many and made "ecology" one of the most important and enduring issues of the decade.

Pollution and its discontents quickly worked its way into the popular culture, and effectively displaced both Vietnam and Black Power as the focus of most "protest" songs. Joni Mitchell's "Big Yellow Taxi," Spirit's "Nature's Way," and Marvin Gaye's "Mercy, Mercy Me (The Ecology)" all rose to the top of the charts on the ecological tidal wave.

The national obsession with nature soon found its way into many people's homes, as an entire generation raised on Sugar Pops seemed to switch to "health foods," such as tofu, whole grain breads, sprouts, lentils, beans, and more beans. Processed sugar, white flour, and chemical preservatives of every stripe became public enemies to many enlightened eaters, as the fine line between processed foods and poison became harder to discern. Entirely new concerns were soon articulated by a new urgent vocabulary. Such words as biodegradable, nitrogen cycle, composting, and enzymes became everyday buzzwords for millions who used to think of environmental

23: U.S. and N. Vietnam announce Vietnam cease-fire.

27: Selective service draft ends.

30: The group Kiss debuts in Queens, N.Y., club.

#1 Singles:
Carly Simon—"You're So Vain"
Stevie Wonder—"Superstition"

Selected Gold Record Albums:
Osmonds—*Crazy Horses*
Donna Fargo—*Happiest Girl in the Whole USA*
Rolling Stones—*More Hot Rocks*

FEBRUARY 1973

8: Senator Sam Ervin named to Senate Watergate panel.

2: NBC's *The Midnight Special* debuts hosted by Helen Reddy.

regulation as a fancy name for air-conditioning.

During the Seventies, concern about the environment replaced the cold war fear of nuclear war as the chief cause of public paranoia. As in many Seventies' disaster and conspiracy movies, the real enemy was from within. You were far more likely to be poisoned by Twinkies or an evil corporation than be nuked by the Soviets while Nixon and Brezhnev were partying with Henry Kissinger and Jill St. John. Eating horribly dry "natural" peanut butter and lentil bread provided millions with a superior, assured feeling that they were not being slowly murdered by "the system."

THE RISE AND FALL
OF SPIRO T.

Frank Sinatra and Spiro Agnew do a reactionary tango.

Spiro T. Agnew remains one of the last unreconstructed villains of the Seventies. Even as most Watergate figures collect their royalties, or appear at reunions, die, or continue being born again, "Ted" Agnew remains completely invisible.

Yet for a brief slimy moment, Agnew was the darling spokesman for President Richard Nixon's silent majority. His alliterative attacks on the media's malaise mongers earned him the affection and regard of the regular Joes of the early Seventies who cringed at the thought of the "Acid, Abortion, and Amnesty" crowd taking over the country.

He golfed with Frank Sinatra and joked with Bob Hope. He was tough on blacks, crooks, and liberals, and the public loved him. Agnew represented a critical part of Nixon's successful strategy to build a permanent Republican majority. As a Greek (Orthodox turned Episcopalian), suburbanite, liberal Democrat turned law-and-order politician, Agnew spoke the language of the disaffected ethnics who fled both the cities and the Democratic party. Unlike

12: "Operation Homecoming" brings home first of 142 American POWs.

12: U.S. annouces 10 percent dollar devaluation.

21: Laotian government reaches cease-fire with Communist rebels.

22: China and U.S. move toward normal relations; open liaison offices.

27: Two to three hundred radical American Indians seize trading post at Wounded Knee, S.D.; take eleven hostages.

8: Woodstock host Max Yasgur dies in Florida.

15: Tennessee court indicts *Deep Throat* producers.

66

TV's *Kojak*, Spiro never flaunted his Greekness; he buried it in a John Wayne toughness that announced his acceptance by WASP and Republican alike.

Agnew's tough-guy image, along with his penchant for beaning bystanders with golf balls, earned him a place as an instant reactionary folk hero. Agnew watches, toys, and T-shirts appeared spontaneously and were the first fad of the Seventies. Spurning a licensing gold mine, Agnew refused to seek royalties for his image and instead requested that the funds go to aid the families of American POWs.

Agnew's image as both reactionary Neanderthal and clubby clown prince made many liberals cringe when they considered the possibility of Nixon's assassination. He was often considered Nixon's insurance policy against such an event. It is no small coincidence that calls for Nixon's impeachment did not gather strong momentum until after Spiro's removal in October 1973.

Set against the conspiratorial quagmire of Watergate, Agnew's demise seemed a simple case of old-fashioned greed. Apparently the champion of the Silent Majority had been accepting kickbacks and bribes for over ten years. Bag men who had paid him off as a local politico and Maryland governor, continued to deliver the cash right to the Vice President's office. The case broke open in August of '73, and by October 10 Spiro was history. Except for two forgettable novels, *Go Quietly or Else....* and *The Canfield Decision*, and a brief stint as a lobbyist for Arab causes, Agnew remains in complete obscurity, untouched by Nixon's resurrection to statesman status, unreborn and unrepentant.

"I AM WOMAN"

Without a doubt, the full integration of women into the American workplace remains the most significant social movement of the Seventies. The movement acheived so many of its goals so rapidly that it is almost impossible to discuss them without stating the obvious. At the same time, so many of these changes—reproductive rights, equal pay for equal work, and the asumption that it is a woman's option to choose career over child rearing—have really yet to be digested by society and are still powerful forces of so-

#1 Singles:
Elton John—"Crocodile Rock"
Roberta Flack—"Killing Me
Softly with His Song"

MARCH 1973

1: N.Y. judge rules *Deep Throat* "irredeemably obscene."

4: Pink Floyd begins *Dark Side of the Moon* concert tour.

4: Chris Evert wins first professional tennis match.

Selected Gold Record Albums:
Elton John—*Don't Shoot Me I'm Only the Piano Player*
The Stylistics—*The Stylistics*
Elvis Presley—*Aloha from Hawaii Via Satellite*

*Gloria Steinem and Pat Carbine
of* Ms. Magazine, *the house organ
of the women's movement.*

cial dissent and disruption.

It is impossible to imagine that in 1970 only a tiny percentage of doctors, lawyers, and business leaders were women. Of course, by 1970 an entire generation raised on television and mass education was coming of age with the idea that they were somehow different from their parents and their *Leave it to Beaver* life-styles.

By 1970 the so-called sexual revolution and the women's movement found common ground in calling for liberalized abortion laws in both the United States and Europe. In 1970 New York and Hawaii became the *only* states to allow abortion on demand. Yet it was becoming clear to politicians and the media that the women's movement was replacing the Black Power and antiwar movements as the force with the most popular momentum. For all of its leftish trappings (including the word liberation, which sounded a trifle too much like the Communists' "liberation" movements in Vietnam and elsewhere), the women's movement cut across party lines. The Equal Rights Amendment (ERA) passed both the House and Senate with a minimum of delay in 1970, and by 1973, the Supreme Court's *Roe* vs. *Wade* decision had struck down all restrictions on abortion. Changes sought for more than half a century had taken place in a few years.

Yet for many, both feminists and their adversaries, these changes had been too much too soon. In a prescient essay in *Newsweek* just weeks after *Roe* vs. *Wade*, Midge Decter argued that the rhetoric of "liberation" had been embraced all too easily by the press and politicians and that this was a clear sign that it was not being taken seriously. "Whatever view one takes of the movement's aims, they are radical aims, to alter no less than work, marriage and parenthood. . . . The ease with which [institutions have co-opted the movement] bespeaks their need not to know what the movement is about."

In many ways, the rapid-fire sucesses of the movement robbed it of much of its grass-roots support and at the same time galvanized its opposition. By

26: *New York Times* reports that White House Aides John Dean and Jeb Stuart Magruder had previous knowledge of break-in.

28: U.S. resumes bombing in Cambodia.

29: Last U.S. combat troops leave Vietnam.

29: In anti-inflation move, Nixon imposes limits on meat prices.

#1 Singles:
O'Jays—"Love Train"

21: *Godspell* opens in N.Y.

29: Dr. Hook appears "On the Cover of the Rolling Stone."

Selected Gold Record Albums:
Helen Reddy—*I Am Woman*
Alice Cooper—*Billion Dollar Babies*

68

granting abortion rights by federal fiat, *Roe* vs. *Wade* stopped statewide political organizing in its tracks while providing a rallying cry for conservatives. This trend became abundantly clear during the battle for ERA ratification. The amendment was swiftly ratified by thirty-three states between 1972 and 1975, only to sputter and die in the second half of the decade. It stalled, in spite of spirited support by first ladies Betty Ford and Rosalyn Carter, because well-organized groups of conservatives convinced enough people that the ERA was the mastermind of radical feminists out to ruin the family as the backbone of America. And despite press reports to the contrary, such oppositon was not only in the Bible belt.

When the ERA was placed on the ballot for ratification in New Jersey and New York, it was defeated by large margins. Arch conservative Phyllis Schlafly's pro-family campaign had distorted the amendment with a fear campaign that told women that husbands would no longer have to support them, that all toilets would become unisex, that women would be drafted, and so on. Yet for all of Schlafly's organizing, the "movement" did not help itself. By the mid-seventies, the very spokeswomen who had sparked the movement, Gloria Steinem, Kate Millet, and Betty Friedan, seemed shrill and elitist to some, and downright cliché to many others. Stienem's *Ms. Magazine*, which had a spectacular '72 debut, settled into a stodgy orthodoxy by the end of the decade. At the same time, the editorial aspirations of *Ms.*—to tell women "not how to make jelly, but to seize control of their lives"—had been widely disseminated into the general culture.

The language and life-styles of women's liberation were quickly adopted by the popular media. Many could argue that television did more than reflect the women's movement, it created a series of women's role models that made a return to the traditional passive wife role unthinkable. *The Mary Tyler Moore Show* and *Maude* made a strong and entertaining case for freethinking women while comedies like *All in the Family* and *Mary Hartman, Mary Hartman* heaped derision and pity on women consigned to traditional housewifely duties.

The 1972 top-forty hit "I Am Woman" quickly became an anthem for many and an embarrassment for others. Its pop sentimentality proved how quickly the movement had become a slogan. At the same time Helen Reddy's spunky delivery translated a certain militantcy to an audience of

Our Bodies, Ourselves: *an owner's manual for the liberated female.*

APRIL 1973

3: Nixon promises S. Vietnam's President Thieu U.S. intervention if cease-fire is violated.

5: Senate cancels any previously arranged reparation payments to N. Vietnam.

8-11: B-52's continue to pound Cambodian capital.

6: Smothers Brothers win $776G suit against CBS.

8: Pablo Picasso dies.

8: Neil Young's film *Journey Through the Past* premieres.

69

women who had previously been put off by the more austere spokeswomen. Reddy wrote the song and performed it as she was pregnant (giving a whole new meaning to "I was just an embryo with a long, long way to go"), a fact that gave the movement a pro-family look.

Perhaps the most celebrated and banal pop-feminist event was the Billy Jean King–Bobby Riggs match. Riggs, an aging tennis star, played the male chauvinist pig role to the hilt and provided an easy target for King, who was at the top of her game. Nevertheless, the mere fact that a woman could beat a man, and an obnoxious one at that, brought the movement to a level that could be discussed on the *Tonight Show* and around every supper table in America.

Women's Movement Timeline

1970

-Hawaii and New York are the first states to enact liberalized abortion laws.
-The U.S. Senate holds the first ERA hearings since 1956.
-Sit-in at *Ladies Home Journal* results in a supplement to the August 1970 issue.
-*Time* and *Newsweek* have cover stories on the Women's Movement.
-New York City ends public accommodations discrimination and liberates Biltmore Hotel men's bar.

1971

-First female Senate pages.
-New York City Board of Education allows boys and girls to compete in noncontact sports.
-Billy Jean King becomes the first female athlete to earn more than $100,000 in a single year.
-Jill Johnston breaks up a symposium by embracing her female lover on stage.

1972

-*Ms. Magazine* publishes its premier issue.
-*Ms.* publishes a letter by fifty-three prominent women who have had an abortion; readers respond with thousands of personal testimonies.
-Actress Marlo Thomas publishes *Free to Be You and Me,* nonracist, nonsexist, multinational children's literature.

17: Nixon agrees to allow aides to testify before Watergate committee.

30: Nixon announces resignations of H.R. Haldeman, John D. Ehrlichman, and John W. Dean.

#1 Singles:
Vicki Lawrence—"The Night the Lights Went Out in Georgia"
Tony Orlando and Dawn—"Tie a Yellow Ribbon Round the Old Oak Tree"

Selected Gold Record Albums:
Led Zeppelin—*Houses of the Holy*
Bread—*Best of Bread*
Bette Midler—*The Divine Miss M*
Pink Floyd—*The Dark Side of the Moon*

-Black Congresswoman Shirley Chisholm runs for President.

1973

-*Roe* v. *Wade* decision.
-The AFL-CIO endorses the ERA.
-The Government Printing Office accepts Ms. as a legal prefix.
-New Jersey Little League is open to girls.

1974

-Supreme Court outlaws mandatory maternity leaves for teachers.
-Ella Grasso is elected governor of Connecticut, the first woman elected in her own right.
-France legalizes abortions.
-Happy Rockefeller and Betty Ford are open and honest about their mastectomies.

1975

-The United Nations declares the International Year of the Woman.
-New Jersey and New York reject the ERA by wide margins.
-The First Women's Bank opens in New York City.
-The Supreme Court approves legal ads for abortions.
-NOW (National Organization of Women) organizes "Alice Doesn't" strike day, which goes largely unobserved.
-NOW denounces "Growing up Skipper" doll that grows breasts when you twist her arms.
-*Time* names ten women as Man of the Year.

1976

-NASA accepts women for astronaut training.
-The Episcopalian Church ordains women and recognizes those who were illegally ordained.

1977

-Sarah Caldwell becomes the first woman to conduct the New York Metropolitan Opera (at Beverly Sills's insistence.).
-Barbara Walters signs a multi-million dollar contract with ABC.
-Dixie Lee Ray is elected governor of Washington.

MAY 1973

2: *New York Times* reports widespread Republican dirty tricks during 1972 campaign.

11: Government drops Pentagon Papers case against Daniel Ellsberg.

15: CIA claims that John Dean had requested assistance in Watergate cover-up.

17: Senate Watergate Hearings open.

4: PBS shows *Steambath* featuring frontal nudity.

1977

-The Girl Scouts endorse the ERA (causing two Austin leaders to burn their uniforms).
-Dade County, Florida, voters reject a gay rights bill after singer Anita Brayant launches a "Save our Children" campaign.
-AT&T allows dual listings for married couples.

1978

-California voters reject Briggs amendment, which would allow Boards of Education to fire all gay teachers.
-More women than men enter college than at any time in history.

1979

-Susan B. Anthony dollar makes its appearance.
-Phyllis Schlafly holds a party to celebrate the "end of ERA."
-Lee Marvin palimony suit.

GEORGE WHO?

In the years since he led the Democratic party to its biggest electoral disaster in 1972, George McGovern has become a symbol for everything vaguely left wing and wacko in politics. It is difficult to imagine how someone as boring as McGovern, a would-be minister from the scintillating plains of South Dakota, could have staged the coup that took over the party of Daley, Humphrey, and LBJ.

Inheriting the passionate and organized remnants of the powerful antiwar movement, McGovern's grass-roots forces rolled over Ed Muskie's inept campaign. Muskie did a good job of self-destructing when he broke down and cried before reporters after a harsh question about his wife. After Ed's waterworks, McGovern had little trouble mowing down a crowded field of candidates, including George Wallace, Scoop Jackson, Hubert Humphrey, and the recently converted John Lindsay who fractured the moderate and conservative opposition. With Wallace's wounding and Humphrey's defeat in California, McGovern had the nomination sewn up.

An entire generation of blue-collar, union, veteran Democrats watched in

22: Nixon denies knowledge of cover-up; reveals history of goverment wire-tapping and of the "plumbers unit" to stop goverment leaks.

23: Columbia Records President Clive Davis fired for misuse of company funds.

Selected Gold Record Albums:
O'Jays—*Back Stabber*
Yes—*Yessongs*
Steely Dan—*Can't Buy a Thrill*
Nitty Gritty Dirt Band—*Let the Circle Be Unbroken*

#1 Singles:
Stevie Wonder—"You Are the Sunshine of My Life"
Edgar Winter Group—"Frankenstein"

JUNE 1973

13: Nixon announces "Phase 3" of wage-price controls.

horror as the Democratic convention unfolded in Miami. With 30 percent of the delegates under thirty, 15 percent black, and a larger percentage of women, the old bosses were clearly written out of the picture. Chicago Mayor Richard Daley, a living symbol of old-style politics, was not even allowed a seat. To many Americans, McGovern's nomination seemed like a meeting of Peace Corps volunteers and lettuce boycotters.

The love fest came to an abrupt halt when it became known that McGovern's genial running mate, Missouri Senator Tom Eagleton, had undergone repeated electroshock therapy. Looking both inept and disloyal, McGovern jettisoned Eagleton after promising to back him "1,000 percent." Having already scared the country by promising everyone a welfare check of $1,000, McGovern should have known not to speak in round numbers. Not even the Kennedy connection of new running mate Sargeant Shriver could salvage much of the campaign. Lacking both machine and union support, McGovern carried only Massachusetts and the District of Columbia, a fact that still stigmatizes both as the last bastions of liberalism.

For many, McGovern remains the last, bland flowering of Sixties' liberal purity, and certainly the last gasp of an antiwar movement that Nixon had all but neutralized by his "Vietnamization" of the war and its casualties. Neither the subsequent Christmas bombings nor the quagmire of Watergate that denied Nixon his "four more years" have done much to absolve McGovern in the eyes of history. He remains the overarching symbol of leftist elitism that destroyed the old Roosevelt coalition by driving all of the South and much of the working class into the arms of Richard Nixon.

Super-stud Warren Beatty typified McGovern's support among the Hollywood liberal elite.

16-25: Brezhnev makes breezy tour of U.S.

20: Ex-dictator Peron returns to Argentina.

22: Crew of Skylab I return to earth after twenty-eight days in space.

25: John Dean testifies for six hours at Watergate hearings; asserts Nixon role in cover-up; says he had warned Nixon of "a cancer growing on the Presidency."

26: Dean reveals existence of White House "enemies list."

: Getty heir dies of drug overdose.

18: Gordie Howe jumps to WHA for $1 million.

21: The group Bread's last concert.

THE ENDLESS ENIGMA
OF RICHARD NIXON

Operation Candor:
A typical Nixonian pose.

Statesman, psycho, visionary, and sleazebag, Richard Nixon has dominated and haunted American postwar politics like no one else. As Eisenhower's pit bull in the Commie-crazed Fifties, Nixon earned the lifelong loathing of a generation of Democrats who would see their children rally to the New Left. After the debacle at the 1968 Chicago convention and the rise of McGovern in 1972, hatred of Nixon was the only thing that kept some Democratic families together. At the same time, Nixon, the ultimate political operator, split the solid South from the Democratic party while integrating southern schools at an unparalleled rate. For all of the talk of Tricky Dick and warmonger Nixon, he managed to disengage American forces from Vietnam, open relations with China, have détente with the Soviets, and end the hated draft.

Having suffered through the hapless administrations of Ford and Carter, and the brazen mental laziness of Reagan, it's difficult not to look back at Nixon with some admiration. Even evil geniuses have some brains! An inveterate writer, Nixon is perhaps the last literate President America will ever have.

Yet before one gets too misty-eyed for the dear deposed Dick, it's always good to remember how he turned the White House into a center of subversion and sleaze that would make Don Corleone blush. This was a man whose political paranoia led him to tape every conversation he ever had. A man who sent memos to his wife and wiretapped his brother; the man who cozied up to a murderously corrupt Teamsters Union and used it to launder and supply hush money for his political hooligans; the man who ordered the Christmas bombings of hospitals in Hanoi; the man who personally kept John Lennon out of the country; the man who insisted on eating ketchup with his cottage cheese!

For those who *still* haven't made up their minds about the Nixon legacy, the following list should explain why even his right hand man, H. R. "Bob" Haldeman described him as "the weirdest man ever to live in the White House."

29: Nixon, Congress reach agreement to end Cambodian bombing by August 15.

#1 Singles:
Paul McCartney and Wings—"My Love"
George Harrison—"Give Me Love
(Give Me Peace on Earth)"

JULY 1973

Selected Gold Record Albums:
Curtis Mayfield—*Curtis*
George Harrison—*Living in
the Material World*
George Carlin—*Class Clown*

Paul Simon—*There Goes Rhymin' Simon*
The Carpenters—*Now and Then*

3: David Bowie announces retirement.

THE YIN AND YANG OF RICHARD NIXON

YIN: Nixon didn't *start* the Vietnam war, he *ended* it.

YANG: Nixon "Vietnamized" the war's casualties by replacing the U.S. ground forces with the most savage bombing campaign in human history. The war killed more than 2 million Vietnamese from '69 to '73; many argue that Nixon could have arranged the same short-lived and hypocritical cease-fire in '69.

YIN: Nixon went to China and ended a generation of nonrelations with the most populous nation on earth.

YANG: Nixon's wacko, hysterical red baiting in the Fifties was *responsible* for a generation of nonrelations.

YIN: Nixon's statesmanship established détente with Soviets and decreased the chances of nuclear war.

YANG: Nixon was behind the CIA's overthrow and murder of President Salvador Allende in Chile.

YIN: Nixon actually increased social welfare spending and began the Food Stamps program.

YANG: Nixon told his hatchet man Chuck Colson to "catch Ted Kennedy in the sack with one of his babes."

YIN: *Every* President since FDR taped his conversations. Nixon just got caught. He could have burned the tapes.

YANG: Nixon "just got caught" subverting an election, laundering mob money, and misusing intelligence agencies to cover up a series of criminal acts. He should have gone to jail.

10-11: Mitchell claims he shielded President from cover-up; blames Ehrlichman and Haldeman.

16: Nixon aide Alexander P. Butterfield inadvertantly reveals White House taping system; committee moves to obtain tapes as evidence.

17: Nixon ends price freeze.

24: Ehrlichman fingers Haldeman as cover-up culprit.

30: Haldeman denies cover-up role.

6: The group Queen debuts in England with "Keep Yourself Alive."

15: Nolan Ryan pitches second no-hitter of the season.

24: Lance Rentzel suspended from football for pot possession.

28: 600,000 attend Watkins Glen (N.Y.) rock festival.

HENRY KISSINGER

Like few other public figures, Henry Kissinger dominated the decade and remained in the spotlight for the whole span of the convulsive Seventies. From the invasion of Cambodia in 1970 to the hostage crisis in 1979, Kissinger remained a central figure.

Originally a Rockefeller man, Kissinger was chosen to be Nixon's foreign policy advisor right after the '68 election. The conspiracy theorists of the left and right never forgot his close connections to the brothers Rockefeller. Until getting the nod from Nixon, Kissinger was best known for a rather terrifying Harvard treatise advocating the limited use of nuclear weapons. Early in the Nixon Administration, Kissinger was kept in the background. His administration handlers never allowed him to be heard on the nightly news lest his deep, guttural German accent provide the networks with ammunition. In the dark days of Kent State, Nixon needed no "Dr. Strangelove" around his neck.

Yet all of this fear of the press would be unfounded. With the press generally predisposed to distrust Nixon and consider him at best a shifty used-car salesman, Kissinger was granted all the credit for Nixon's foreign policy successes. If the United States opened the door to China, it was Kissinger's crafty art of realpolitik; if the administration opened its door to détente, it was Henry's great statescraft. In the coverage of the war, Kissinger was negotiating a peace, Nixon was prolonging the war. Kissinger's self-styled "shuttle diplomacy" negotiated a peace between Israel and Syria while at the same time disengaging Egypt from the Soviet orbit. By the end of Nixon's first term, Kissinger so completely overshadowed the real secretary of state that it came as no surprise when he got the job just before Watergate broke wide open in the early months of '73.

If the press's buildup of Henry's diplomatic skills was not enough, he was also seen as a ladies' man. In an administration hardly known for its libinious overdrive, Kissinger was seen squiring models and actresses, including Marlo Thomas and Jill St. John. There was even a rumor that he had dated a pre-*MS*. Gloria Steinem.

For all of Henry's skills, he was not immune to the streak of paranoia surrounding the Nixon Whitehouse. It was his furious reaction to leaks sur-

#1 Singles:
Billy Preston—"Will It Go Round in Circles"
Jim Croce—"Bad, Bad Leroy Brown"

Selected Gold Record Albums:
Isaac Hayes—*Live at the Sarahara Tahoe*
Chicago—*Chicago VI*
Jethro Tull—*Passion Play*
The Doobie Brothers—*The Captain and Me*

AUGUST 1973

14: Two Texas teenagers admit to murdering and torturing twenty-seven young men over three years.

9: Film version of *Jesus Christ Superstar* released.

Kris Kristofferson and Rita Coolidge marry in Malibu.

15: Nixon claims that it is "time to put Watergate behind us."

28: 1962 joke rock tune "Monster Mash" hits charts for third time.

rounding the American "tilt" toward Pakistan in the '71 war with India that resulted in the infamous "Plumbers" unit of leak-plugging bag men. His personal loathing for *Pentagon Papers* leaker Daniel Ellsberg was said to have been a chief reason for the infamous break-in to the office of Ellsberg's psychiatrist.

Once the maelstrom of Watergate began swallowing the Nixon gang, Kissinger the superstar was as powerless as any Nixon crony. For Kissinger, 1973 was going to be "The Year of Europe," a time to reassess our relationship with our allies in a post-Vietnam environment. Instead, it became obvious that the administration was fatally hemorrhaging. After Agnew's exit and the "Satruday Night Massacre" made impeachment a real possibility, Kissinger became a symbol of stability for the government itself. Vice President Gerald Ford may have been a nice guy, but most people slept a little better having Henry around. There were even veiled regrets that Kissinger's foreign birth kept him from ever assuming the presidency.

As secretary of state, Kissinger accepted Nixon's resignation. He also spent the night before the resignation listening to a broken, boozy Nixon ranting, crying, and raving. Nixon even asked Henry to kneel down and pray before a painting of Lincoln.

Although Kissinger was a cornerstone of the early Ford administration, his mantle as diplomatic genius was not wearing so well. By April 1975, the "peace" in Vietnam had become a Communist victory. To many, particularly right-wing Republicans who had always considered him a stalking horse for Rockefeller and any number of dark conspiracies, Henry's détente with the Soviets had become a liabilty. During the 1976 primary elections, Ronald Reagan almost beat Ford out of the nomination by making an issue of Henry's deal with the Communists.

During the Carter years, Kissinger loomed large as figure of experienced, hardboiled reason that contrasted well with Carter's preachy, moralistic approach to foreign policy. At the decade's end, Kissinger was once again a shadowy figure in the news as it was revealed that he and his friend David Rockefeller were instrumental in getting the Shah of Iran into the United States for medical treatment—the act that precipitated the seizure of the U.S. Embassy in Tehran. The Seventies ended as they began, with Kissinger in the center of controversy, fending off rumors about how this myste-

"Power is the ultimate aphrodisiac."
—Henry Kissinger

"9: Judge John Sirica rules Nixon must turn over tapes.

#1 Singles:
Maureen McGovern—"The Morning After"
Diana Ross—"Touch Me in the Morning"
Stories—"Brother Louie"

SEPTEMBER 1973

6: Patrick Buchanan admits White House dirty tricks campaign.

11: Military junta overthrows Chile's Marxist President Salvador Allende Gossens.

Selected Gold Record Albums:
Soundtrack—*Cabaret*
Grand Funk Railroad—*We're an American Band*
John Denver—*Farewell Andromeda*

The Allman Brothers—*Brothers and Sisters*

6: FBI claims all New York City track trifecta races were fixed.

77

rious foreigner could have assumed so much influence over our foreign policy.

TANIA HEARST, SUPERSTAR

One day she was just a skinny heiress making macramé plant hangers for her scrawny, ex-math teacher fiancé Steve Weed, the next day she became the object of the most celebrated person-hunt in history. The kidnapping of Patty Hearst, the granddaughter of "Citizen Kane," sent shockwaves across the country. By February 1974, many felt that most of the crazy radical stunts were over. The nation seemed to be settling into a particularly tasteless phase of self-absorption with the Carpenters, streaking, and the "Ooga Chaka" version of "Hooked on a Feeling."

Patty's captors were the oddly named Symbionese Liberation Army. Just who were the Symbionese, and what *did* they want? The SLA was hatched in the hothouse atmosphere of Berkeley and Oakland, California, where the Black Power forces and the antiwar movement still made noise out of proportion to their numbers. To this day, Berkeley continues to have an almost Sixties theme park atmosphere to it, outdoing all other college towns for its tie-dyed and radical quotient.

For all of their outrageous rhetoric, SLA members were heavily armed and murderously dangerous. Having murdered an Oakland educator only months before Patty's abduction, they had proven their unhinged revolutionary zeal. In lieu of a simple ransom, the SLA demanded that the Hearsts, "corporate monsters and upholders of the fascist beast," give away hundreds of millions of dollars to the poor. Patty's father, William Randolph Hearst, attempted to placate them by giving a few million of a Hearst trust fund to the "People in Need" food giveaway program. In his book, *My Search for Patty Hearst*, Stephen Weed describes the program as a crazy quilt of Black Panthers, Black Muslims, common criminals, and a smattering of Bay Area activists. Most of the food was spoiled before it was delivered, and much of the money was siphoned off by any number of shakedown artists. Oddly enough, one of the most earnest organizers of the program

23: Juan Peron elected Argentine President after eighteen-year exile.

27: Carlos Santana changes name to "Deva-dip."

25: Skylab II completes fifty-nine days in space.

28: Rolling Stones perform "Angie" on first U.S. TV appearance since 1967.

#1 Singles:
Marvin Gaye—"Let's Get It On"
Helen Reddy—"Delta Dawn"
Grand Funk Railroad—"We're an American Band"

Selected Gold Record Albums:
Carly Simon—*Anticipation*
Rolling Stones—*Goat's Head Soup*
Focus—*Focus 3*

OCTOBER 1973

2: White House announces heating oil fuel rationing.

was ex-activist accountant Sara Jane Moore. She reportedly grew so disillusioned with the program that she became an FBI informant and then made an unsuccessful attempt to kill President Ford in September 1975.

The giveaway program quickly became moot when Patty announced that she was was joining the SLA. She denounced her parents as "corporate liars," part of a plan to "murder all black and poor people down to the last woman and child." She took the revolutionary name "Tania," after a slain Bolivian comrade of Che Guevara. She called the SLA "an environment of love in the belly of the fascist beast."

Even after this outrageous announcement, most people still sympathized with Patty. The *Berkeley Barb* hailed her "liberation," while many felt that her statements were typical of a kidnap victim who has begun to identify with her captor. All sympathy ceased on April 15, when Patty and her SLA gang robbed the Hibernia Bank in San Francisco. Patty appeared in fatigues and SLA cap with a machine gun in tow. She seemed completely in earnest when she told the bank customers to "get down or I'll blow your motherfucking heads off." Fellow SLA member Nancy Ling shot a bystander in the hip as the gang made off with over $10,000.

Things got even uglier when the the L.A. SWAT team descended on the SLA's hideaway in May. A two-hour shoot-out became the biggest firefight on U.S. soil in history. The entire SLA except Patty Hearst and SLA members Bill and Emily Harris were incinerated in the blaze.

After another year and a half on the lam, Patty was captured, convicted, retried, jailed, and finally pardoned by Jimmy Carter. Her trial was a bit of an anticlimax after her fiery career as Tania. For millions of Americans, particularly those sympathetic to the radical left, Patty Hearst lived out a revolutionary fantasy. She didn't just have a Che poster in her room, she was living his dream! Here she was, a rich kid playing terrorist for real. Patty provided a cathartic trip into radical gangsterism and showed everyone how ugly it could be. It's not surprising that most of the Bonnie and Clyde antihero criminal worship vanished from the popular media soon after her arrest. Yet at the same time, the image of a self-assured nice white girl toting a submachine gun remained too-powerful a symbol to ignore. Within two years of Patty's capture, the TV show *Charlie's Angels* was letting loose with the firepower and getting number-one ratings to boot.

Tania: The pinup girl of the S.L.A.

3: Senate Watergate committee begins hearings on White House "dirty tricks" campaign in 1972.

6: Arab nations launch all-out attack on Israel during Yom Kippur.

9: Nixon friend Charles "Bebe" Rebozo admits accepting bribes from Howard Hughes.

9-11: Egyptian forces overrun Israel's defense line.

10: Vice President Agnew resigns from office.

12: Nixon names Rep. Gerald Ford to replace Agnew as V.P.

9: Elvis and Priscilla Presley divorce.

79

GERALD RUDOLPH FORD

The administration of Gerald R. Ford, the thirty-eighth—and only unelected—President of the United States, was twenty-seven of the most exciting months of our lives. Ford was the designated hitter for both Spiro Agnew *and* Richard Nixon.

Who can forget the thrill of knowing that the man in the White House actually toasted his own English muffins for breakfast? That he promised that "our long national nightmare" was over, and then, a month later, he pardoned the unindicted co-conspirator who had preceded him?

Funny Lady Barbra Streisand meets funny guy Gerald Ford.

Remember the *Mayaguez*? WIN Buttons? *The New York Daily News* headline that proclaimed: "Ford to NY: Drop Dead!"? Chevy Chase impersonating him on *Saturday Night Live*? Ford himself appearing on *Saturday Night Live*?

From August 1974 to January 1977, we marveled as on a state visit to Austria, he slipped and fell to his hands and knees while debarking from a plane. In Sacramento, he was struck by an elevator gate. On a golf course, caddies often dove from some of his errant shots. He was the man some skeptics claimed couldn't walk and chew gum at the same time.

Truth be told, he could do both. In fact, President Ford had Jack Armstrong-like credentials: He was the first Eagle Scout to become President, he was an All-American football player at the University of Michigan, and he was a Yale Law School graduate.

Let's face it, the guy had bad luck. Once a carload of teens smashed into his limousine in Hartford—the only President to be in a traffic accident during his term in office. There were other more serious scrapes—Ford escaped two assassination attempts. The first was by a Manson follower named Lynette "Squeaky" Fromme, followed a mere seventeen days later by an attempt by an FBI informant, Sara Jane Moore.

On a more serious note, Ford did help heal the nation of its Vietnam-Watergate trauma, and history may treat him kinder than he was treated during those twenty-seven months.

15: Soviets vow support for Arab allies.

15: NBC premiere of *Tomorrow* Show with Tom Snyder.

18: Egyptians set back in Sinai; Soviet premier in Cairo.

18: *The Way We Were* released.

19: Dean pleads guilty to Watergate cover-up count.

20: Nixon fires Watergate special prosecutor Archibald Cox, prompting "Saturday Night Masssacre": resignations of Attorney General Richardson and his assistant William Ruckelshaus.

22: U.S. and Soviets iron out UN ceasefire, ending MidEast fighting.

23: In reaction to "Saturday Night Massacre," Congress considers impeachment proceedings for the first time.

FUN FORD FAX

- His real name was Leslie Lynch King, Jr., and he was born in Omaha. But two years after his birth, his parents were divorced and his mother married a paint salesman named Gerald Rudolf Ford. He eventually adopted young Leslie and changed his name. (The young man later changed the spelling of his middle name.)
- He is ambidextrous.
- He appeared on the cover of *Cosmopolitan* magazine in 1942 dressed in his navy uniform, with his then-girlfriend Phyllis Brown.
- While Vice President, he donned a T-shirt emblazoned with the phrase "Keep on streaking" and raced the length of the vice-presidential jet.
- And if that isn't funny enough, consider this joke he made about Ronald Reagan, who opposed him for the 1976 GOP nomination: "Ronald Reagan and I have one thing in common—We both played football. I played for Michigan. He played for Warner Bros."

Betty and Jerry brought warmth back to the White House

BICENTENNIAL MINUTIAE

From the moment the first "Bicentennial Minute" ticked on the air on July 4, 1974, until the last tall ship passed through New York Harbor on July 4, 1976, America was engaged in an orgy of marketing, patriotism and star-spangled lunacy. The bicentennial celebration became the prototype for such subsequent historical lovefests as the 1984 Summer Olympics, the 1986 Statue of Liberty Centennial, and whatever anniversaries the hype-masters devise for us to celebrate in the future.

Lest you forget, let us remind you of some of the merchandise one could buy during 1975 and 1976:

- A Los Angeles designer created a bicentennial polyester bikini.
- The watchmaker Elgin marketed a Liberty Bell alarm clock with two Minutemen to strike the gong and George Washington, John Hancock, and Thomas Jefferson to mark time at midnight and noon.
- A Miami firm invented a Spirit of '76 lamp made from a parking meter.
- Mobil Oil took out an ad in *The New York Times* claiming Sam Adams as

Bicentennial Czar John Warner
speaks to an enraptured audience.

an early ally of the petroleum industry.
● The Revere Copper and Brass Co. (descended from Paul Revere's own company) sold a bicentennial omelette pan and in its ads trumpeted "the customers are coming."

Enough! shouted some latter-day Tom Paines who called themselves "The People's Bicentennial Commission" and decried the commercialization of the event. This group of Sixties activists (which included Jane Fonda, Tom Hayden and Jesse Jackson) pulled such stunts as dumping oil barrels in Boston Harbor as a protest against petroleum companies and hanging Ronald McDonald in effigy in Ann Arbor, Michigan. In another stunt, they printed up excerpts of the Declaration of Independence and presented them as a modern-day petition to 1,744 residents of Delaware. Eighty-seven percent didn't recognize the words as those of our founding fathers. Fifty percent refused to sign it, believing that all this talk about the pursuit of happiness might be leftist propaganda.

All of the hype and antihype was overshadowed on July 4, 1976, when the bicentennial reached its climax. It became a national healing—after all in the early Seventies, if you sported an American flag lapel, it marked you as a Nixonian crypto-fascist. But by 1976, the rest of America had finally won back the right to wave the flag without being branded as an extremist. This was no mean feat.

On that day, the "Op Sail" display of the tall ships of 30 nations in New York Harbor was the most stunning of the hundreds of celebrations going on across the country. President Gerald Ford—who thought he would be the beneficiary of the outpouring of good feelings—had a busy day. He rang the Liberty Bell on the deck of an aircraft carrier in New York harbor. Earlier in the day, speaking at Valley Forge, Pennsylvania, he reminisced about the homemade ice cream and the fireworks of his Grand Rapids boyhood, and opened a time capsule from the centennial celebration of 1876. Among the other events on that memorable day:
● In Chicago, 1,776 new U.S. citizens were sworn in.
● The residents of Lake City, Pennsylvania, decided they'd rather look forward two hundred years than look back to the past, so the town dedicated a landing pad for UFOs.

7: Congress overrides Nixon's veto of War Powers Act.

16: Nixon signs Alaska oil pipeline bill.

17: At Disney World, Nixon declares "I am not a crook."

21: White House discloses 18½-minute gap in subpoenaed Watergate tape.

25: Nixon bans Sunday gas sales and enacts fifty-mph speed limit.

26: Oil embargo and recession fed sends Dow to eleven-year low.

- A Detroit woman, dubbed the "mad patriot," played "The Stars and Stripes Forever" on the telephone to total strangers. "I'm not mad," she explained. "I'm just trying to make other people aware of how happy they should be."
- Richard Nixon, who had expected the bicentennial to be the capstone of his political career, instead watched a local fireworks display from his compound-in-exile in San Clemente, California.

Maybe it was justice. On Independence Day, 1971, President Nixon had announced a unilateral change of dates of the bicentennial celebration so that the hoopla would not mark the anniversary of the American Revolution but rather of the signing of the Declaration of Independence, which would place the anniversary right in the final year of his second administration. And before Watergate toppled him, many Americans thought that the bicentennial would be a Republican partisan celebration, akin to the red, white, and blue excesses orchestrated for Nixon's 1972 Republican convention. Thus, the positive and excited feelings that many Americans experienced on July 4, 1976, were both surprising and rewarding.

As political columnist Elizabeth Drew observed: "The feeling of the day sort of crept up on us, took many of us by surprise. For those of us who had been in despair about the Bicentennial, who feared the worst, the surprise was a very pleasant one...No doubt the good feeling observed today, even the patriotic feeling, comes out of the country, as distinguished from confidence in our government."

GAY LIBERATION

Like the women's movement, the gay liberation movement of the Seventies resulted in a revolution in many people's everyday lives—changes that would seem inconceivable just a few years before. In June '69, homosexual patrons of New York's Stonewall Tavern refused to put up with police harassment and, to everyone's surprise, turned on the police in a violent riot. Before Stonewall, a public gathering of homosexuals was essentially an illegal affair. Gay bars existed with speakeasy-

Post-Stonewall, pre-clone: an early Seventies march for gay rights.

#1 Singles:
Eddie Kendricks—"Keep on Truckin'"
Ringo Starr—"Photograph"

DECEMBER 1973

4: William Simon becomes new Energy "Czar."

4-7: Truckers block highways to protest gas cutbacks and speed limit.

8: Nixon reveals financial records and questionable income tax payments.

elected Gold Record Albums:
m Croce—*Life and Times*
arry White—*I've Got So Much to Give*
ohn Lennon—*Mind Games*
e Walsh—*The Smoker You Drink, The Player You Get*
arth Wind and Fire—*Head to the Sky*

2: Members of the group The Who jailed overnight for $6,000 hotel destruction.

16: O. J. Simpson is first to rush for more than 2,000 yards.

83

like secrecy and were regularly raided (and exploited) by vice squads. Public attitudes toward gays wavered between pity and contempt, as gays were commonly considered to be perverts, deviants, and psychopaths. When the Stonewall riots erupted, the headline in New York's *Daily News* read: "Homo Nest Raided, Queen Bees are Stinging Mad."

Stonewall sparked a nationwide organizing movement that quite literally took many gays "out of the closet" and onto the streets and television screens of America. A nation that had largely ignored gays or had consigned them to certain seedy neighborhoods was now facing a national phenomenon: Many of its sons and daughters were openly, and at times militantly, admitting their homosexuality. Once organized, gays became a political force to be reckoned with. Certain cities, most notably New York and San Francisco, became magnets for gays. Whole neighborhoods emerged as "gay ghettos," self-defined and protective enclaves where many could escape the scorn, snickers, and ever-present violence. Voting as a block, gays joined other ethnic and special interest groups in exercising their political power. Singer Anita Bryant's celebrated gay-bashing campaign in Florida ("The Normal Majority") probably did more to galvanize pro-gay sentiment than anything else. By the late Seventies, an outspoken gay activist named Harvey Milk had emerged as a major political power in San Francisco, while New York voters elected Ed Koch, an unmarried bachelor, as mayor, in spite of some ugly gay-baiting innuendos, including the infamous primary slogan, "Vote for Cuomo, not the Homo."

The gay liberation movement was most strongly reflected in Seventies' pop culture. Unlike the closeted stars of the past, Seventies' pop idols Elton John and David Bowie proved that they could be both bisexual and enormously popular. The rapid rise and fall of the glitter rock movement revealed a worldwide pop flirtation with bisexuality. Mick Jagger swaggered through most of the early Seventies with more makeup than his wife Bianca. Disco, however, provided gays with the most visible manifestation of their ability to set trends and dominate pop culture. Many of the trendiest discos, including New York's Studio 54, had overwhelmingly gay clienteles. The late-Seventies' disco attitudes, including that of almost athletic sexual activity, were an outgrowth of the gay club scene. With the disco movement, mainstream America accepted and participated in a huge pansexual orgy

13: Rocked by coal strike, England enacts three-day work week.

20: Bobby Darin dies of heart failure.

18: N.Y. Governor Rockefeller resigns to pursue two national committees.

25: OPEC doubles price of oil; ends embargo for all nations except U.S. and Netherlands.

25: *The Sting* released.

28: Alexandr Solzhenitsyn's *The Gulag Archipelago* published in Paris.

#1 Singles:
The Carpenters—"Top of the World"
Charlie Rich—"The Most Beautiful Girl"
Jim Croce—"Time in a Bottle"

Selected Gold Record Album
Steve Miller Band—*The Jo*
Soundtrack—*American Gr*
Anne Murray—*Snowbird*
Loggins and Messina—*Full*

set to some of the dumbest and most danceable music imaginable. By decade's end, a band as banal as The Village People could openly brandish a collection of gay stereotypes (The "Leather Man," the "Indian," and the "Biker") and sell some of the most popular singles of the period.

While the decade ended light-years removed from the pre-Stonewall era, a visible backlash was underway. The assassination of Harvey Milk (along with San Francisco Mayor Moscone) by disgruntled city employee Dan White was symptomatic of the violent contempt many still felt for gays. White's amazingly light sentence (prompted by the infamous "Twinkie defense"—the argument that he had been rendered mentally unstable by a diet of junk food) resulted in the most violent gay riots since Stonewall. The occasionally violent "disco sucks" movement also had more than its share of anti-gay sentiment. Yet for the most part, the Seventies proved to be a kind of gay golden age, the period between liberation of Stonewall and the staggering tragedy of AIDS.

JERRY BROWN

The award for the ultimate politician of the Seventies has to go to Jerry Brown. His father served two terms as governor in the hard-boiled style of Democratic bosses, and in 1962 he humiliated Richard Nixon into his infamous "You won't have Nixon to kick around anymore" concession speech. Jerry Junior rebelled, studied Zen, and spent four years as a Jesuit seminarian trying to "find himself."

In 1973 he found himself succeeding Ronald Reagan as governor of California. Brown quickly replaced Ron and Nancy's Hollywood conservatism with his own mystical call for "lowered expectations"—a slippery Zen aphorism that worried traditional Democrats and stole the thunder of the tax-cutting right until Proposition 13 erupted in 1978 and caused Brown to match his lowered expectations with lowered revenues.

Like New York's Mayor John Lindsay, Brown was far better at managing images than balancing a budget or running a government. Most of his speeches were completely extemporaneous and studded with Carl Sagan-esque calls for the colonization of space as a way to integrate the races on earth. He called California "the meeting place of the inner and the outer

The Village People *flaunted a parade of gay stereotypes and still endeared themselves to millions of middle Americans.*

4: Nixon rejects Senate subpoena for more than five hundred tapes.

6: *How to be Your Own Best Friend* reaches best-seller list.

24: Oil companies report huge profits from OPEC price rise.

21: Georgia Governor Jimmy Carter invites Bob Dylan to dinner.

30: ABA sues NBA for $600 million in antitrust case.

universe."

Long before Jimmy Carter donned his cardigan and carried his own luggage, Brown mastered the art of symbolic frugality. He replaced his official limousine with a powder-blue Plymouth Satellite and shunned the new governor's mansion (built to Nancy Reagan's specifications) for a monastic $250-a-month bachelor pad.

Brown's erratic and eccentric rule proved popular during a decade when millions of Californians and fellow travelers turned from tradional politics and religion to est, Transcendental Meditation, Rolfing, and myriad New Age solutions. Brown made a late and impressive run for the White House in '76, beating Jimmy Carter in a few final primaries as the southerner limped to the nomination. There was never any love lost between Carter and Brown. Brown's people called Carter "a political hemophiliac." Carter's aides characterized Brown as a jellyfish: "it stings at first, but it's totally transparent."

By 1979 Brown not only embraced Proposition 13 but openly advocated many of the positions of the Reagan right, including a constitutional call for a balanced budget. Yet for all his political conservatism, Brown remained a New Age enigma. On the brink of challenging Carter in April '79, Brown took off for a ten-day African safari with singer Linda Ronstadt. Ronstadt—who changed musical styles as often as Brown changed political spots—was

Governor Jerry Brown and lovely Linda Ronstadt embark for their disastrous African safari.

#1 Singles:
Steve Miller Band—"The Joker"
Al Wilson—"Show and Tell"
Ringo Starr—"You're Sixteen"

FEBRUARY 1974

Selected Gold Record Albums:
Jim Nabors—*The Lord's Prayer*
Eagles—*Eagles*
Carly Simon—*Hot Cakes*
O'Jays—*Ship Ahoy*

2: Keith Emerson injured when trick piano explodes prematurely.

4: Heiress Patricia Hearst kidnapped by Symbionese Liberation Army.

6: House votes to begin impeachment proceedings.

8: Skylab crew returns after eighty-four days in space.

12: SLA demands $230 million in food poor as Hearst ransom.

86

a perfect beard for the bachelor Brown. In the words of a close aide, the sexy rock star "humanized" the brainy gov, whom many had begun to suspect as a cold guru, or perhaps worse. Jerry's dad hoped all the fuss would prove that Jerry II was a "regular man" after all.

If the sight of a would-be president shacking up with a rock star wasn't controversial enough, Jerry's safari turned out to be as much fun as Francis McComber's. Hounded by the press and broiled by the sun, Ronstadt barely avoided fistfights with reporters while Jerry exchanged embarrassing banalities with African dignitaries. Brown aides confessed that the whole trip had been cooked up to demonstrate foreign policy finesse and appeal to black voters. In their words, Brown "needed a metaphor that embraced black concerns." In the end, the safari left Brown looking like an ass and exposed his relationship with Ronstadt as a ridiculous press gimmick.

His 1980 presidential bid never recovered from this flaky bit of grandstanding, and Brown faded away as the Reagan era replaced his age of limitations with a faith in unbridled capitalism. In retrospect, Brown does provide a fascinating missing link between the hippie and the yuppie, between the "New Left" and the Reagan revolution. Brown's capacity to embrace and exploit any number of intellectual and spiritual trends, to coin and co-opt the buzzwords of the emerging "New Age" was both his greatest skill and his most despised characteristic. He adopted and discarded "concepts" the way yuppies consumed products from the *Sharper Image* catalog. His grasshopperlike jump from one "belief system" to another was the consummate Seventies' sport.

Vice-President Rocky discards decorum to respond to students' gestures of affection.

GREAT EXPIRATIONS: ROCKY IN THE SEVENTIES

During a decade when all politicians took a beating, no one seemed more pathetically out of sorts than Nelson Rockefeller. Starting the Seventies as New York's "liberal" Republican governor, Rocky quickly read the writing on the wall and made a beeline for the right. He sponsored a draconian drug law with unenforceable penalties for first-time pot and coke users. And finally, on September 13, 1971, Rocky bloodily won his tough-guy credentials when he sent state troopers to quell the Attica prison riot. Nine hos-

13: Soviet Union expels novelist Alexandr Solzhenitsyn.

15: Seven states and Washington, D.C., ration gasoline by using odd-even system.

18: Hearst agrees to $2 million food giveaway. SLA asks for more.

#1 Singles:
Barbra Steisand—"The Way We Were"
Love Unlimited Orchestra—"Love's Theme"

Rolling Stone reports that David ie has turned down offer to write st Gay National Anthem."

21: Norman Mailer signs $1 million deal to write book about "the whole human experience."

Selected Gold Record Albums:
Joni Mitchell—*Court and Spark*
Yes—*Tales from Topographic Oceans*
The Pointer Sisters—*The Pointer Sisters*
Barry White—*Stone Goin'*

tages and thirty-three prisoners died; Rockefeller refused even to visit the site.

As the stench of Watergate grew, Rocky suddenly and mysteriously resigned from the governorship to pursue two commissions that nobody had ever heard of. When Agnew resigned, Rocky made it clear that he was up for the job. But it was not until Ford assumed the presidency that Rocky got the nod. Ford's choice immediately set the Republican right against him. To the right, Rockefeller was the living embodiment of Wall Street's soft elite that had sold out the party and the country to détente, deficits, and liberalism.

As symbols of stability after the Watergate debacle, both Rockefeller and his former employee Henry Kissinger were public enemy number one for the thousands of conspiracy buffs on both the left and the right. After all, how could so much have gone wrong so fast—defeat in war, energy shortages, economic chaos, governmental collapses, Soviet advances on every continent—if not spawned by some vast network of traitors? And here was Nelson Rockefeller, an unelected Vice President, one heartbeat away from the office of unelected President.

For all of his scheming to get the job, Rockefeller was clearly miserable as Vice President. He got so frustrated during one campus speech that he gave the finger to jeering students. With Ronald Reagan and the Repubican right breathing down the President's neck, nobody was surprised when Ford jettisoned Rocky from his '76 ticket.

Upon retirement in 1977, Rocky settled down to his full-time hobby—art collecting. Yet when Rocky breathed his last in January 1979, he was not just examining his etchings. After a preliminary cover-up, it became clear to everyone that Rocky expired in the company of a young art assistant who just happened to be wearing a nightgown at the time. For all of his money, power, and connections, Nelson Rockefeller suffered the most embarrassing death of the decade.

JIMMY CARTER

How did it happen? Of all the strange and embarrassing Seventies' binges: macramé, pet rocks, double-knit, the Bay City Rollers—none comes close to the inexplicable enigma of Jimmy Carter. How did this man, who came

MARCH 1974

1: Seven of Nixon's closest aides indicted by Watergate grand jury; Nixon considered "unindicted co-conspirator."

6: Nixon concedes knowledge of Watergate hush money.

9: In taped message Patty Hearst criticizes her father; SLA criticizes quality of food given away.

18: OPEC ends embarg against U.S.

2: Stevie Wonder wins five Grammy awards.

12: John Lennon and Harry Nilsson bounced from L.A.'s Troubador Club.

88

out of nowhere and who has since returned to the blessing of relative obscurity, become President of the United States?

Like all of the fads, fashions, and short-lived passions of the mid-Seventies, Carter was a creature of his time. In his case, a short window of historical coincidence—that meteoric moment of post-Watergate idealism and born-again fervor—created the ripe conditions for our first and only peanut farmer President.

After the ashes of Watergate and Ford's sneaky pardon of Nixon, the common wisdom was that the Democrats could nominate any *Homo sapien* and still win. The trick was to win the nomination. Carter won it by copying the campaign styles of the two biggest vote getters in the '72 contest—George Wallace and George McGovern. Like McGovern, he entered early, ran often, and adopted a preachy minister's style to appeal to idealists who were turned off by Nixon's Don Corleone style of governing. Like Wallace, he ran as a good ol' boy from the Deep South. Beyond Wallace, he appealed to the burgeoning numbers of Southern Baptists just as the country was going through a religious revival. In many ways, Carter won by pandering to just about every crowd. To Baptists he preached purity, to the "kids" he quoted Bob Dylan and spoke of the inspring music of Led Zeppelin and the Allman Brothers, for blacks he hung up a picture of Martin Luther King in the Georgia State House, for wary whites he promised to respect the "ethnic purity" of urban neighborhoods.

In many ways Carter's entire career peaked with the Democratic primaries. From the moment his nomination was assured to the last day of his administration, the entire nation seemed to be wondering "Who is this guy, and how did we get stuck with him?"

Elected largely by the poor, the black, and the South, Carter came to power in a last spasm of Seventies' populism just as public attitudes and popular culture were beginning to shift toward more elitist concerns. Carter's habit of wearing blue jeans, carrying his own luggage, attending stock car races, hosting talk radio shows, and discussing his hemorrhoids carried all the right countercultural symbols at exactly the wrong time. By 1977, the exclusive élan of Studio 54 and *designer* jeans were taking hold in a culture just a little bit tired of the egalitarian ethos of Woodstock nation.

And if Jimmy's White House square dances weren't corny enough, there

The Carters entertain the Shah and the Empress of Iran.

was his family. America might have learned to love Miss Lillian and even his faith-healing sister Ruth Stapleton, but Jimmy's pudgy brother Billy was simply too white trash for most. Nixon's brother Donald might have been owned by Howard Hughes, but even he never had the gall to use his name for a brand of beer, bad-mouth Jews, or become a Libyan agent! Billy did all of this and more in one of the strangest sibling rivalries on record.

In the field of foreign affairs, Carter took the moral high ground. This might have won points with a nation tired of carpet-bombing Vietnam and CIA assassinations, but the rest of the world was aghast. Within six months of his inauguration Carter had soured relations with both the USSR and most of the NATO allies. Brezhnev was livid while Germany's Willy Schmidt accused Carter of behaving "like a faith healer, conducting foreign policy from the pulpit." A world grown used to Kissinger's realpolitik was in no mood for Carter's born-again bantering.

To his credit, Carter made the most of Egyptian President Anwar Sadat's peace initiative and put his personal stamp on the Middle East with the Camp David meetings of autumn '78. Yet the political capital of this coup was quickly dissipated as both the economy and foreign policy ran beyond the grasp of Carter's preaching. After the overthrow of the Shah of Iran, Carter faced his last year in office with double-digit interest rates and inflation and a gas shortage as critical as Nixon faced in '73.

Matters weren't helped by Carter's habit of preachy political theater. During July of 1979 he literally disappeared into a mountain retreat and summoned a council of "wise men." All of this unfolded during a week when the economy lapsed into a recession, the Skylab space station crashed, Chrysler seemed on the brink of bankruptcy, and Sandanista rebels assumed control of Nicaragua. Rumors spread of a mental breakdown, resignation, or a deal with a renegade Ted Kennedy. Instead, Carter descended from the mountaintop and criticized America for its "crisis of confidence." Quickly dubbed "The Malaise Speech" by pundits and Republicans, this speech provided Ronald Reagan fuel for more than ten years of Carter bashing. It proved that Carter's revival-tent tactics no longer had much appeal.

Carter was actually buoyed by the hostage crisis in fall '79. For the first few months he rode the crest of the yellow-ribbon-flying, patriotic binge.

3: In taped message, Patty Hearst avows SLA membership.

8: Hank Aaron breaks Babe Ruth's home run record.

10: Golda Meir resigns; takes blame for Yom Kippur war fiasco.

15: Patty Hearst participates in bank robbery.

16: Daryle Lamonica joins exodus to WFL.

18: Sadat announces end of Egyptian reliance on Soviet arms.

24: Ray Stevens releases "The Streak."

25: Military coup in Portugal.

Ford or Carter?

*Match wits with the two one-term wonders of the Seventies
by matching the appropriate response to the right President.*

Mayaguez	*Malaise*
WIN (Whip Inflation Now)	*MEOW (Moral Equivalent of War)*
Burt Lance	*Earl Butz*
James Schlesinger	*James Schlesinger*
"An inordinate fear of communism"	*"Russia does not dominate Poland"*
Son smoked pot in the White House	*Brother cozied up to Qaddafi*
Looked dumb when flustered	*Looked mean when flustered*
"Ethnic purity"	*"I'm a Ford not a Lincoln"*
Attended stock car races	*Entertained Queen Elizabeth with The Captain and Tenille*
Made own English muffins	*Carried own luggage*
Kissed Brezhnev	*Partied with the Shah*
Wife photographed with mass murderer	*Wife mixed pills with booze*

The public quickly tired of his blatant manipulation of the crisis, however,
and of his ineffectual "Rose Garden Strategy." After the Desert One helicopter rescue mission crashed 1980, Carter was all but finished. Having been
elected trying to undo the "Imperial Presidency," Carter succeeded in making people want a strong leader so badly that they turned to a California
actor in landslide numbers. At least Reagan could "act presidential."

30: White House releases 1,200
pages of tape transcripts.

#1 Singles:
Blue Swede—"Hooked on a Feeling"
Elton John—"Bennie and the Jets"
MFSB and the Three Degrees—"TSOB"

MAY 1974

2: Spiro T. Agnew disbarred.

7: Republican Senate leaders say tape transcripts
reveal "deplorable, disgusting, shabby, immoral
performances by all concerned."

: Jim Morrison's widow, Pam, dies
heroin overdose at 27.

Selected Gold Record Albums:
The Doobie Brothers—*What Once Were Vices Are Now Habits*
Herbie Hancock—*Head Hunters*
Love Unlimited Orchestra—*Rhapsody in White*

Fads and Trends of the Seventies

I n the Seventies we dressed for excess. We tottered on platform shoes (the better to balance our elephant bells), centered ourselves on Earth Shoes, sloshed on water beds, and ran naked through crowds. Mood rings got us in touch with our feelings, and jogging got us in touch with the bodies we subjected to so much partying and those inevitable "munchies." Somewhere along the line the recession and the need to get a job put men back in touch with the three-piece suit, and women learned to "dress for success." The disco look, the preppy look, the punk look, and the gay "clone" look all existed simultaneously as styles proliferated to keep pace with "life-styles."

A decade that began with the miniskirt revolt against designer-dictators ended with a slavish devotion to designer *anything* that plagues us to this day. Although most Seventies' garments and gadgets still lay in a synthetic heap at the corner thrift shop, they reflect the wild, uninhibited, and tastelessy exuberant spirit of those uncertain times. In fact, in all their harvest gold outlandishness, they stand as a stark reminder of just how staid and stuffy things have become since.

HAIR

Long hair is usually thought of as a Sixties' phenomenon. But during the Sixties, it was really only an elite group—the hippies, college students, and their camp followers—who let their hair grow long. It wasn't until the early Seventies that long hair spread to all segments of American society.

If you need proof that something happened to hair between 1970 and 1971, check out a high school yearbook for the class of '70. You'll see that

This tortured Disco Wedge permanent was as far from the "Natural Look" as you could go.

17: Six SLA members killed as SWAT team storms headquarters.

18: India explodes nuclear device.

9: Critic Jon Landau writes: "I have seen the future of rock and roll and his name is Bruce Springsteen."

24: Duke Ellington dies.

24: *The Conversation* wins top honors at Cannes.

26: Teenage melee at London Dav Cassidy show leaves two dead.

the majority of boys had relatively short hair, sort of a modified version of the Bobby Sherman over-the-forehead sweep. But by the time the class of '71 was posing for their mug shots, hirsute hell had broken loose. Most of the boys now looked like Led Zeppelin's roadies.

Shortly thereafter, the trend toward long hair began to filter down to adults. Middle-age men who should have known better grew out their crew cuts, sprouted sideburns, and began getting their hair "styled" at joints that just a few months earlier had been regular old-fashioned barber shops.

There was no turning back; the Golden Age of Hair was upon us—as you'll see as you take this tonsorial tour of the hairiest decade ever:

The Uneasy Rider: Middle-parted, unruly, and unkempt; this "style" was especially popular among blue-collar guys who secretly envied hippies but resisted growing their hair long until they knew no one would hassle them about it. See: Mark Farner.

The "Baretta" Bad Guy/Lounge Lizard: What happened when the Uneasy Rider decided to clean up his act. Parted in the middle, but shagged, styled, and blow-dried, usually shoulder-length. It cost $25 at better unisex hairstylists. A thick mustache is essential for balance. See: Tony Orlando, Freddie Prinze. Best worn with a Qiana shirt, whose collars extended over a wide-lapeled jacket like the wings of the Concorde, with flared or elephant-belled pants.

The Tony Manero: Hair gets swept off the forehead for the first time since 1963 with this blow-dried version of the Fifties' pompadour ("The Dry Look"). First sighted around 1974 in bridge-and-tunnel discos, it was marketed to the world three and a half years later by John Travolta in *Saturday Night Fever*. Especially favored by white, urban ethnics.

The 'Fro: Black pride gets taken to the max with these huge well-sculptured naturals. Good-bye, Dixie Peach, hello, Afro Sheen. Among the best: Angela Davis, Julius Erving, and the members of most funk bands. Goes best with wine-colored jump suits, five-inch platform shoes, and applejack caps. White guys who for years thought they were cursed with too-curly hair got in on the act with their knockoff version called the Isro, in honor of those many members of the Hebrew faith—such as Gabriel (Kotter) Kaplan and Art Garfunkel—who sported one.

The Shag: Around 1971 when long-haired women got tired of the has-

The Glitter 'Fro: for that otherworld look of orgasmic abandon.

sles of tending to such lengthy locks, they modified their looks with this style popularized by Jane Fonda in *Klute*. The style allowed them to keep their hair long, even if it made them look like extras from *Planet of the Apes*.

▼ ***The Farrah Flipout:*** Inspired by Farrah Fawcett-Majors, the star of *Charlie's Angels*, this blow-dried, curling-ironed spectacular, which first surfaced around 1977, is still seen today on junior high students in suburbia and on Oliver North's secretary.

▼ ***The Wedge:*** Olympian Dorothy Hamill inspired this 1976 shortish 'do, which was worn with ease by both young girls and older matrons.

▼ ***The Punk:*** By the end of the decade, as the influence of Johnny Rotten and his ilk spread to the States, high school kids were getting suspended once again because of problems associated with their hairstyles. Unlike the late-Sixties' long-hair paranoia, this time principals got pissed because the kids' hair was too short. Not crew-cut short, but spiked, dyed, or Mohawked—on both boys and girls. Ten years later Joan Rivers is wearing an upscale version of Sid Vicious's 'do.

HOT PANTS

James Brown sang about 'em. Jane Fonda wore 'em in *Klute*. David Bowie wore them on his first American tour.

We're talking about hot pants, those thigh-high short shorts that adorned the legs of many of the young women of America during the better part of 1971.

The pants first appeared in Europe in late 1970 as a way of letting women show their gams again—this in the wake of the great midiskirt controversy, which was threatening to cover up all those lovely legs that the miniskirt had exposed.

When they arrived in America in February 1971, American women clamored over the new garments, which were available in satin, denim, cotton, leather, and velvet. "The way women are buying them and men are acting," sniffed one New York boutique manager, "it would seem that legs have been out of sight for ten years, not ten months."

Not all people responded well to hot pants. Both the Metropolitan Life Insurance Company and New York's Irving Trust Company forbade their female employees from wearing them because they "lacked the necessary decorum." Many high schools also ruled against them—most of those institutions had allowed girls to wear regular pants to class just a couple of years earlier, so what did you expect?

Other corporations were more tolerant. Allegheny Airlines, for instance, designed blue hot pants for its stewardesses' new spring ensembles, and the National Bank of Washington, D.C., saw no problems with its women wearing them.

Where they were prevalent was in the swinging singles bars, which were then in their *Love, American Style* heyday. At a joint called the Pewter Mug in Atlanta, the management allowed in "all the hot pants we can get."

You knew the fad was nearing its end—ironically in summer, when legs would look their leggiest—when some clothing manufacturers came up with hot pants for men. They flopped and soon women lost interest too. Today in most major cities you can still see plenty of women wearing hot pants. These women, however, stand on street corners and charge for their services. Not the kind of high-fashion devotees its designers had in mind back in 1970.

FASHION
SEVENTIES' STYLE

Go to any Salvation Army in any town in America and you can find them: acres and acres of shiny fabrics in outrageous shapes and colors. Hot pants, leisure suits, fake leather, fake fur, rabbit fur, wedgies, clogs, Earth Shoes, platforms, safari jackets, spandex disco pants, leg warmers, bow ties, lycra stretch pants, chocolate brown double-knit blazers, "Lurex" sparkle T-shirts, Qiana scarves, Vibram-soled hiking boots, down jackets, Levi's Panatela suits, "Afternoon Delight" sparkle T-shirts, Frye boots, polyester plaid shirts, remnants of the urban cowboy look, the clone look, the punk look, the dress-for-success outfit. . . .

One could go on forever. Seventies' style began with the confluence of two mighty movements. The sexual and the synthetic revolutions combined forces to produce some of the ugliest and most outrageous clothes ever seen.

The first few years of the decade saw a revolt against taste and tradition

You had to be sure of your "New Man" status to wear this hot-pants-and-cape ensemble.

2-3: Nixon in Moscow; summit fails to dispel Watergate cloud.

15-25: Greek and Turkish troops clash over Cyprus.

24: Supreme Court rules Nixon must give up all tapes.

24-30: House Judiciary Committee votes three counts of impeachment against Nixon.

2: Soviet ballet star Mikhail Baryshnikov defects to Canada.

9: Crosby, Stills and Nash begin reunion tour.

18: 3,000 strikeouts for Bob Gibson.

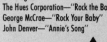

and the dictates of Paris designers. The same sentiment that drove women to spurn midis for hot pants during the coldest winter in years produced the following aberrations:

Platform shoes: These were a kinky orthopedic nightmare popularized by glitter rockers and bad-assed funk fanatics. Heels of up to seven inches gave men and women alike a look of teetering androgeny. The most legendary pair featured a glass heel filled with water and a live goldfish. Like glitter and funk, platforms reflected a carefree decadent reaction to the prevailing "back to nature" mood of the early Seventies.

Tube tops, halters, the "braless" look: In surely the strangest incongruity of the period, the natural look collided with the women's movement to "liberate" the young breasts of Seventies' America. Playtex sales plummeted to many a mom's horror and many a man's delight. The jogging boom and the dress-for-success look of the late Seventies brought most breasts back under wraps.

Granny dresses/the peasant look: After lashing out at the midi, American women settled into a dowdy, "natural," full-length look that seemed to take its fashion cues from Granny on the *Beverly Hillbillies*.

Knitted caps: Ali MacGraw and Marvin Gaye looked good in them, but the list stops there.

Elephant bells: Skin tight at the thighs, these pants blossomed to unreal widths at the hem. When worn with a tight Qiana shirt and platforms, one assumed the strange, compartmentalized look of a larval beetle.

No makeup: This was the trademark of millions of women as they got back to basics in the early Seventies. Even soapy shampoos were shunned as things got "organic." One's hair became part of the ecology as you applied herbs and "enzymes" where once only Breck would go.

Patches: These adorned many a shredded and filthy pair of jeans. Long before designers and stone washers got their hands on Levis, American teenagers were bleaching, bashing, and torturing denim to achieve a perfectly disheveled look. Once jeans were sufficiently mutilated, they were adorned with a crazy quilt of patches, stitchings and parts of other pants.

High-waisted, Forties-style pants with platform shoes defined a look that was at once freaky and nostalgic.

AUGUST 1974

#1 Singles:
The Hues Corporation—"Rock the Boat"
George McCrae—"Rock Your Baby"
John Denver—"Annie's Song"

2: John Dean sentenced to one to three years for cover-up role.

5: Nixon releases "smoking gun" tape revealing knowledge of burglary and cover-up.

29: Mama Cass Elliot dies in London.

Selected Gold Record Albums:
Soundtrack—*The Great Gatsby*
Dylan/Band—*Before the Flood*
David Bowie—*Diamond Dogs*
Edgar Winter Group—*Shock Treatment*

7: Faye Dunaway marries Peter Wolf of J. Geils Band.

96

The ubiquity of the happy face soon insured a market for commercially designed patches that popularized such Seventies' slogans as "Don't Bug Me," "I'm Okay, You're Okay," and "Have A Nice Day." Other favorite patches included peace signs, Mr. Natural, the "Zig Zag" man, and the Rolling Stones' mouth-and-tongue logo.

Overalls: Particularly the Osh Kosh by Gosh variety of overalls were a perfect combination for girls with a tube top or for guys with a thermal underwear shirt.

Red Snaps Day-Glo hip huggers: For the *Brady Bunch*-imitating set, these pants were not complete without a hairbrush prominently stuck in the back pocket. If your mom didn't let you wear hip huggers, she might outfit you in red, white, and blue "Vote" fashions from Sears' Lemon Frog Shop. (For boys' fashions, you could go down to The Put On Shop and buy a sleeveless belted sweater vest. If your mom didn't trust her ability to match all these crazy colors, Sears supplied *Grrr-animals*, a mix-and-match variety of interchangeable kids' clothes with numbers to indicate which piece went with what.

Too many bouts of the munchies? The shapeless Granny dress (center) covered a multitude of sins.

7: Nixon aides and key Republicans insist that he cannot survive.

8: Nixon announces resignation.

9: Nixon resigns; Gerald Ford takes oath.

12: In first address, Ford calls inflation public enemy number one.

16: Pro-Soviet Ethiopian military coup.

20: Ford chooses Nelson Rockefeller as vice president.

16: Ramones debut at New York club CBGB's.

29: ABA's Utah Stars sign high schooler Moses Malone.

Simple, conservative, boring—the string-tie virtually defined the "Dress for Success" look.

Toe socks: Usually purple with multicolored toes, these were the least-worn gift item of the Seventies.

Leather: Before leather was sexy, it was clunky. *Thick leather barrettes* were held with a wooden stick and held many a ponytail. *Clunky etched leather pocketbooks* gave you that Western crafts look. Of course, for those craft do-it-yourselfer, *decoupage* provided hours of enjoyment, and resulted in millions decoupaged pocketbooks and purses, which gave every girl that personal collage look.

Earth Shoes: Designed by Danish Yoga instructor Anne Kalso, Earth Shoes were based on the perfect poise of Brazilian Indians who walked barefoot in the soft jungle soil. U.S. distributor Raymond Jacobs used such natural credentials to sell millions of negative-heeled shoes. To Jacobs and others, Earth Shoes were not a style, but how "nature intended you to walk."

By middecade, the fashion scene took its cue from the economy and settled into an exhausted conservatism. As early as '73, *GQ* wondered aloud if many young dudes weren't creating a "credibility gap" between their wardrobe and their careers. After all, it's hard to climb the corporate ladder when you come to work looking like Superfly. The recession and stagflation of 1974–1976 sent many young boomers out into the work force with slim pickings. Many women and former flower children were entering the job market for the first time. The resulting crunch resulted in a radical shift in fashion emphasis.

The return of the three-piece suit: Suit sales leaped by almost 40 percent in '76. Designer John Weitz observed that "a whole generation is trying to look businesslike with a capital B." Vests, which had been abandoned for years, made a huge comeback as millions of boomers went whole hog for the corporate look.

The dress-for-success look: Women entered the work force in unparalleled numbers and forged a new dress code that has undergone only slight modifications in the intervening years. In an energetic attempt to look as sexless as possible, many women adopted the plain blue blazer with the string-tie look. This harsh, almost schoolmarm style became most prevalent in legal and government circles, and was best popularized by such female groundbreakers as New York City Council President Carol Bellamy and Congresswoman Liz Holtzman. A more subdued female executive look included a nice floral blouse, navy or neutral blazer, and matching skirt topped off by a scarf in place of the string tie. Mary Tyler Moore's use of affordable designer Norman Todd gave millions of women fashion tips for the office.

The Annie Hall look: This swept the country in 1977 with its own funky variation on the dress for success look. Adopting oversized men's shirts, floppy hats, long skirts, baggy pants, clunky boots, and owlish glasses, Diane Keaton's adorable character created an instant antistyle that allowed women to look both kooky and conservative at the same time. By exaggerating the reverse drag of office wear, the Annie Hall look projected an air of whimsical vulnerability and allowed women to be both innocent and seductive without looking silly or sleazy—a tall order given many Seventies' fashion statements.

Specialized sportswear: The Seventies' boom in consumer sports like tennis ("inner" and otherwise), skiing, dancing, hiking, and jogging produced a whole new world of fashion and footwear alternatives. Before the Seventies, there were two kinds of sneakers: high tops and low tops, and maybe an occasional tennis sneaker. By decade's end, running shoes had become a kind of spiritual and technological status symbol. Jogging outfits became acceptable wear in the mall and on the track. Hiking shoes and down vests gave an outdoorsy look to the deskbound. Dance shoes, leotards, and body stockings boomed as disco and roller skating demaded a combination of flexibility and sexuality. While many might exercise in their corporate T-shirt, others had to have their endeavors endorsed by Adidas to feel they were getting their money's worth. La Coste shirts proliferated wildly in '78 and '79 as the whole country seemed to go all gator crazy. These comfort-

Sewn-on patches added a multitude of signs and symbols to the subtleties of body language.

Unsafe at any speed: Platform shoes were condemned as health hazards by **Consumer Reports.**

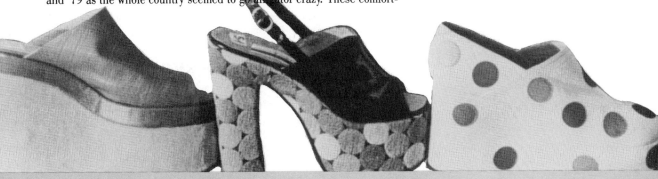

23: Kissinger to OPEC: oil shock could bring "breakdown of world order and safety.".

23: Ted Kennedy rules out 1976 White House bid.

23: Nixon hospitalized with phlebitis.

28: Betty Ford undergoes mastectomy.

23: Robbie McIntosh of Average White Band overdoses.

#1 Singles:
Eric Clapton—"I Shot the Sheriff"
Barry White—"Can't Get Enough of Your Love, Babe"
Andy Kim—"Rock Me Gently"

Selected Gold Record Albums:
Rick Wakeman—*Journey to the Center of the Earth*
Bad Company—*Bad Company*
Barry White—*Can't Get Enough*

99

able, sensible, and conspicuously nonsynthetic clothes told the world that you were looking for an elite sports look. This La Coste craze combined with the already popular L. L. Bean look (down vests, duck boots, and hunting jackets) to result in the critical mass that would become known as the preppie look in the late Seventies and early Eighties.

Disco wear: While the leisure suit may have launched a million gags among the rich and famous, its stretchy, synthetic, pastel, wide-collared combination of sportswear and office attire reincarnated itself on the disco floor. As John Travolta made obvious, disco was the working stiff's chance to strut his stuff in spandex. Disco's outrageous variation contact dance was matched by an equally garish stab at "dressing up." For all of its libidinous excess, disco was essentially a conservative return to zoot suits, flappers, and the conventions of a pre-rock-and-roll past.

The punk look, the black dress, the "attitude" look: Punk's embrace of black and white (and occasional hot pink) represented a violent rejection of the mellow "natural" look and the playful pastels of the disco crowd. In its rejection of style for black shirts, short hair, mutilated earlobes, and an air of maladjusted disdain, punk has emerged as the longest lasting fashion trend of the Seventies. This can still be seen in every city in America, where hordes of seventeen year olds still clamor to look like Siouxie and Sid Vicious.

The deification of the designer: After fighting the establishment, Americans ended the Seventies with a passion for brand names and instant status. After a shaky decade of fashion disasters, millions embraced their Calvins, Halstons, Armanis, Yves St. Laurents, and Vanderbilts as totems against uncertainty. Americans wanted to be led again, and this paved the way for the Eighties, a decade dominated by such leaders as Ronald Reagan and Ralph Lauren.

THE SEXUAL REVOLUTION

Everybody got laid in the Seventies, the high-water mark of the one-night stand. You could get away with anything and no one cared. Condoms? Curious leftovers from the Fifties that were advertised in the back pages of stroke books. Biological clocks? Something that told bears when to hibernate. To

OCTOBER 1974

8: Ford asks Americans to "Whip Inflation Now." Distributes WIN buttons.

15: Mexico announces discovery of huge oil reserve.

27: Margarett "Happy" Rockefeller undergoes mastectomy.

1: Wilt Chamberlain retires.

13: Ed Sullivan dies.

17: Oakland A's win third straight World Series.

be married was to be chained. To be married with children was to be doubly chained. To be single or only casually "committed" was the most desirable state. Marriage and children were virtually foreign countries to many latter-day boomers. Pop songs and movies showed the hellish drudgery of mindless marriage and extolled the virtues of the sexually uninhibited. Songs like Carly Simon's "That's the Way I Heard It Should Be" made matrimony seem like a drag. The Eagles' "Already Gone" celebrated breaking up with a "victory song."

For all of their sexual stamina, latter-day boomers were not born hornier than past generations. Despite all the tut-tutting of many elders, the sexual revolution was not a matter of morals but demography, destiny, and chemistry. After all, here you had the largest group of babies ever born coming of age at the same time that the pill and antibiotics had eliminated pregnancy and venereal disease as the logical outcome of promiscuity. Given the same chance, every generation would have behaved the same way.

Return with us then for this sixty-second guide to the sexual mayhem of in the Seventies.

Singles bars (early 1970s): An opening line, a couple of tequila sunrises, a line or toke in the car, and you were in. Was life really that simple? Or was it the glint from thousands of gold chains that hypnotized a generation of women into easy submission?

The Peterson-Kekich Wife-Swap (1972-73): *Bob and Carol and Ted and Alice* meets the Game of the Week when New York Yankees pitchers Fritz Peterson and Mike Kekich announce publicly that they have swapped wives and families. One marriage lasts, the other doesn't. For this heroic act, their baseball cards should be in Cooperstown, but inexplicably aren't.

The Single's Pad: And where did those bar prowlers crash when they weren't inquiring about some prospective bed partner's astrological sign? Where else but those ultra-modern apartment complexes filled entirely with these lean and hungry Lotharios. In these high-rise summer camps for the terminally adolescent, nary a wedding band could be seen. Many of these complexes have now been converted into co-ops, but they can be glimpsed, preserved on tape, on a handful of *Love, American Style* episodes.

Plato's Retreat: This Manhattan club offered cut-rate orgies for the un-

28: Arab nations announce unconditional support of PLO.

29: Nixon in shock after surgery, near death.

#1 Singles:
Olivia Newton-John—"I Honestly Love You"
Billy Preston—"Nothing From Nothing"
Dionne Warwick and the Spinners—"Then Came You"

1: Unemployment reaches three-year high.

NOVEMBER 1974

30: Ali KOs Foreman in Zaire, regains heavyweight title.

Selected Gold Record Albums:
Rolling Stones—*It's Only Rock and Roll*
John Lennon—*Walls and Bridges*
Olivia Newton-John—*Let Me Be There*
Quincy Jones—*Body Heat*
Black Oak Arkansas—*Black Oak Arkansas*

2: Hank Aaron traded to Milwaukee Brewers.

101

washed masses. Ordinary, if overly horny, couples would plunk down $12.50 and head for the "mattress room," which they'd turn into a tapestry of tangled arms, legs, and other body parts, with more collective grunting and groaning than WrestleMania. "Sex is not the main factor people come here," claimed the club's owner. "This is a mellow atmosphere, a nice place." Oh. That still doesn't explain why it was one of the first places closed by the New York City Department of Health during the early days of the AIDS scare.

Hustler magazine: Columbus, Ohio, publishing magnate Larry Flynt's raunchy mag made even *Playboy*'s Hugh Hefner and *Penthouse*'s Bob Guccione blush. Famous for publishing a comic strip called Chester the Molester, as well as nude photos of a sunbathing Jackie Onassis, Flynt later would be shot and paralyzed by an unknown assailant and would become, thanks to Jimmy Carter's evangelical sister Ruth, a born-again Christian. First decision: to change that comic strip's name to Chester the Protector.

Last Tango in Paris (1973): The porn aesthetic hits the legitimate screen as a post-*Godfather* Marlon Brando bares his fanny for Bernardo Bertolucci's camera. Truth be told, *Deep Throat* is eminently more amusing and a hell of a lot less pretentious.

Co-ed Dorms: The panty raid became passé as more and more colleges said to hell with *in loco parentis* rules. It now became easier for guys to watch women perform intimate acts, such as shaving their legs. Too bad so few did.

Water Beds: An essential piece of furniture in the bedrooms of swinging singles. One's sex life or at least one's sacroiliac was said to improve dramatically by rolling around these slosh piles. That is if you didn't slide off onto the shag-carpeted floor attempting some esoteric technique suggested by *The Joy of Sex*.

Living together: Millions of Americans moved from dating to cohabitation without benefit of a marriage license, or a second thought. For many liberated women, the arrangement transcended the whole "marriage as chattel" trip, and told the world that she was as tentative about the whole thing as he. The biggest problem for many wasn't the arrangement, but what to call your significant other. Your partner? Lover? Mistress? Roommate? Friend? Old man? Old lady? One new word would be invented in the Seven-

Sex clubs like **Plato's Retreat** *franchised the sexual revolution and provided instant orgies for those willing to pay the cover charge.*

8: Lt. Calley paroled.

20: U.S. sues to break up AT&T.

21: Walter Mondale withdraws from 1976 presidential race.

24: Ford, Brezhnev meet in Vladivostok, USSR, for arms talks.

26: Japanese Prime Minister Tanaka resigns in money scandal.

13: *Trial of Billy Jack* released.

27: George Steinbrenner suspended from baseball.

102

ties, however, to describe what happens when said significant other decided to split. That word is palimony.

Sex books: Sexual manuals (or more properly, marriage manuals) used to be clunky works, whose clinical language was one step removed from a third-year anatomy text. Available only by mail order, they usually remained buried in your parents' night table. In the Seventies, thanks to such epics as *The Joy of Sex*, *The Sensuous Man*, *The Sensuous Woman*, and their various sequels and spin-offs, sex became as easily explainable as a Venus paint-by-number set. These tomes were proudly displayed on both *The New York Times* best seller list and your coffee table.

Of all the sex manuals, *The Joy of Sex* most dramatically expressed the clinical detachment and completely nonjudgmental attitudes of the era. *Joy* celebrated sex as "the safest of all human activities," and assured its nervous readers that "good hand and mouth work practically guarantee you a good partner.'

With *Joy*'s cookbook motif, sex is reduced to a menu of choices, with an accent on the "top grade," "cordon bleu," and "high quality," making sex, like drugs and stereos, one of the first quality commodities that many proto-yuppies were taught to crave.

Joy includes the following observations that sum up the many Seventies' attitudes towards sex:

On children: "Children can limit the sex play of adults by being around."

On bondage: "Chains create a tied up and tinkling look—fashionable now and they look good on naked skin."

On pain: ". . . the idea of being beaten unquestionably turns some people on, and if it does, you should try it."

On bisexuality: "All people are bisexual."

On rape: "Lovers will play rape games without end, but the real thing is a frightening turn-off."

On fidelity: "We've deliberately not gone into the ethics of lifestyles."

Fear of Flying: No conversation about the sexual revolution would be complete without discussing Erica Jong's controversial best-seller. A turn-on to men and a breakthrough for women, *Flying* discusses female sexual longing and fulfillment with the same bawdy abandon as male literary lechers Henry Miller and Norman Mailer. Miller called it "the feminine coun-

The singles bar: How many Tequila Sunrises did it take to get from "what's your sign?" to "your place or mine?"

#1 Singles:
Stevie Wonder—"You Haven't Done Nothin'"
Bachman Turner Overdrive—"You Ain't Seen Nothing Yet"
John Lennon with Elton John—"Whatever Gets You Thru the Night"
Billy Swan—"I Can Help"

2: House leader Wilbur Mills in affair with stripper, Fanne Fox.

12: Jimmy Carter begins 1976 White House campaign.

DECMEBER 1974

Selected Gold Record Albums:
David Bowie—*Bowie Live*
Helen Reddy—*I Don't Know How to Love Him*
Jethro Tull—*War Child*
Paul Anka—*Anka*
Joni Mitchell—*Miles of Aisles*

12: *The Godfather Part II* released.

12: Mick Taylor leaves Rolling Stones.

terpart of *Tropic of Cancer*. For all the wild plot gyrations, it is Jong's subject, female sexual fulfillment, that makes *Flying* a Seventies' classic. After all, before women's liberation and the 1970s, female sexual anatomy was barely discussed. Even girly mags like *Playboy* denied the existence of the vagina and airbrushed it into gauzy oblivion. Yet with the Seventies, one could barely turn around without reading the unending debate about female orgasm and its attendant myths and misses. In the Seventies, women were no longer "submitting" to sex, but going at it with as much desire and abandon as men.

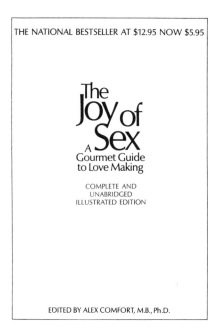

THE NATIONAL BESTSELLER AT $12.95 NOW $5.95

The
Joy of
Sex
A
Gourmet Guide
to Love Making

COMPLETE AND
UNABRIDGED
ILLUSTRATED EDITION

EDITED BY ALEX COMFORT, M.B., Ph.D.

Half cookbook, half instruction manual, The Joy of Sex provided a guilt-free guide to cordon bleu sex.

DRUG CULTURE

No discussion of Seventies' pop culture is complete without mentioning the D word. Like much of the counterculture, drugs—particularly pot—passed from revolutionary to merely de rigueur during the early Seventies. What

19: Rockefeller sworn in as Vice President.

13: George Harrison lunches with Gerald Ford at the White House.

21: *New York Times* reveals wide-spread CIA domestic spying.

#1 Singles:
Carl Douglas—"Kung Fu Fighting"
Harry Chapin—"Cat's in the Cradle"
Helen Reddy—"Angie Baby"

Selected Gold Record Albums:
Jackson Brown—*Late for the Sky*
Harry Chapin—*Verities and Balderdash*
Bobby Vinton—*Melodies of Love*

JANUARY 1975

5: Ford names Rockefeller to investigate CIA abuses.

6: Boston mayor cancels Led Zeppelin show after fans riot.

had been considered a revolutionary act, a "statement," became a normal, adolescent ritual. Drugs: finding them, taking them, hiding them, and talking about them were to the Seventies what making out and cruising were to the Fifties. In many ways, drug culture was made for the Seventies. After all, drugs are the perfect consumer item for a culture dominated by teens and adolescents. With peer pressure, hedonism, and expressive conformity being the driving force of most teen behavior, drugs were made for the boomer-intensive times. After all, the "just say no" Eighties did not begin until most of the formerly indulgent boomers had become parents.

For all the sex going on during the so-called sexual revolution, getting high was still the most dominant preoccupation of the decade. In most previous decades most of the best slang and popular songs involved elaborate code words and obscure song lyrics to talk about sex. With sex so out in the open, most of this linguistic energy went into drug lingo, creating an elaborate slang that dominated youth culture for much of the decade. If you weren't holding, then getting a joint/jay/doobie/bone/ace/hooter was your main concern. Of course, if you didn't have any papers, you could use a chillum/spliff/hookah/bong/lock-pipe/one-hitter/party bowl/shotgut, or just make do with a screen perched on a beer can for a poor man's makeshift water pipe.

Many of the behavioral, political, and social changes of the late Seventies were reflected in the changes in the drug culture. As the drug of choice shifted from pot, with its hazy introspection, to cocaine, with its high-priced hedonism, social mores changed from the communal to the exclusive. Studio 54's choosy admission policy was a perfect reflection of the coke culture going on inside. Only the right people—those rich enough to take a toot in the bathroom stalls—were allowed in. Coke and all the cash behind it made much of the seamier side of drug culture apparent to many. Major coke dealers were no longer happy Cheech and Chong-like dopers, but high-powered movers and shakers who played like moguls and consorted with gangsters. Not since prohibition days were so many millions of Americans dependent on organized crime for their buzz of choice. More than Ralph Lauren, inflation, or Ronald Reagan, cocaine provided the missing link between the Seventies' frazzled self-absorption and the money- and status-obsessed Eighties.

POT CULTURE VS.
COKE CULTURE

Ideal Party:
❀ Pot: Sharing drugs with 400,000 people at Woodstock or Watkins Glen.
❀ Coke: Sitting and snorting alone on a toilet, while everyone wonders where you went.

Car of choice:
❀ Pot: VW
❀ Coke: BMW

Dealer Profile:
❀ Pot: Philosophy major with friends in the country with an acre of home-grown.
❀ Coke: A frantically stylish friend of a friend with YSL jeans and connections to the Gambino family.

Biggest Material Risk:
❀ Pot: Spilling bong water on the shag rug.
❀ Coke: Blowing your life savings so you can keep on tootin'.

Biggest Existential Risk:
❀ Pot: Spending ten years without getting anything done.
❀ Coke: Waiting another ten seconds before getting another rush.

Biggest Ambition:
❀ Pot: Pondering the interconnectedness of all living things.
❀ Coke: Making a killing in the options market.

Design/Style:
❀ Pot: Victorian
❀ Coke: High-Tech

FEBRARY 1975

3: Federal budget announced with largest peacetime deficit.

4: British Tories elect Margaret Thatcher party chief.

6: Henry "Scoop" Jackson enters presidential race.

17: Sen. Lloyd Bentsen enters presidential race.

#1 Singles:
Neil Sedaka—"Laughter in the Rain"
Ohio Players—"Fire"
Linda Ronstadt—"You're No Good"
Average White Band—"Pick Up the Pieces"

Selected Gold Record Albums:
Bob Dylan—*Blood on the Tracks*
Jefferson Starship—*Dragon Fly*
Todd Rundgren—*Something/Anything?*
Olivia Newton-John—*Have You Ever Been Mellow*

DRUGS AND MUSIC OF CHOICE

In the Seventies, drugs and records were more than something your bought, they *said* something about who you were, and where your "head" was at any particular time. Of course some drugs and music went together better than others. The following is an entirely speculative table, charting the changes in drug and music culture through the decade.

	Drug of Choice	Music of Choice
1970	$20/oz. Pot	"Truckin' "—Grateful Dead
	Acid	"Spill the Wine"—Eric Burdon
	Speed	"Whole Lotta Love"—Led Zeppelin
	Barbituates	"Closer to Home"—Grand Funk Railroad
	Colt 45	"Knock Three Times"—Dawn
	Mateus Rose	"Bridge Over Troubled Waters"—Simon and Garfunkel
	Bud	"Okie From Muskogie"—Merle Haggard
	Sugar Smacks	"I Think I Love You"—Partridge Family
1971	Acapulco Gold	"Layla"—Eric Clapton
	Acid	*Aqualung*—Jethro Tull
	Smack	"Sister Morphine"—Rolling Stones
	Reds	"Iron Man"—Black Sabbath
	Valium	"Rainy Days and Mondays"—Carpenters
	Jesus	"Spirit in the Sky"—Norman Greenbaum
	Boone's Farm	*New Riders of the Purple Sage*
1972	Homegrown	*Court and Spark*—Joni Mitchell
	Acid	"Roundabout"—Yes
	Speed	"School's Out"—Alice Cooper
	Smack	"Tumblin' Dice"—Stones
	Almaden White	"Summer Breeze"—Seals and Crofts

MARCH 1975

7: Unemployent reaches 8.2 percent.

13-25: S. Vietnamese troops in full retreat; refugees press south.

18: CIA reveals Howard Hughes's attempts to salvage Soviet submarine.

20: Foreign embassies flee Cambodia as Khmer Rouge encircle Phnom Penh.

1: Best New Vocalist Grammy for Olivia Newton-John.

2: Linda McCartney busted for pot possession in L.A.

	Drug of Choice	**Music of Choice**
1973	Colombian	"Smoke on the Water"—Deep Purple
	Night Train	"Super Fly"—Curtis Mayfield
	Ludes	*Dark Side of the Moon*—Pink Floyd
	Speed	"We're an American Band"—Grand Funk
	Spanish Fly	"Pillow Talk"—Sylvia
	Amyl Nitrate	"Leader of the Pack"—Bette Midler
1974	"Blond" hash	"The Joker"—Steve Miller
	Champale	"Can't Get Enough of Your Love Babe"—Barry White
	Ludes	*Not Fragile*—Bachman Turner Overdrive
	Coke	"Dr. Wu"—Steely Dan
	Speed	*Diamond Dogs*—Bowie
	Rum and Coke	"Let Me Be There"—Olivia Newton John
	Tequila/Lemon/Salt	"Midnight at the Oasis"—Maria Muldaur
	Harvey Wallbangers	"Rock Your Baby"—George Macrae
1975	"Really Fine" Colombian	*Hissing of Summer Lawns*—Joni Mitchell
	Coors Beer	"Thank God I'm a Country Boy"—John Denver
	'Shrooms	*The Lamb Lies Down on Broadway*—Genesis
	Ludes	*Energized*—Foghat
	Speed	*Welcome to My Nightmare*—Alice Cooper
	Poppers	*Young Americans*—Bowie
	Tequila sunrise	"Lyin' Eyes"—Eagles
1976	Thai stick	*Bustin Out*—Pure Prairie League
	Acid	*Mothership Connection*—Parliament
	Ludes	*Love Hurts*—Nazareth
	Paul Masson Zinfandel	*Silk Degrees*—Boz Scaggs
	Champale	"Boogie Fever"—Sylvers
	Coke	"You Sexy Thing"—Hot Chocolate
	Valium	"I Write the Songs"—Barry Manilow
	White wine spritzer	"The Four Seasons"—Vivaldi

25: Saudi King Faisal assassinated by nephew at Palace ceremony.

24: Ali defeats Chuck Wepner to retain title.

26: Congress passes tax cut to stimulate economy.

29: All six Led Zeppelin albums are on the charts.

#1 Singles:
Eagles—"Best of My Love"
Olivia Newton-John—"Have You Ever Been Mellow"
Doobie Brothers—"Black Water"
Frankie Valli—"My Eyes Adored You"
Labelle—"Lady Marmalade"

Selected Gold Record Albums:
Led Zeppelin—*Physical Grafitti*
B. T. Express—*Do It (Till You're Satisfied)*
Minnie Ripperton—*Perfect Angel*

APRIL 1975

1: Unemployment reaches post-Depression high of 8.7 percent.

Drug of Choice	Music of Choice	
Last year's pot	*Year of the Cat*—Al Stewart	**1977**
Jack Daniels	*Tejas*—Z. Z. Top	
Colt 45	"Car Wash"—Rose Royce	
Speed	"The Things We Do for Love"—10CC	
Poppers	"Don't Leave Me This Way"—Thelma Houston	
Smack	"Anarchy in the UK"—Sex Pistols	
Valium	"Dreams"—Fleetwood Mac	

Sinsemilla	"Deacon Blue"—Steely Dan	**1978**
Screwdrivers	"It's a Heartache"—Bonnie Tyler	
Budweiser	"My Way"—Elvis Presley	
White Russians	"Just the Way You Are"—Billy Joel	
Ludes	"Baker Street"—Jerry Rafferty	
Jack Daniels	*The Sound In Your Mind*—Willie Nelson	
Coke	"Lay Down Sally"—Eric Clapton	
Speed	"Hot Blooded"—Foreigner	
Poppers	"If I Can't Have You"—Yvonne Elliman	
Valium	*Greatest Hits Album*—Abba	

Paraquat Green	Rust Never Sleeps—Neil Young	**1979**
Rolling Rock	Candy O—Cars	
Mescalin	Armed Forces—Elvis Costello	
Champale	*I Will Survive*—Gloria Gaynor	
Glue	*Rock and Roll High School*—Ramones	
Speed	"Heart of Glass"—Blondie	
Poppers	"Y.M.C.A."—Village People	
Coke	"Hot Stuff"—Donna Summer	
Tab	"No More Tears"—Barbra Streisand & Donna Summer	

: Ford announces symbolic Saigon airlift.

15-20: Vietcong press on Saigon, destroy nearby airbase at Bienhoa.

16-17: Cambodian capital falls to Khmer Rouge.

21: Gen. Nguyen van Thieu resigns; all U.S. military advisors leave S. Vietnam.

12: *Tommy* (the film) released.

17: Ford is first President to visit Ford Theater since Lincoln.

19: "The Hustle" enters charts.

#1 Singles:
Minnie Ripperton—"Loving You"
Elton John—"Philadephia Freedom"
B. J. Thomas—"Another Somebody Done Somebody Wrong Song"

RELIGIOUS CULTS
AND MOVEMENTS

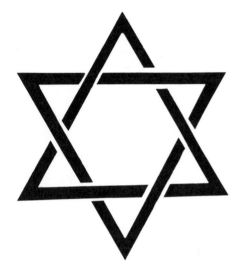

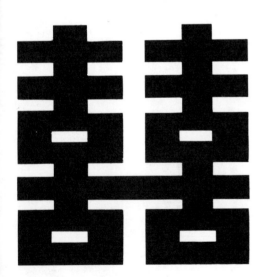

Raised on television, sex, drugs, and rock and roll, millions of impressionable baby boomers abandoned organized religion in the Seventies to dabble in a spiritual salad bar of fads, cults, and movements. Having failed to achieve "the revolution," many former flower children embraced a search for self and a quest for the divine, and many convinced themselves they were one and the same.

The decade began with a literal explosion of spiritualism, both Eastern and Western. In '71, *Life* magazine reported that "the wilting flower child [has] blossomed into the Jesus Freak." Pop culture was saturated with such "God-rock" songs as "Spirit in the Sky," "My Sweet Lord," "Put Your Hand in the Hand," and "The Lord's Prayer," while Broadway featured both the clown-Christ *Godspell* and acid-drenched passion play *Jesus Christ Superstar*. Feeding on the fervor and naïveté of young middle-class idealists, Christian cults, such as the Children of God, led many to abandon their lives and families for what many considered to be zombielike servitude. By '73, professional kidnapper Ted Patrick billed himself as the first certified "deprogrammer" of Jesus freaks. When asked for his secret, he replied: "Get that Bible away from them as soon as possible!"

Of all the cults, none caused as much concern and outrage as the Reverend Sun Myung Moon's Unification Church. Arriving from Korea in '73, Moon wasted no time in amassing huge amounts of money from his cult members and in ingratiating himself with members of Congress and the Nixon administration. "Moonies" were recruited by an almost scientific method of ego stroking, and "love bombing," and rhythmic chanting that appealed to a seemingly endless supply of confused kids. After years of drugs and "Inna Godda Da Vida," perhaps Moon's rhythmic, *Manchurian Candidate*-like brainwashing techniques seemed a relief.

Moon's curious brand of Christianity included group sex with new initiates ("blood cleansings") and an endless search for power. Moon claims his teachings supercede the Bible and that Jews were in league with Satan to betray Christ. In spite of such published outrages, Moon won favor with his fierce anti-Communist stance and courted Nixon during the darkest days of

29: Ford orders total evacuation of S. Vietnam.

30: Eighty-one U.S. helicopters remove last Americans and refugees from Saigon; Vietcong enter city within hours.

MAY 1975

14: U.S. forces rescue container ship *Mayaguez* from Cambodians.

16: Congress votes $405 million to resett Vietnamese refugees.

Selected Gold Record Albums:
Tony Orlando and Dawn—*Tuneweaving*
Phoebe Snow—*Phoebe Snow*
Aerosmith—*Get Your Wings*

4: Moe Howard, last of Three Stooges, dies.

5: South Africa legalizes television.

10: Stevie Wonder performs at Wa ington, D.C.'s, "Human Kindr Day."

Watergate. He went so far as to call him an "Archangel," and met with Nixon in January of '74 after leading a rally with Nixon's daughter Tricia and her husband. By the mid-Seventies, Moon controlled a munitions factory in Korea, a growing real estate empire in the U.S., and was beginning to dabble in newspapers. By '78, a House subcommittee linked Moon with the Korean Central Intelligence Agency and declared him a foreign agent. None of this bad press did anything to stop him from gaining thousands of new adherents and in arranging a gigantic mass "wedding" of his followers in New York's Madison Square Garden.

On the left side of the cult spectrum, the Divine Light Mission of Guru Mararaj-ji received its biggest boost when former Chicago Seven defendant Rennie Davis declared that following the fifteen-year-old guru was "the practical method to end poverty, racism, sexism and imperialism.... I would cross the planet on my hands and knees to touch his toe."

From '71 to '73, this post-adolescent "Perfect Master" amassed more than 60,000 U.S. followers, two huge estates, and several Rolls-Royces, Jaguars, and Mercedes. His menu for "Divine Light" involved three simple steps:

—Divine light: Sparks of inspiration and pain caused by pressing on your eyeballs as hard as you can.

—Nectar: Tilt your head backward with your tongue curled backward until you taste your own nasal drippings (a.k.a. snot)

—The Word: Plug your ears as hard as you can until you are overwhelmed with an inner buzz.

The "Perfect Master" outdid himself in November 1973 when he rented the Astrodome for "Millennium '73," a rally humbly billed as "The most significant event in human history." UFOs were expected to arrive for an interplanetary tailgate party. Neither aliens nor crowds materialized. A sex scandal in '74 sent the less than Perfect Master packing and greatly diminished his following.

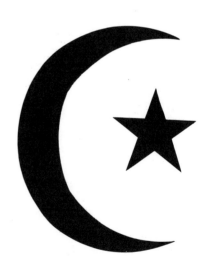

Rennie Davis was not the only Chicago Seven defendant to embrace the new consciousness of the Seventies. In his book *Growing Up At 37*, Jerry Rubin provides a veritable Michelin guide to the human potential movement. According to Rubin, the movement from revolution to inner dimensions was natural. "Instead of being *the movement*, we have become part of

27: Ford imposes second one-dollar increase on imported oil.

27: Alaska okays private marijuana use.

28: Ford reassures NATO allies in face of Indochina collapse.

29: Duke President Terry Sanford enters presidential race.

25: *The Bermuda Triangle* tops New York Times best-seller list.

Selected Gold Record Albums:
Styx—*Styx II*
Electric Light Orchestra—*Eldorado*
Steely Dan—*Katy Lied*
Elton John—*Captain Fantastic and the Brown Dirt Cowboy*

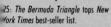

111

the flow." Rubin provides readers with a no-holds-barred account of his journey through est, gestalt, bioenergetics, Rolfing, massage, health foods, tai chi, Esalen, hypnotism, Silva mind control, Arica, acupuncture, sex therapy, and Reichian therapy—"a smorgasbord course in new consciousness." At times, Rubin treads a fine line between self-discovery and masturbation: "breathing on my cock and feeling energy throughout my system is inspiring." In the end, he embraces Werner Erhard's est. By '78, Erhard and Rubin become a road-show attraction, presenting a New Age fusion of Sixties' and Seventies' pop legends.

Although Rubin described est as a force "stronger than marijuana" that would "weaken the will of the people to compete, achieve and dominate," est proved to be a catalyst for the cut-throat competitive business culture of the Eighties.

Werner Erhard's est (Erhard Seminar Training) provided its adherents with an extreme combination of Dale Carnegie, Napoleon (Think and Grow Rich) Hill, and Zen Buddhism. After a couple of failed careers where he defrauded a few companies and abandoned his wife and children, Erhard finally got "it" while driving down a California freeway. "It" encompassed the selfish worldview that est would give to its thousands of willing, paying adherents. On weekend retreats, est trainees were denied freedom, food, even bathrooms as their resistance to "It" was broken down. "It" meant realizing that the world had no meaning or purpose, that you are the architect of everything you do, that you are the sole cause of everything that happens to you. Erhard's brand of radical self-reliance and self-absorption dispensed with the niceties of compassion and social responsibilities that weighed too many people down with guilt trips. By the late Seventies, est had gained hundreds of thousands of adherents and was in the throws of "The Hunger Project," a fund-raising effort that did not pretend to feed people. Its sole object was to perpetuate the "idea" of the end of hunger.

Most of est's self-evident pomposities made it a ripe target for satire of every stripe. TV's Mary Hartman joined STET, and Kris Kristoferson preached the word in *Semi-Tough*. Nevertheless, est provided many a polyester clad salesman with a quasi-mystical sense of cut-throat chutspa that Dale Carnegie never could.

Scientology received a huge boost during the spiritual quest of the Seven-

Rev. Moon called Nixon an "Archangel."
Congress called Moon a secret
agent for the Korean C.I.A.

#1 Singles:
Tony Orlando and Dawn—"He Don't Love You"
Earth, Wind and Fire—"Shining Star"
Freddy Fender—"Before the Next Teardrop Falls"

JUNE 1975

3: Ozzie Nelson dies.

9: CIA report reveals assassination attempts; domestic spying, and widespread use of LSD on unwitting "volunteers."

10: New York City narrowly avoids financial default.

23: Alice Cooper falls off stage and breaks several ribs.

112

CELEBRITIES AND THEIR CULTS

est:		*Scientology*	*The 15-Year-Old*
John Denver	Jerry Rubin	John Travolta	*Perfect Master*
Valerie Harper	Bucky Fuller	Karen Black	Rennie Davis
			(Chicago 7)

ties, gaining celebrity adherents John Travolta and Karen Black, as well as a certain countercultural cachet when Scientology workers broke into IRS offices to steal thousands of documents. Founded in the Fifities when sci-fi writer L. Ron Hubbard's *Dianetics* reached the best-seller lists, Scientology embraced many of the vaguely Buddhist doctrines of past lives and varying degrees of "clearness" (read: *karma*) that you could determine only by means of expensive "audits." Auditing released you of negative "memories/ images/facsimilies" and freed you to higher stages of spiritual powers. In addition to their IRS break-in, Scientologists lashed out with lawsuits against everyone who questioned their legitimacy.

By 1975 Transcendental Meditation had grown so mainstream that the Maharishi was appearing on Merv and the cover of *Time* magazine, which declared TM as "the turn-on of the 70's—a drugless high even the narc squad might enjoy." In '75, TM centers were giving out 30,000 new mantras per month at $125 a pop. Involving twenty minutes of meditation each day—with no wrong way to meditate—TM was a pantheistic grab bag. For many it was simply a way to relax and be quiet. Stevie Wonder, the Beach Boys, even congressmen meditated. Some physicians saw it as a way to lower blood pressure. Many religious leaders saw TM as "creeping Hinduism." Many Buddhists saw TM as a shallow relaxation technique, more suited to the personnel department than a search for enlightenment. Considering that TM was adopted and subsidized by such diverse corporations as AT&T, General Foods, Blue Cross/Blue Shield of Chicago, and Folsom Prison, it's hard to argue with their assessment.

Despite the benign acceptance of TM and good-natured lampooning of est's excesses, many harbored serious reservations about certain cultists' flight from freedom toward total adulation of messiahs and charlatans. The mass suicide of 911 cultists at the People's Temple in Jonestown, Guyana, in November 1978 provided a grisly coda to the Seventies' cult movement. *Time* called Jonestown "the Altamont" of cults. In many ways, Jonestown provided a brutal example of the hippie ethos gone haywire. Combining the charismatic allure of an evangelical preacher with the rhetoric of the radical

From Jesus Freaks to Perfect Masters, millions of Americans embraced a "Cults R Us" lifestyle during the Seventies.

26: Indira Gandhi suspends democracy, arrests political foes.

#1 Singles:
John Denver—"Thank God I'm a Country Boy"
America—"Sister Golden Hair"
Captain & Tennille—"Love Will Keep Us Together"

JULY 1975

3: Unemployment rate declines.

8: Ford announces reelection bid "to finish the job I started."

29: Overdose death for folk singer Tim Buckley.

Selected Gold Record Albums:
Wings—*Venus and Mars*
O'Jays—*Survival*
The Carpenters—*Horizon*
Lynyrd Skynyrd—*Nothing Fancy*
Eagles—*One of These Nights*

1: Ali tops Joe Bugner in Kuala Lumpur title bout.

Sri Crimnoy	**Born-Again Christians**		**Bahai Faith**	**Jim Jones**
John McLaughlin	Charles Colson	Jimmy Carter	Seals & Crofts	Mark Lane
Carlos Santana	Larry Flynt	Demond Wilson		

left, Jim Jones had taken his San Francisco-based People's Temple to Guyana to found a perfect state. Although Jones and his wife came from lily-white Indiana, most of his followers were poor and black. In San Francisco, Jones had gained a reputation as an organizer. He even received a letter of commendation from Vice President Walter Mondale for his help in the 1976 campaign. Yet even before moving to the jungle, Jones had begun to snap and sink into messianic delusions. "Too many people are looking at the Bible instead of me."

Tales of abuses had appeared in *New West* magazine and the *San Francisco Chronicle* in 1977. When San Francisco Congressman Leo Ryan went to visit the People's Temple, he was shown a perfectly happy, orderly ant farm. When members tried to leave with Ryan, however, the congressman and his party were shot, and Jones beseeched his membership to commit mass suicide with poisoned Kool-Aid. Amazingly, many of his followers did so voluntarily while he exorted them to die like good "Marxist Leninists." Unwilling members were shot or injected with poison. Jones himself was shot in the head. Only a handful escaped, including Jonestown lawyer Mark Lane, whose 1966 book *Rush to Judgment* was one of the early, celebrated accounts of a Kennedy assassination conspiracy. Coming only days after the Moscone/Milk murders, Jonestown sent the city of San Francisco into a state of shock and made many wonder what had become of the home base of "the summer of love."

FADS

Mood rings and pet rocks were two of the most irrational fads of the Seventies. Both became popular in late 1975. What does that say about that year?

Mood rings were invented by a New York meditation student named Joshua Reynolds in the summer of 1974 and became a marketing sensation the following year. One estimate claimed that more than 20 million of the damn things were sold in '75.

17: U.S. and Soviet astronauts join in Apollo/Soyuz space mission.

20: *Breach of Faith* tops best-seller lists.

31: N.Y.'s Mayor Beame lays off thousands to avoid bankruptcy.

#1 Singles:
Wings—"Listen to What the Man Said"
Van McCoy—"The Hustle"

 AUGUST 1975

1: Thirty-five nations sign Helsinki accords, officially ending World War II.

The perfect trinket for the Me Decade, mood rings were clear quartz "stones" filled with liquid crystals that changed color according to one's body temperature. But the rings weren't just for looking pretty—they were eyes to the soul that reflected the wearer's mood. Colors spanned the rainbow. Blue showed inner tranquility; green, stability; purple, happiness. But beware if your ring turned black. That meant you were tense. You couldn't expect anyone to get behind you then, you negative energy freak. (That happened once to Sophia Loren. At a press conference, her mood ring turned black, so she took it off, lest the reporters get wise to her inner turmoil.)

No doubt Miss Loren was wearing one of the classier varieties of mood rings, like the $45 silver version or the $250 14-carat gold version sold at Bonwit Teller. That may have been acceptable for her or celebrities like Muhammad Ali and Joe Namath, who also wore the rings, but we peasants would have to shell out as little as $2.98 for the baubles. The liquid crystals in the rings were supposed to last two years and then turn black forever. But by '77, when most of those 20 million rings were turning black, few people were wearing them anymore.

Mood rings you could almost . . . almost understand. After all, in the mid-Seventies people were looking into their souls, getting in touch with their feelings, meditating, and the like. But pet rocks? That's a toughie to figure out. Chalk it up to gullibility of people for a cute novelty item and the marketing genius of Gary Dahl, a Los Gatos, California, advertising executive.

How about a pet that would require no paper-training, no walking in inclement weather, no payments for food and medical care? Quicker than you can say Fred Flintstone, Dahl created the pet rock. It was an instant success and became the hot gift for Christmas 1975.

Dahl bought 2 1/2 tons of rocks from a Mexican beach and eventually was shipping 3,000 to 6,000 a day to stores like Bloomingdale's, Macy's, and Lord and Taylor. Packaged in their own individual cardboard carrying box, nestled in excelsior, they sold for $5.

The Pet Rock was the ultimate goof gift of a fad-intensive times.

#1 Singles:
Eagles—"One of These Nights"
Bee Gees—"Jive Talkin'"
Hamilton, Joe Frank and Reynolds—"Fallin' in Love"
KC and the Sunshine Band—"Get Down Tonight"

FBI joins hunt for missing Teamster boss Jimmy Hoffa.

9: Seagram heir Samuel Bronfman reported abducted.

8: *Nashville* opens in Nashville.

16: Peter Gabriel leaves the group Genesis.

Selected Gold Record Albums:
Rolling Stones—*Made in the Shade*
Captain & Tennille—*Love Will Keep Us Together*

Marshall Tucker Band—*Marshall Tucker Band*
Ohio Players—*Honey*
Jefferson Starship—*Red Octopus*

SEPTEMBER 1975

And that wasn't all. In each box, Dahl included a care-and-training manual, which let you know how to treat your new pet upon first entering your home. "Place it on some old newspapers. The rock will never know what the paper is for and will require no further instruction." Dahl claimed you could also teach the rock how to roll over, heel, and play dead. The latter would be an especially popular talent of the pet rock.

Dahl's manual also claimed the pet rock could be used for attack training: "Reach into your pocket and purse as though you were going to comply with the mugger's demands. Extract your pet rock. Shout the command: 'Attack' and bash the mugger's head in."

STREAKING

During the 1970s, many Americans were into running. A small minority of them, however, preferred to do their running for very short distances—without their clothes on. This peculiar habit, which flourished during the winter and spring of 1974, was given the curious name of streaking.

The fad began in late January 1974 on college campuses—a sure sign that the student protest movement was over. Kids weren't running around naked to protest anything (although several student groups did sponsor "streaks for impeachment"). They were doing it just to have fun and to see what they could get away with. Streaking was the Seventies' equivalent of the panty raid of the 1950s, and it verified what many Sixties' veterans had been thinking: that the next generation of students had a decidedly apolitical bent.

Students across the nation took up streaking with a vengeance. At the University of Georgia, a few 'Dawgs parachuted out of a plane stark naked. At the University of South Carolina, several students streakers biked through Columbia. Even at staid Harvard, streaking took on a decided Ivy League cast: A group of Crimson streakers wearing only surgical masks dashed through a room where classmates were taking an anatomy exam. Twelve hundred University of Colorado students streaked at one time, breaking the old record of 1,000 and earning a dubious place in the *Guinness Book of World Records*.

Streakings were reported at such diverse places as the Eiffel Tower in

Half street-theater and half jogging, streaking proved to be the perfection transition fad between the Sixties and the Eighties.

5: Manson follower Lynette ''Squeaky'' Fromme attempts to shoot President Ford in Sacramento, CA.

5: *Jaws* becomes biggest grossing film to date.

10: Lt. Calley's conviction reinstated.

18: Patty Hearst captured by FBI.

20: Bay City Rollers' American debut.

22: Political activist Sara Jane Moore shoots pistol at President Ford in San Francisco; shot deflected by hero bystander.

Paris, St. Peter's Square in Rome, and in Kenya, South Korea, Brazil, and Taiwan.

The most famous streaking incident occurred on April 2, 1974, at the Academy Awards when Robert Opel, a thirty-eight-year-old advertising executive, ran completely naked past host David Niven, showing his body beautiful to a live, national television audience. Niven's comeback was a classic: "I suppose it was bound to happen . . . the only laugh that man will ever get in life is stripping off his pants and showing shortcomings." When the commotion had quieted, Liz Taylor, whom Niven was about to introduce, came on stage to present the Oscar for Best Picture to *The Sting*. Unlike Niven, she was flustered. Her reaction: "That's a pretty hard act to follow. I'm nervous—that really upset me. I'm jealous."

For his part, Opel (who had a legitimate press pass) explained his thirty seconds of fame: "It just occurred to me that it might be an educative thing to do. You know, people shouldn't be ashamed of being nude in public. Besides it's a hell of a way to launch a career."

The fad even had its own anthem. Five days after the Oscar telecast, "The Streak," a tune written and performed by veteran singer Ray Stevens ("Everything Is Beautiful," "Ahab the Arab"), entered the Billboard charts. Five weeks later it was number one, and would be so for the next three weeks.

But by then streaking was winding down. By late May and June, anyone caught streaking was as outmoded as, well, an anti-Vietnam protestor.

No one quite knew why the fad took off, so to speak—and why it just seemed to fade away a few months later, although media guru Marshall McLuhan weighed in with his assessment: "Streaking is a put-on, a form of assault," he said. "It's an art form of course. All entertainment has elements of malice and power in it. Streaking has a political point, too. It's a form of activism." Good try, Doc. But we think a Princeton student scoped out the situation more keenly: "I never really understood why we did it in the first place," the undergrad explained. "And I couldn't say why we're not doing it now."

FIFTIES' NOSTALGIA

One of the most enduring legacies of the 1970s is the veneration of the 1950s as a kind of golden age of innocence. The 1950s revival started in the

25: OPEC raises oil price by 10 percent.

#1 Singles:
Glen Campbell—"Rhinestone Cowboy"
David Bowie—"Fame"
John Denver—"I'm Sorry"

25: Jackie Wilson suffers heart attack, enters coma.

28: Four Oakland A's pitch in combined no-hitter.

30: HBO begins nationwide programming.

Selected Gold Record Albums:
Aerosmith—*Aerosmith*
Richard Pryor—*Is It Something I Said?*
Janis Ian—*Between the Lines*

*John Travolta
in* **Grease**

early Seventies and hasn't stopped since. Not for nothing did it coincide with the rise of Richard Nixon, the ultimate living 1950s revival. In fact, some pundits claimed that the overwhelming Nixon victory over George McGovern in 1972 was a desire to return to those preturbulent days before the Sixties. The Fifties' revival also grew out of the hopelessness and frustration of many people as it became apparent that the agenda of the Sixties was not going to be accomplished.

The revival may have been spurred by those who came of age during the decade, but those who were mere kiddies then became its most visible proponents. On college campuses and at high schools, kids held Fifties' parties at which long-haired boys slicked Vitalis on their skulls and pushed their hair behind their ears, while long-haired girls tied their Joni Mitchell manes into ponytails, as both jitterbugged to earlier rock-and-roll hits.

For those who recalled the Fifties as a time of McCarthyism, Cold War anxieties, and sexual repression, this revival seemed mighty strange. But of course it wasn't *those* Fifties that were being revived. Like most forms of nostalgia, the most negative aspects were filtered out. The new party line—and the one that we've lived with into the Nineties—is that the Fifties were a time of innocence, where teens wiled away their days at sock hops and malt shops.

The first "rock-and-roll revival" concert was held in October 1969. By 1973 they had become a cottage industry. They were inexpensive to produce and didn't have the decibel-bending levels of contemporary rock concerts. Such artists as Fats Domino, Bill Haley, the Coasters, and assorted doowop groups were now making more money for a couple of gigs than they did during entire years of their heydays.

Music-wise, the high-water mark of this first wave of Fifties' nostalgia was on October 21, 1972, when Chuck Berry's "My Ding-a-Ling" hit number one (just a week earlier *Newsweek* had splashed Marilyn Monroe on its cover for its story about the Fifties' revival entitled "Yearning for the Good Old Days.")

As for Berry: The most influential rock guitarist of all time never had a

OCTOBER 1975

9: Soviet dissident Andrei Sakharov wins Nobel peace prize.

19: Chinese warn Kissinger against detente with USSR.

20: U.S. and Soviets agree to five-year grain accord.

21: Birch Bayh joins pre dential race.

1: Ali defeats Frazier in "Thrilla in Manila."

1: Al Jackson of Booker T and the MGs shot to death in Memphis.

9: Yoko Ono gives birth to Sean Ono Lennon.

11: *Saturday Night Live* debuts; George Carlin hosts.

118

number one hit during his prime. Such rock classics as "School Days," "Johnny B. Goode," or "Sweet Little 16″ never topped the charts. Instead, Berry reached that mark with "My Ding-a-Ling," a stupid kiddie rhyme with a third-grader's attitude about sex. That same week, two other Fifties' survivors, Elvis Presley and Rick (Don't Call Me Ricky) Nelson both had top-ten songs, "Burning Love" and "Garden Party," respectively. Nelson's song, ironically, dealt with the rude reaction he received from a Madison Square Garden rock-and-roll revival audience when he dared to perform some of his new material. Meanwhile, a still-slim Elvis was at the height of his post-comeback fame.

The revival didn't enrich only the Fifties' retreads. Sha Na Na, a group of Columbia University students who dressed in Fifties' styles (in reality, all were preteens during the original Fifties) became extremely popular. Considered little more than a freak show when they performed at Woodstock in 1969, they would eventually become stars of their own syndicated TV show and would be the prototype for dozens of other faux-Fifties' bands.

The revival spread to other media as well. *Happy Days* brought the 1950s to TV. On the big screen, *American Graffiti* captured the decade's ambience in a big way, and it was followed by other nostalgic films, such as *The Lords of Flatbush* and *American Hot Wax*.

The biggest perpetrator of the Fifties' myth, however, was *Grease*. The musical about life at Rydell High School opened off-Broadway on February 14, 1972, moved to Broadway a few months later, and would run into the early 1980s. The 1978 movie version starring Olivia Newton-John and John Travolta was that year's box-office smash.

Little did we know that Fifties' nostalgia would become a permanent feature of the American cultural landscape. Jeff Greenfield, then a twenty-nine-year-old writer and now of ABC News, was prescient when he told *Newsweek* in 1972: "The generation that grew up in the Fifties is now equipped to revive itself. We are now old enough to be TV producers and film distributors. In ten years, people will be reminiscing about the '60s. It's not surprising that the '50s are back now. All it means is that a new generation is feeling its age."

The Fifties' "revival" has lasted two decades longer than the decade itself. Now, in an age of doo-wop commercials for everything from transmis-

29: Ford nixes federal aid to New York City; New York *Daily News*: FORD TO CITY: DROP DEAD.

#1 Singles:
Neil Sedaka—"Bad Blood"

10: Portugal abandons colony of Angola as civil war rages.

10: UN votes resolution equating Zionism with racism.

NOVEMBER 1975

26: *Ragtime* tops best-seller list.

Selected Gold Record Albums:
Allman Brothers—*Win, Lose or Draw*
Bruce Springsteen—*Born to Run*
Jackson Browne—*For Everyman*

6: The group Sex Pistols debut in London.

The Greatest (Muhammad Ali) engages in a bit of personal summitry with the Brezhnev.

sion repairs to shoes, Fifties'-themed restaurants and diners, covers of 1950s' tunes, and obsession with Elvis and Marilyn, maybe it's finally time to say: Enough.

SPORTS IN THE SEVENTIES

Weird leagues: With lots of well-heeled folks willing to invest their spare cash in fly-by-night sports ventures, rival leagues sprang up to challenge the long-established leagues. The World Football League's biggest legacy will be teams with such singular nicknames as the Philadelphia Bell and the Chicago Fire. The World Hockey Association was notable for luring swinger Derek Sanderson from the NHL and giving new life to ancient Gordie Howe. But the coolest alternate league was the American Basketball Association, which began play in 1967 but reached its zenith in the early Seventies. It featured a red, white, and blue ball and a wide-open anything-goes style of play, characterized by the one and only Dr. J, Julius Erving.

Million-dollar athletes: In the 1970s, it became possible to buy a pennant. Thanks to free agentry, by the end of the decade the third-string designated hitter of the Seattle Mariners was making more than the combined salaries of the President of the United States, the Vice President, and several cabinet members.

Mark Spitz: This moustachioed dental student won seven gold medals in swimming at the 1972 Olympics and became a best-selling poster boy. Schick offered him $25,000 to shave off his mustache—and he refused.

The Bronx Zoo: Cleveland shipbuilder George Steinbrenner bought the New York Yankees in 1973, the first act in a dugout soap opera that is still playing seventeen seasons later. The histrionics reached fever pitch midde-cade: Reggie Jackson vs. George, Reggie vs. Thurman Munson, Billy Martin vs. George, Billy vs. Thurman. Somehow the Bronx Bombers managed to win three consecutive American League titles, as well as the 1977 and 1978 World Series.

Monday Night Football: "Isn't it absolutely incredible what wondrous verbiage flows from my mouth?" exclaimed Howard Cosell, and he wasn't kidding. Rarely had a sportscaster generated so much controversy as did the toupeed, nasal-voiced Cosell, one-third of the announcing team on

Jim Bouton's tell-all book turned him into an instant TV personality (with Ben Davidson (left) on the set of TV bomb Ball Four).

12: George Wallace joins Democratic presidential race.

17: Black Panther Eldridge Cleaver arrested.

18: Commander Cody and Lost Planet Airmen appear on *Police Woman*.

20: Spain's dictator Generalissimo Francisco Franco dies.

21: Ronald Reagan announces he will run against Ford.

26: "Squeaky" Fromme convicted.

27: Ford okays federal aid for New York City.

ABC's fall classic. It became a ritual after its debut in 1970, although during the first few games viewer mail ran against Cosell, nine to one. When the action on the field became dull, Cosell and his partners, Frank Gifford and Dandy Don Meredith, would get into some off-the-wall digressions that often sounded like last call at the local men's club.

Muhammad Ali: After the Supreme Court overruled his draft evasion conviction in 1970, Ali went on to supply the world with plenty of drama: The first Ali-Joe Frazier battle (1971); the rumble in the jungle against George Foreman (1974), in which Ali regained the heavyweight crown; and the thriller in Manila (1975), in which he avenged his earlier loss to Frazier. The champ reached his low point, however, in 1976 when he "fought" Japanese wrestling champ Antonio Inoki to a draw and collected $6 million for his troubles.

Mark Fidrych: This Detroit Tiger pitcher was the Peter Frampton of baseball. Just as 1976 was the year Frampton came alive, so it was the year that the Bird was the word. One of the flakiest of all baseball players, he talked to the ball, fell to his hands and knees to pat down the dirt behind the mound, and drew sell-out crowds wherever he went. He compiled a 19-9 record and was named American League rookie of the year, but tendonitis in his shoulder forced him out of baseball just a few seasons later. He still plays ball—in a Stan Musial League in Marlboro, Massachusetts.

Big Mouth Jim: In 1970, after his promising big-league career was cut short by an injury, ex-Yankee hurler Jim Bouton wrote *Ball Four: My Life and Hard Times Throwing the Knuckleball in the Big Leagues.* This inside account of the 1969 season dared to reveal that ball players (even the married ones) chased women and liked their booze and pills. Fellow players were not amused, but the book became the most commercially successful sports book in publishing history and helped usher in the era when athletes would be seen as less than demigods.

CAR CULTURE IN THE SEVENTIES

Until the Seventies, cars had been an essential part of America's self-image. From the flapper with her fliver to the sexy Mustangs and GTOs of

Mark Spitz won seven gold medals, only to see his achievement overshadowed by the PLO's Munich massacre.

the Sixties, cars have always been a kind of national libido, a symbol of affluence, freedom, and industrial superiority.

The Seventies were different. It was a decade that began with Earth Day when earnest protesters buried Chevys to protest the pollution of the internal combustion engine. It was a time of gas shortages, massive recalls, Nader-esque seat-belt laws, and design decisions made in hell. It was the decade Detroit took a beating from Osaka.

The decade began with a sixty-five-day strike at General Motors and went downhill from there, ending with a last-minute compromise guaranteeing a federal bail-out of Chrysler. In the interim, the Japanese took over America's growing import market, capturing 90 percent of the 2.3 million cars that the nation imported in 1979.

Like most of the fashions of the period, most Seventies' era cars are still camp classics at best. Yet amid the bland and downright ugly hulks of this schizoid era, some standouts must be mentioned.

Who can forget the decade's first subcompact? American Motors' Gremlin was actually introduced in 1969. It was one of the four 1970 models priced under $2,000. The Gremlin's sawed-off design was soon in competition with Ford's tiny Pinto. Before tests proved its habit of blowing up during rear-end collisons, the tiny hatchback with rack-and-pinion steering sold quite well—more than 328,000 during its debut year. Chevy soon answered with its long-awaited Vega. Its celebrated aluminum block engine would never quite work out.

Other highlights of the early Seventies include Ford's German-made import, the Mercury Capri, a nice little car it hawked as "a sexy European." GM introduced the sporty Opel, and Chrysler brought in its own boxy Colt from Mitsubishi, the folks responsible for the Japanese Zeros that bombed Pearl Harbor.

The energy crisis of '73–'74 sent big-car sales plunging while the Big Three retooled. Of all the "downsized" cars, none challenged America's machos more than the "castrated" Cadillac Seville of 1975. Cadillac had the nerve to shed more than 1000 pounds and twenty-five inches of length on the Seville and raise the price to $12,500.

Yet no sooner did Detroit emerge with smaller, "downsized" cars than oil prices relented, sending consumers on a big car binge. In 1977 V-8s cap-

19: Senate nixes U.S. role in Angola.

21: PLO terrorists attack OPEC meeting in Vienna.

#1 Singles:
Staple Singers—"Let's Do it Again"

JANUARY 1976

8: China's Chou En-lai dies at age 78.

9: Robert Byrd enters presidential race.

20: Joe Walsh joins The Eagles.

30: N.Y. Film Critics top award to *Nashville*.

Selected Gold Record Albums:
Kiss—*Alive!*
Earth, Wind and Fire—*Gratitude*
Who—*Who By Numbers*
Barry Manilow—*Trying to Get the Feeling*

10: Blues great Howlin' Wolfe dies at age 65.

11: *Pacific Overtures* opens on Broadway.

tured more than 77 percent of the American market. This was followed by yet another oil shock that sent Americans scrambling for tiny Festivas, Rabbits, Chevettes, Dodge Omnis, and millions of Japanese imports.

Although always dead last in sales, AMC stood out with the most outlandishly designed cars. In the spirit of Yankee pride and ingenuity, AMC announced the "Denim" version of its 1973 Gremlin. Complete with blue jeans, "landau" roof, and stitched and studded denim interior, this AMC classic is perhaps the ultimate in Seventies' style. AMC's 1975 Pacer provided American drivers with the glassiest car on the road. Its rounded "solarium" rear end was complemented by the unique feature of a driver's door four inches longer than the passenger's. AMC also wins the prize for the ugliest car of the decade with its Matador, a bloated midsized monster with guppy-eyed headlights.

Japanese Datsuns and Toyotas dominated America's import market by providing cheap, dependable, and energy-efficient transportation at a time when Detroit was churning out an unusually high percentage of lemons. Japan's luck was increased by Volkswagen's decision to replace the lovable Bug with the untested Rabbit. The VW "Thing" won few fans but does stand out as the weirdest car of the Seventies—a sporty combination of a dune buggy and a Nazi staff car. With few exceptions, Japanese cars were extremely functional. They worked in a soulless sort of way. No one ever composed a surfing song about a Datsun B-210 or "My Little Corolla." At the same time, the Datsun 240-Z still stands out as the most exciting car of the decade. Designed in Germany, this beautifully light and powerful sports car was as sleek as a Porsche and slicker than a Corvette and still cost less than $4,000 when introduced in '71. Subsequent Z's increased in price and speed, but lacked the compact beauty of the original.

For all the fits and starts of the oil companies, the bad cars, and speed limits, American drivers took to the roads with a peculiar gusto in the Seventies. It was the decade of bumper sticker statements. From "Honk If You Love Jesus," "Honk If You Think He's [Nixon] Guilty," to "Beep, Beep Yer Ass," Americans used their cars for the first time as a political and personal statement.

Of all these expressive drivers, none did it with more artistry and enthusiasm than van owners. In the mid-Seventies, vans became a sociological

19: Former Georgia Governor James E. Carter tops Iowa caucuses.

27: Western-backed forces flee Angolan capital.

31: Pope Paul VI blasts feminism.

25: Bob Dylan plays benefit for jailed boxer Rubin "Hurricane" Carter.

#1 Singles:
Bay City Rollers—"Saturday Night"
C. W. McCall—"Convoy"
Barry Manilow—"I Write the Songs"
Diana Ross—"Theme from Mahogany"
Ohio Players—"Love Rollercoaster"

Selected Gold Record Albums:
Harold Melvin and the Blue Notes—*Wake Up Everybody*
Rufus—*Rufus Featuring Chaka Khan*
Bob Dylan—*Desire*

C. W. McCall—*Black Bear Road*
Donna Summer—*Love to Love You Baby.*

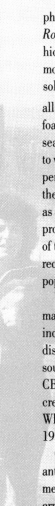

phenomenon. An entire generation of drivers weaned on Kerouac's *On the Road* were now living, smoking, partying and fornicating in these boxy vehicles first designed for plumbing contractors and electricians. By 1977 more than 2 million vans were on the road, and over 570,000 were being sold every year. Vans provided a way of getting away from it all while taking all the comforts of home with you. Many were appointed with the tackiest foam, the deepest of shag carpets, paneling, TVs, wine cellars, space-age seats, and, of course, the eight-track tape deck. Customization was the key to vanthropological expression. Portholes in the shapes of keys, arrows, and penises provided needed light and air. For all of the comforts inside the van, the paint job *on* the van was the biggest statement of all. Some cost as much as $3,000 and required thirty or more passes of the airbrush to complete the proper effect. Most van art parodied the sex and drug fantasies of album art of the period. At the same time, this public painting of private vehicles directly influenced the subway vandal art that would become so prevalent and popular in the early Eighties.

While the gas shortages and speed limits of the early seventies were a major inconvenience for most drivers, they threatened the jobs of America's independent truckers. In a 1973 television documentary, striking truckers discussed how they communicated via citizen's band radios to find out sources of gas and to keep abreast of the whereabouts of "smokeys." Sales of CBs soared as gas shortages and the fifty-five-mile-an-hour speed limit created an atmosphere of right-wing rebellion among American truckers. While only 1 million people had gotten CB licenses in the years between 1958 and 1973, more than 2 million licenses were issued in 1974 alone.

CB culture was one of the more strident and peculiar examples of the antiestablishment movements of the Seventies. Fed up with big government, police, and the apparent collusion of oil companies and foreign governments to gouge the American driver and consumer, the CB phenomenon created the image of the trucker as the last American cowboy, the rugged individual roaring down the road with a massive eighteen-wheeler at his command. While Teamsters, and particularly their union boss Jimmy Hoffa, had always enjoyed an outlaw reputation, the CB/trucker subcult caught the imagination of a public that felt powerless in the face of political and economic chaos.

For millions, running was the perfect escape from an imperfect world.

FEBRUARY 1976

7: Hua Kuo-feng named new Chinese premier.

3: Ingmar Bergman suffers nervous breakdown after tax bust.

12: Soviet-backed Angolan forces claim victory.

12: Sal Mineo murdered.

17: Ford announces reform of CIA.

18: EPA bans Mercury pesticides.

19: Centers for Disease Contr swine flu danger.

CB songs invariably told of clashes with police. CBers took on the antipolice attitude of the Sixties, hippie, but from a fiercely individualistic point of view. Smokey was not an enemy of the people, but merely an impediment to the trucker's freedom to roll as fast as possible. "Crashing the gate doing 98″" touched a chord in gas-line America that sent C. B. McCall's "Convoy" to a number one.

The CBer's new and unique language emerged almost spontaneously as the medium flourished. CB terms, such as "handle," "10–4," "Smokey," and "Bear," have entered the permanent language. CB culture reflected a way of life under siege, an atmosphere of paranoia and defiance on the American highway that was in its own way as genuine and influential as any campus rebellion.

RUNNING

In the Seventies, running, which had been considered a terrible form of drudgery, associated in many minds with such sadistic pursuits as military service or high-school gym, became transformed into a near-mystical experience shared by 40 million Americans. So much for the loneliness of the long-distance runner. The marathon, a 26.2-mile ordeal whose oddball participants always made good copy, became a chic, must-do event. Roads became clogged with sweating joggers in multicolored running shoes who embraced the activity with evangelical fervor. You couldn't attend a cocktail party (with nonalcoholic cocktails, of course!) without some thick-legged blowhard boasting about his "personal best" or his plans, revealed in excruciating detail, for conquering the marathon.

We may not have known what we were running away from, but we certainly knew why we were running. As one writer said, "We can drain off tensions and negative emotions, heighten creativity and enter altered states of consciousness. . . . Running is a positive addiction which builds character, enhances individuality, reinforces long-term goals and helps you kick whatever nasty habits you currently employ." That sense of near immortality must have propelled one runner who ran the last sixteen miles of a 1978 marathon with a .22-caliber bullet in his head, fired by an unknown assailant as he pounded through the streets of Allendale, Michigan. He thought

21: Nixon makes "private" visit to China.

24: President Ford and Jimmy Carter first in New Hampshire primary voting.

#1 Singles:
Paul Simon—"50 Ways to Leave Your Lover"
Rhythm Heritage—"Theme from S.W.A.T."

22: Former Supreme Florence Ballard dies destitute at 32.

23: Daniel Schorr fired from CBS News for leaking House document.

29: *Helter Skelter* is number-one best-seller.

Selected Gold Record Albums:
Fleetwood Mac—*Bare Trees*
Natalie Cole—*Inseparable*
Peter Frampton—*Frampton Comes Alive*

David Bowie—*Station to Station*
Bad Company—*Run with the Pack*

125

that someone had merely thrown a stone at him and, after the race, offered this excuse: "I've had worse races."

All these exhibitionists, physical cultists, and sweat hogs were seeking one thing: the "runner's high," a groovy sensation that was supposed to replace the high brought on by artificial stimulants. (Coincidentally, one popular form of running was called LSD for long slow distance.)

Running was a cheap form of self-entertainment, perfect for tough, self-centered times. You could run anywhere, with little cost (except for a $50 pair of sneakers, now known as running shoes), and it required little talent, save for discipline and the ability to withstand pain.

Running was the cutting edge in a revival of physical fitness, which encompassed everything from biking to tennis to aerobics. Even the sedentary got into the spirit by wearing the all-purpose warm-up suit, which suddenly became acceptable garb in suburban shopping malls.

Why did this all happen, though?

"I think the U.S. is in a terribly inward-looking, narcissistic frame of mind," said the unlikely guru of the running boom, a formerly overweight ex-magazine editor named Jim Fixx. "We've lost faith in a lot of the important institutions in our society, like government and marriage." Fixx's book, *The Complete Book of Running*, which featured the author's bulging quadriceps on its cover, was a number-one best-seller for four months in 1978 and '79 and was de rigueur reading among the sweat-for-success set. Alas, poor Fixx died while running in 1984, which helped dampen enthusiasm for the boom and provided a kind of I-told-you-so sense of silent satisfaction for the legions of duff-sitters.

And the running boom certainly attracted its celebrity adherents. *People* magazine routinely displayed sweating actors and actresses gliding along Santa Monica or Malibu or some other Southern California beach. Jerry Brown jogged indoors, forbidding photographers to shoot him while sweaty, saying "I'm entitled to my private space." Aging Senator William Proxmire ran to work daily through the streets of Washington and proclaimed that running is a "super feeling—like being immortal." And the mania even hit the White House. President Jimmy Carter attracted national attention when he collapsed during a 6.2-mile race in 1979, which supplied a ready-made metaphor during those less-than-heady days of malaise.

MARCH 1976

9: Ford takes Florida primary; Carter tops Wallace.

11: New York City bans Concorde flights.

18: New trial set for "Hurricane" Carter.

20: Patty Hearst convicted of armed robbery.

2: *Bubblin' Brown Sugar* opens on Broadway.

6: Dorothy Hamill wins World figure skating title.

Today folks are still running, but most *People* magazine celebrities are shown pumping iron rather than pounding pavement. And a lot of those Seventies' runners now find themselves sore of knee and tight of hamstring and have returned to walking, their marathoning days a fading, wistful memory.

GADGETS, BRANDS, AND THE BIRTH OF YUPPIE CULTURE

The gadgetry nearest and dearest to the growing boomer was his stereo. Stereos, FM radios, and album culture were the formative influence on many a future yuppie. In a world where everyone was created equal, you immediately formed judgments based on the kind of albums one played on which receiver with what kind of speakers, and so on. Drugs quickly provided another form of brand identification and assignment of caste. Colombian was better than Mexican, brown was better than green; ludes were for losers, and coke meant you had the money to get it.

Into this strange acquisitive culture arrived a staggering array of new and undreamed-of gadgetry. In 1972, the word *digital* meant the kind of alarm clock that had little panels of numbers that would mechanically flip over as the minutes passed. Adding machines were mechanical, and computers were the kind of huge machines they had on *The Time Tunnel* that read millions of paper cards with little square holes.

No gadget is more associated with the Seventies than the *blow dryer*. It's hard to believe, but before the Seventies, hair dryers were those cone-head devices women like to gossip under. The penis-as-a-pistol blow dryer of the early Seventies made everyone his own hairdresser and allowed both men and women to enter uncharted hair dimensions. The "Dry Look," the "Mark Spitz look," and the "Farrah look" would have been impossible without it.

Desk and pocket calculators took the country by storm. Two and half million of these huge, clunky, simple machines were sold in 1972, when a machine that did simple arithmetic could fetch more than $100. By 1973, competition and demand were driving down the price. Pocket calculators dominated the electronic gift show and Christmas of '73, when the average

23: Reagan upsets Ford in North Carolina; Carter outdraws Wallace.

24: Ford announces national swine flu immunization program.

31: N.J. Supreme Court okays Karen Quinlan's right to die.

#1 Singles:
The Miracles—"Love Machine Pt. 1"
Four Seasons—"December 1963"

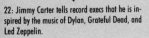

22: Jimmy Carter tells record execs that he is inspired by the music of Dylan, Grateful Dead, and Led Zeppelin.

29: *One Flew Over the Cuckoo's Nest* sweeps Oscars.

Selected Gold Record Albums:
Queen—*Night at the Opera*
Captain & Tennille—*Song of Joy*
Willie Nelson—*Red Headed Stranger*
Wings—*Wings at the Speed of Sound*
Pure Prairie League—*Bustin' Out*

hand-held model retailed for $40. Commodore chairman Jack Tremiel promised that by '74, calculators would cost less than $20. In many ways, the calculator boom of 1971 to '74 set the pattern for emerging gadget technology such as digital watches and personal computers.

Along with pet rocks, *digital watches* were the hit of Christmas 1975. Priced anywhere from $30 to $3,000, these bulky timepieces fell into two types. Liquid crystal watches emitted a weak, constant beam that had to be viewed a certain angles. Light-emitting diode (LED) watches could be seen only if a certain tiny button was pushed. Anyone without a penpoint or minuscule fingers was often at a loss to tell the time. For all their accuracy, these watches were hideous to look at and impractical to use. They sold like mad.

After trekking through Europe with their *Let's Go* guides and backpacks, many boomers returned to the States with a taste for *wine*. In the early Seventies, wine was a jug affair, and Gallo was verboten among those observing Cesar Chavez's grape and lettuce boycott. Brands like Almaden, Mateus, and Italian Swiss Colony dominated the classier *pot luck dinners*, while pitchers of Yago added the fruity continental taste of sangria to many a party. Boone's Farm and Ripple remained the wines most likely to be drunk by the younger set. By the late Seventies, consumers were growing ever more sophisticated about varietals, breeding a huge wine boom in both Europe and California.

The wine boon soon affected soda, as millions turned to *Perrier* for the perfect taste of carbonated "nothing." The Perrier success amazed many and seemed to prove that you could sell anything if you gave it a French name. The bottled water battle heated up as more competition moved in, including Evian and Poland Springs. Craig Claiborne shocked everyone when his taste test revealed a preference for Canada Dry Club Soda! Yet for all of the water wars, by 1979 bottled water comprised less than 1 percent of all soft drink sales.

When affluent boomers weren't drinking expensive water, they were parboiling themselves in it in their *hot tubs*. In a perfect combination of Sixties' and Seventies' life-styles, hot tubs combined polymorphous perversity with conspicuous consumption. With a hot tub, you could keep up with the Joneses and hang out naked with Mrs. Jones at the same time. Of course, a

APRIL 1976

5: Howard Hughes dies without official will.

6: "Scoop" Jackson tops Carter in N.Y. primary; Ford wins.

7: Hua ousts Deng in Chinese power struggle.

26: Senate asserts right to oversee CIA.

9: Phil Ochs hangs himself.

18: Best Musical Tony for *A Chorus Line*.

22: Ingmar Bergman flees Sweden and its tax laws.

22: Barbara Walters becomes first woman news anchor; signs $1 million deal.

hot tub wasn't merely a gadget but a way of life. According to the book *Hot Tubs* by Leon Elder, you should "sink into the tub, and you'll begin to shed the dead skin of your previous persona and find a smoother one underneath. It happens when you sit around with naked friends and neighbors for a few hours. Suddenly you realize you are looking at persons instead of bodies." Although basically a California phenomenon, more than 300,000 hot tubs were in use by 1979, when tales of the health hazards (and poached people) put a dent in their sales.

By the late seventies, many of the gadgets that were the mainstays of Eighties' "couch potato" existence were in their germinal state. *Microwaves* had been around since the beginning of the decade but were shunned as cancerous poodle killers. In 1977 New York's Citibank launched an aggressive campaign to win consumers with hundreds of "Automatic Teller Machines" (ATMs). By 1978 ads for Sony's *Betamax* were already asking you to "get involved" with your television set. Steve Jobs was messing around in his legendary *Apple* garage in '77, and Tandy/Radio Shack released its first crude, 64K PC as early as '78. Drivers in the know were already flocking to *BMWs*, and would-be business tycoons were already fretting about Japan's superiority and reading Erich Vogel's *Japan as Number One*. With the possible exception of hot air popcorn poppers, little has emerged in the Eighties that isn't a variation on a Seventies' theme.

A RANDOM GLOSSARY OF THE QUINTESSENTIALLY SEVENTIES

Acupuncture: Nixon's Ping-Pong diplomacy brought a new brand of mystic needle medicine to the gullible West.

Astrology: While many settled for the midcult wisdom of *Linda Goodman's Sun Signs* and the use of "what's your sign?" as a quicker picker upper, others went in for the wisdom of the Tarot and the *I Ching*. On the more highbrow front, Jung edged out Freud as the guru of choice, as dream workshops, mandala-drawing parties, and talk of "synchronicity" dominated pot luck dinners from Bowdoin to Berkeley.

27: Carter ends Jackson momentum with Pennsylvania victory.

29: Mormon officials announce discovery of Hughes will leaving them $100 million.

#1 Singles:
Johnnie Taylor—"Disco Lady"

30: Porno star Harry Reems arrested for obscenity in Memphis.

Selected Gold Record Albums:
Frank Zappa—*Apostrophe*
Parliament—*Mothership Connection*
Rolling Stones—*Black and Blue*
Barbra Steisand—*Lazy Afternoon*

MAY 1976

1: Reagan takes Texas; ahead of Ford in delegate count.

Bandanas: From Choate to the Bowery, bandanas provided an eclectic look of total empathy with the Zig Zag Man. Upscale dog owners put bandanas on their black Labradors and drove them around in pickup trucks.

Candles: Where incense went, big bulky candles were never far behind. Sand candles, scented candles, peace sign candles, Nixon candles, and penis candles gave every room that "whore house/Hindu funeral parlor" look so essential to getting out of it and getting it on.

Death: Like divorce and orgasm, death became just another "experience" in the touch-feely Seventies. Is this why so many people had so much trouble with Karen Ann Quinlan's inability to let go?

Drug-culture candy: Hot on the heels of the frenetic promotion of Screaming Yellow Zonkers, candies like Zotz and Space Candy exploded in your mouth, providing a "rush" for the preadolescent eager for any sensuous experience.

Drug toys: Casual or intense, drug use bred its own brand of self-absorbed toys, including plastic wave machines, clacking metal pendulum balls, and those metal pivoting magnets that could provide hours of fun as they reeled from repulsion to attraction. For the graphically inclined, Escher prints were the ultimate mind game.

Earth tones: These colors dominated interior designs as cork walls and harvest-gold shag carpeting created a little bit of Middle Earth in many singles-only apartment complexes.

Hamburger Helper: This item proved to be the budget stretcher of the "Phase II" era, as price quotas sent the meat supply into a nosedive.

The Happy Face: Claimed by many, but copyrighted by none, the insipid, yellow, grinning icon swept America in '71. New York button wholesaler N. G. Slater sold more than 20 million buttons in that year alone. Tired of be-

11: Reagan tops Ford in Nebraska.

25: Ford and Reagan split six state contests.

25: Rep. Wayne Hays admits affair with secretary, Elizabeth Ray.

3: Saul Bellow wins Nobel prize for literature.

ing divided into hawks and doves, black and white, and young and old, America embraced this innocuously pleasant symbol with a mindless, religious fervor. As stoned and happy as the "DooDah Man" and as harmless as a phone company logo, the Happy Face played a peculiar and essential role in America's post-Sixties reconciliation.

Herbal teas: These teas provided a nonstressful, uncompetitive way to greet the first day of the rest of your life. An earthen mugful of Red Zinger, Morning Thunder, or Camomile with your granola could get you through the day, while Sleepy Time never got in the way of nodding out.

High tech: For younger boomers, no post-college experience was complete without a stint at loft living. Lofts allowed boomers to carve out suburban-size living spaces out of the post-industrial ruin of recession-wracked urban America. No loft was complete if it was not sufficiently high-tech—outfitted with all the creature comforts of a Luftwaffe hangar. Gray plastic matte and black rubber were all you needed for that design-by-Devo look. The most perfect use of this look can be seen on the album jacket of the Talking Heads' wonderful ode to paranoia, *Fear of Music.*

Incense: In all its variations, incense added an earthy touch to even the most suburban bedroom. It did a good job of masking that spilled bong water smell too.

IUDs: Copper, natural, as old as the Egyptians, the intrauterine device was the Seventies' contraceptive of choice.

Kahoutek: The comet that no one expected that didn't show up after all, providing the biggest bust of a disappointment-obsessed decade.

Laetrile: Spurning common sense and modern science, countless cancer victims trekked to Mexico to pay thousands for a bogus peach-pit "cure."

Macramé: Suburban girls became "dream weavers" as they knotted miles

28: U.S. and Soviets ink underground nuclear testing agreement.

31: Martha Mitchell dies.

#1 Singles:
Bellamy Brothers—"Let Your Love Flow"
John Sebastian—"Welcome Back"
The Sylvers—"Boogie Fever"
Wings—"Silly Love Songs"
Diana Ross—"Love Hangover"

8: Carter clinches nomination.

JUNE 1976

28: *Taxi Driver* wins top honors at Cannes.

31: *Guinness Book of World Records* names The Who as world's loudest rock band.

Selected Gold Record Albums:
Doobie Brothers—*Takin' It to the Streets*
Mac Davis—*All the Love in the World*
Aerosmith—*Rocks*
America—*Hideaway*

5: Ramones release first album.

131

of cord and string into the largest assemblage of plant hangers the world has ever known.

Musk cologne: Whether extracted from the glands of a Mongolian yak or concocted in some New Jersey chemical plant, Musk for Men colognes gave men that earthy, unisex odor that helped them convince themselves they were God's gift to the fern bar.

Mysteries of the universe: As the borders of science and technology closed in on millions, many took to the study of such eternal mysteries as Big Foot, the Bermuda Triangle, and of course, The Loch Ness Monster.

Natural foods: Raised on Wonder Bread and TV dinners, many boomers embraced the natural world with a taste for food far more Middle Eastern than Middle American. Seemingly overnight, millions of Americans exhibited a taste for pot luck dinners consisting of tofu, tahini, moussaka, banana bread, lentil loaf, zucchini bread, alfalfa sprouts, quiche, avocados, and an explosion of salad varieties that resulted in that most Seventies of restaurant creations: the salad bar. Heathful substitutes became the rage. Sugar and white flour became as politically incorrect as nuclear power and apartheid during the Seventies. Brown rice, honey, carob (for chocolate), and whole grain everything gained currency as boomers loudly rejected everything they were raised on.

The organic bathroom: Herbal Essence shampoos, oatmeal soaps, and naturally abrasive loofas replaced Mr. Bubble as the cleanser of choice as millions sought out the organic life-style. Skin Trip and Bonne Bell Ten-O-Six were essential in a girl's pursuit of that *Waltons* complexion. Dr. Brauner's Shampoo provided a few thousand words of incomprehensible philosophy with every bottle. And who didn't get at least one unwanted Christmas present of Soap on a Rope?

Patchouli: This scent announced your reeking embrace of the countercul-

10: Wayne Hays recovers from coma after sleeping pill overdose.

10: Karen Anne Quinlan returns home to die.

16: Rioting in South African township of Soweto.

26: Food riots rock Polish Communist regime.

30: Italian Communist party breaks with Moscow.

17: NBA and ABA merge.

19: "Roots Rock Reggae," Bob Marley's first hit, enters charts.

30: Neil Diamond in L.A. pot bust; autographs albums for arresting officers.

132

ture's ethos of sex and drugs and incense. For girl teeny boomers too young for suggestive perfume, Max Factor Kissing Gloss provided a sheen and a scent of strawberry and bubble gum to tell the world (or at least their girlfriends) that they were ready from some heavy kissing action.

POW bracelets: This was the jewelry that allowed "silent majority" youth to make a statement too. You could adopt your own POW/MIA and still stay stylish in the precious metals-obsessed early Seventies. POWs were copper. MIAs were bronze.

Puka Shells: Nothing looked better tucked in your halter than that puka shell necklace from that certain someone.

Seventies coins: These flops include the largely ignored bicentennial quarter and the disastrous Susan B. Anthony dollar.

Silver and turquoise homemade jewelry: Nothing accented that Mexican wedding blouse and peasant skirt ensemble like some silver turquoise jewelry made by a local "craftsperson" totally in tune with Wounded Knee.

Solar Panels: These panels captured all of the sun's natual goodness and lowered your heating bills. America's search for "energy independence" lead to tax breaks for these ugly collectors. Neither solar energy nor Carter's call for synfuels (synthetic oil) survived long in the Reagan era.

Tiger Balm: This provided a virtual orgy for the pores during the hedonistic Seventies. After a hard day of getting your head together, nothing spoke to your uptight muscles like a gentle hit of this sensuously unguent rubbed on by lover or willing stranger.

Windfall profit taxes: Hard to believe it, but we once had a government that thought some companies made too much money. These taxes were levied on oil companys' profits gained from OPEC's price hikes.

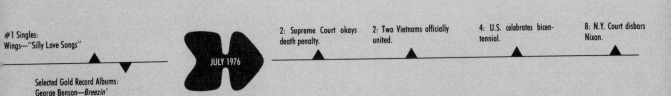

#1 Singles:
Wings—"Silly Love Songs"

JULY 1976

2: Supreme Court okays death penalty.

2: Two Vietnams officially united.

4: U.S. celebrates bicentennial.

8: N.Y. Court disbars Nixon.

Selected Gold Record Albums:
George Benson—*Breezin'*
Neil Diamond—*Beautiful Noise*
Elvin Bishop—*Fooled Around and Fell in Love*
Daryl Hall and John Oates—*Sara Smile*

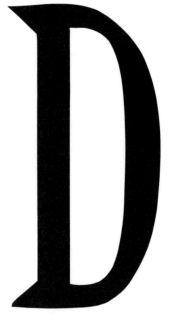D iversity was the key to rock in the Seventies. As audiences grew and splintered, a bevy of musical styles emerged: art rock, southern rock, glitter, heavy metal, and funk. By the end of the decade, disco divided popular taste and punk promised yet another revolution. The rise of FM radio accelerated the division of musical markets and audience taste. Followers of "progressive" rock stations would no longer be caught dead listening to top-forty stations. And on top forty, musical tastes gyrated radically and gave rise to the extraordinary blandness of such Seventies' superstars as Abba, the Carpenters, and The Captain and Tennille, not to mention such one-hit wonders as Blue (Ooga Chaka) Swede. More than any other medium, rock suffered most severely from the Sixties' hangover, and from a desire for the "next big thing." Having dominated the Sixties with their talent, the Beatles haunted much of the Seventies with their absence, as every fan and critic looked for the next Fab Four in such diverse sensations as David Essex, T. Rex, Elton John, Bruce Springsteen, and of course, the Knack. It seemed the decade was almost over before the wild abandon of punk and disco caused most to stop looking over their shoulders for a shadow of the past. For those happy enough to experience the present, the Seventies provided some of the best rock and roll of all time—be it the searing virtuosity of a Duane Allman solo, the jaded studio genius of Steely Dan, or the unabashed funk weirdness of the Parliament/Funkadelic.

POSTBREAKUP BEATLES

The Beatles' breakup provided the rudest reminder that the Sixties were

8: Pat Nixon suffers stroke.

12-15: Democratic convention nominates Carter and Mondale.

20: Viking 1 sends back photos of Martian surface.

28: Chinese earthquake kill over 100,000.

9: Tanzania is first of twenty-one nations to boycott Montreal Olympics.

11: Frank Sinatra marries Barbara Marx (Zeppo's ex).

22: Romania's Nadia Comaneci dominates Olympic gymnastic competition.

31: Six Eastern block athletes defect to Canada.

really over. The demise of the Fab Four into acrimony and lawsuits was but one indication that the Age of Aquarius was not all it was cracked up to be. While the Beatles as a group were the most cogent symbols for everything "the Sixties" were supposed to represent, it is interesting to note how the movement of the Liverpool lads away from each other and into their own fields shed light on the many and myriad movements of the Seventies.

John Lennon: No one, with the possible exception of Jerry Rubin, embraced the Seventies with as much narcissistic abandon as the thinking man's Beatle. John's early solo albums, particularly his *Plastic Ono* album, catalog his self-absorption, Primal Scream therapy, and self-deification. His long descent into public drunkenness (with Harry Nilsson, no less) followed his regrettable collaboration with Elephant's Memory, which produced "Woman Is the Nigger of the World," among other forgettable tunes. Spending most of his time fighting off deportation and listening to Yoko sing wonders like "Don't Worry Kyoko (Mama's Only Looking for a Hand in the Snow)" didn't leave John much time to be a hitmaster before retiring to five years of house husbandry in the Dakota. Both critical and popular success eluded John's newer work during the entire decade. "Imagine" made it to no higher than number three on the charts. John's only number-one hit came in tandem with the very hot Elton John: "Whatever Gets You Through the Night." He also co-wrote "Fame," which Bowie took to number one in '75.

Paul McCartney: As John's solo career straddled the line between the uncommercial and the unbearable, Paul laid down a decade-long string of singable ditties and silly love songs that would make him one of the richest men in England. Always the melodic Beatle, the yin to John's yang, Paul had demonstrated an early penchant for the treacly and whimsical with such numbers as "Ob-La-Di" and "Her Majesty." Left to his own devices, he blazed a trail of such insipid hits as "Uncle Albert/Admiral Halsey," "Listen to What the Man Says," and the unforgettable "Mary Had a Little Lamb."

Having settled into the role of family man with former photographer/groupie Linda Eastman, Paul moved as far as he could from John and Yoko's life-style as political and conceptual artists. During the first few years of the decade, it seemed Mr. and Mrs. Mc were never seen without evidence of their ever-growing brood and flocks of sheep to keep everyone company. Of

George Harrison, the quiet Beatle, began the decade with the bang, but soon settled into a metaphysical rut.

#1 Singles:
Starland Vocal Band—"Afternoon Delight"
Manhattans—"Kiss and Say Goodbye"

7: Mobster John Roselli murdered. Had testified at Senate committee on mob links to JFK assassination.

16-19: Ford and Sen. Robert J. Dole nominated at Republican Convention.

AUGUST 1976

Selected Gold Record Albums:
Boz Scaggs—*Silk Degrees*
The Carpenters—*A Kind of Hush*
Natalie Cole—*Sparkle*
Phoebe Snow—*Second Childhood*

15: Black gangs attack whites at Detroit rock concert.

135

John Lennon and Yoko Ono engage in a bit of primal screaming.

the ten Seventies' albums by McCartney and his band Wings, *Band on the Run* remains a favorite of those who see Paul as the keeper of the Beatles' flame. It runs smoothly and perhaps too cutely together, like the legendary second side of *Abby Road*. It reflects Paul at the height of his one-man-band period, as he plays all the instruments on its three strongest numbers, "Jet," "Helen Wheels," and "Band on the Run."

George Harrison: The Beatles broke up just as George was hitting his stride. It is clear in a few scenes of *Let It Be* that he is growing fed up with Paul's domineering ways. "While My Guitar Gently Sleeps" remains one of the most powerful numbers on the erratic *White Album*. In 1969 George's "Something" became the first Beatle gold record not written by John and Paul. Long interested in Eastern music, George had been messing around with a sitar sound since the kitchy raga rock numbers on the *Help!* album. Some of these Hindu dirges turned into the Beatles' most forgettable and regrettable numbers, including "Within You Without You" and "The Inner Light," the rarely played flip side of "Lady Madonna." With these behind him, few figured George to emerge as perhaps the dominant ex-Beatle of the early Seventies. "All Things Must Pass" led the pack of "God-rock" records of '70–'71 with the snappy "My Sweet Lord." George reached his high tide with the concert for Bangladesh. While John and Paul fought it out in the tabloids with cheap shots like "How do you sleep?" George united a rock-and-roll pantheon (including Eric Clapton, Bob Dylan, Billy Preston, Ringo Starr, and Leon Russell) for Bengali relief. Unfortunately for George, the public's penchant for religious rock did not long outlive 1972. His later albums, *Living in the Material World*, *Extra Texture*, and *33⅓*, offered little to dispel his image as a droning mystic given to muddy arrangements and occasional guitar virtuosity. Though never as didactic as John, George's brand of mysticism often sounded downright silly coming from someone with Rolls-Royces and a paisley mansion. Near hits like "Material World" and "Crackerbox Palace" did little more than preach to the converted. The late Seventies found George farther into a hitless obscurity that would be broken only by "All Those Years Ago," his sad but catchy elegy to John in 1981.

Ringo Starr: Never one to take himself too seriously, Ringo's Seventies' solo efforts wavered between the mawkishly sentimental and downright awful. "It Don't Come Easy," "Photograph," and "You're Sixteen," aside, Ringo's solo singles went nowhere. His first album, *Sentimental Journey*, was a collection of crooner oldies reportedly recorded "for his mum." By decade's end, it seemed that only his mum was buying his records, for *Ringo The 4th* never even reached the top two hundred.

ROCK-AND-ROLL GRAVEYARD

The early Seventies saw rock and roll fall into a major identity crisis as critics and musicians struggled with the "Is rock dead?" question. If rock didn't die, many of its spawn wasted no time in doing so. Rock stars seemed to drop like flies in the Seventies. As the music entered its third decade, and some of its old-timers began looking just a little long in the tooth, a lifestyle of hard drugs and fast living was quickly taking its toll. Death by Valium, vomit, heroin, handguns, motorcycle, and occasional plane crash robbed the rock world of the up-and-coming as well as the down and burned out.

†With only three years of superstardom behind him, **Jimi Hendrix** was only twenty-seven when he fell victim to his own vomit on September 18, 1970. Hendrix's manic riffs had single-handedly revolutionized the electric guitar while his husky, bluesy voice packed a potent sexual force. His outlandish outfits, unabashed black identity, and voracious appetite for all that sex, drugs, and rock and roll could bring made him one of the few enduring originals in an art form crowded with poseurs and has-beens. He remains unique as a black artist with an avid following among the all-white "album-oriented" FM listenership that flourished in the Seventies.

†Jimi was barely out of this astral plane when **Janis Joplin** checked out. The body of the queen of raunchy bluesrock was found crammed between a wall and the bed in a room in Hollywood's Landmark Hotel on October 3, 1970. The twenty-eight-year-old singer had signed her will only three days earlier, and controversy erupted over whether her overdose was an accident or suicide. Like

#1 Singles:
Elton John and Kiki Dee—"Don't Go Breaking My Heart"

SEPTEMBER 1976

1: Wayne Hays resigns.

3: Unemployment rises to 7.9 percent.

9: Mao Tse-tung dies.

Selected Gold Record Albums:
David Bowie—*ChangesOneBowie*
Seals and Crofts—*Get Closer*
Loggins and Messina—*Native Sons*

4: FBI director announces engagement to a former nun.

8: Steve Ford invites Peter Frampton to "hang out" at the White House.

137

Jimi, Janis had harnessed a bluesy and blatantly sexual wildness to the psychedelic scene of late Sixties' San Francisco. Released the spring after her death, "Me and Bobby McGee" provided her with a posthumous number-one hit.

✝ Lost in the aftershocks of Jimi's and Janis's departure, Canned Heat's **Al Wilson** o.d.'d on sleeping pills while camping out in the backyard of fellow band member Bob Hite. The owlish, reclusive Wilson was best known for his raspy renditions of the band's best-known numbers, "Goin' Up the Country" and "On the Road Again."

✝ **Jim Morrison** was reported to have had the body of a seventy-year-old man when he was found dead in a Paris bathtub in July '71. Morrison's penchant for drugs, drinking, bad Baudelaire, and indecent exposure had taken a toll on his health and reputation by the time he decided to cool out in the City of Lights. While some argue that Morrison was on his way toward has-been status when he ceased living, the Doors' "L. A. Woman" remains one  of the most popular (and overplayed) numbers in the FM radio repertory. Morrison in death remains a bigger cult figure than ever. The fact that his death was not announced for six days after the fact has resulted in rumors and myths of almost Elvis-size proportions. His simple gravestone in Père Lachaise cemetery (which he shares with such rock and rollers as Oscar Wilde, Edith Piaf, Molière, and Héloise and Abelard) remains a cult gathering ground and is regularly festooned with flowers, bad poetry, and pills.

✝ **Duane Allman** was on a legendary roll when a motorcycle accident killed him in October 1971. His hot licks on *Layla* and *The Allman Brothers Band Live at the Fillmore East* were quickly making Duane and his brother's band a popular and critical favorite. Though the band would flourish after him (and after band member Berry Oakley's spookily similar crash only three blocks from Duane's crash site), it clearly lacked the wicked virtuosity of his slide guitar. Brother Gregg kept the band together as it grew to supergroup status with *Eat A Peach* and playing before 600,000 at Watkins Glen. The magic was clearly gone without Duane though, and Gregg slid

23: Presidential debate marred by twenty-seven-minute technical glitch; candidates stand in awkward silence.

29: Britain requests aid from International Monetary Fund.

29: Nixon sells memoirs for $2 million.

#1 Singles:
Bee Gees—"You Should Be Dancing"
KC and The Sunshine Band—"(Shake, Shake, Shake) Shake Your Booty"
Wild Cherry—"Play That Funky Music (White Boy)"

Selected Gold Record Albums:
Bob Dylan—*Hard Rain*
Steely Dan—*Royal Scam*
Steve Miller—*Fly Like an Eagle*
Peter Frampton—*Frampton*

deeper into a world of despair, drugs, and Cher.

✝ **Jim Croce** was just taking off with a couple of hit singles when his plane failed to clear a tree in Natchitoches, Louisiana, in 1973. The sad-eyed mellow balladeer with Groucho mustache and cigar was on tour to support his number-one hit "Bad Bad Leroy Brown" when he died. Soon after his death the cloying "Time in a Bottle" became a posthumous hit.

Best known for their strung-out solos, interminable jams, and the psychedelic excess of mid-Sixties' San Francisco scene, **The Grateful Dead** owed much of their early hard-assed outlaw image to the great unwashed **Ron "Pig Pen" McKernan.** For all of the Dead's trippy aura, Pig Pen remained a hardcore drinker. So much that by the early Seventies, his doctors told him his liver would not endure much more of the lush life. Pig Pen did not let a little thing like mortality get in the way of accompanying the Dead on their classic Europe '72 tour. And so when his liver and his life finally gave way to cirrhosis in March '73, it came as no one's great surprise. **Jerry Garcia** summed up his partner's fate: "He was a juicer, man. It did him in."

✝ A lot of folks had their troubles adjusting to the Seventies, but **Phil Ochs** literally died of an overdose of the decade. In the kinder, gentler years of the early Sixties, when you could still make a loud statement with an acoustic guitar, Ochs cut quite a niche for himself as an issues-oriented folk singer. In the Seventies, rejection sent Ochs on a downward spiral of depression and drinking. As the war wound down and the movement mellowed, Ochs found himself without cause or audience, or apparent reason to go on. He hanged himself at his sister's house in 1976.

✝ As the earthy, girthy Mama at the vocal center of the **Mamas and Papas, Cass Elliot** had won a broad spectrum of fans. By the early Seventies, Cass had grown fatter and desperate for a comeback. Things got so bad that she even did a stint on *Hollywood Squares.* She was in the midst of a solo comeback when she was found dead in Harry Nilsson's apartment in July '74. Though official reports waver between a heart attack and heroin, the rumor of her choking on a ham sandwich has cruelly emerged as the unofficial cause of death.

OCTOBER 1976

4: Interior Secretary Earl Butz resigns for racial slurs.

7: At presidential debate, Ford remarks that Poland is not dominated by USSR.

12: Swine flu program suspended.

15: V.P. candidates Dole and Mondale meet in acrimonious debate.

20: Film debut for Led Zeppelin's *The Song Remains the Same.*

21: Americans win all seven Nobel prizes.

✝**Elvis**'s descent from the sensual "King Creole" to a bloated "Hunka Hunk of Burning Love" is as grotesque as it is well documented. By the time he died atop his toilet in Graceland (reading *The Scientific Search for the Face of Jesus*), the King was a hundred pounds overweight and described as "a walking pharmaceutical shop." Just weeks before the fatal binge, Elvis's bodyguards released the best-selling *Elvis: What Happened?* a tale of drugs, sex, cruelty, and paranoia. The public couldn't get enough of the book's revelations of Elvis's fascination with guns, his late-night visits to morgues, his belief in his own mystical powers, and his voracious appetite for sex and pills. This myth-shattering account and Elvis's sudden death proved too much for his millions of fans, many of whom still believe that he walks among us, haunting the Burger Kings and malls of this mortal world.

✝**Keith Moon's** irrepressible acts of practical joking and hotel smashing were an integral part of the eccentric image of **The Who.** By the time Keith expired in '78, his drinking had turned the rock-and-roll imp into a middle-age slob. Ironically he was trying to sober up when he expired from an accidental overdose of a prescription drug he was taking to overcome his addiction to booze. In a spooky rock-and-roll twist of fate, he spent his last night screening *The Buddy Holly Story*.

✝While Elvis spent more than twenty years destroying his mind and body, it took **Sid Vicious** less than twenty-four months to soar from the headlines to the graveyard. What Sid lacked in talent he more than compensated for in exuberance. Sid's addiction to heroin and to groupie Nancy Spungen did not help the already raunchy reputation of the **Sex Pistols.** Sid and Nancy were already far from functional when they set up housekeeping in New York's notoriously hip Chelsea Hotel. That Sid could not recall whether he had murdered Nancy or had witnessed her suicide was not surprising given their shared obsession with self-obliteration. Sid's murder rap became a moot point when he killed himself with an intentional overdose in winter '79.

AND LEST WE FORGET

Tammi Terrell, Motown soloist, cancer, March 1970.
Gene Vincent, rockabilly superstar, depression/alcohol/ulcer, October 1971.

Sid Vicious's talent for excess exceeded his musical gifts.

NOVEMBER 1976

#1 Singles:
Walter Murphy and the Big Apple Band—"A Fifth of Beethoven"
Rick Dees and His Cast of Idiots—"Disco Duck (Pt 1)"
Chicago—"If You Leave Me Now"

Selected Gold Record Albums:
Linda Ronstadt—*Hasten Down the Wind*
Marlo Thomas and Friends—*Free to Be You and Me*
Parliament—*Clones of Dr. Funkenstein*

4: Carter elected with narrow margin; declares mandate for change.

4: New York's Mayor Beame hosts honorary lunch for Bee Gees.

14: Carter's hometown church drops ban on black members.

140

Keith Relf, Yardbirds, electrocution by guitar, May 1976.

Paul Williams, Temptations, suicide, August 1973.

Rory Storme, Ringo's ex-bandmate (Rory Storme and the Hurricanes), double suicide (with his mother!), June 1972.

Bobby Darin, crooner, heart attack, December 1973.

Gram Parsons, Flying Burrito Brothers, overdose, September 1973.

Robbie McIntosh, Average White Band, accidental overdose, September 1974.

Tim Buckley, folk singer, accidental overdose, June 1975.

Marc Bolan, glitter rocker, car wreck, September 1977.

Ronnie Van Zandt and Steve Gaines, Lynyrd Skynyrd, plane crash, October 1977.

Donnie Hathaway, soul singer, fall from a window, January 1979.

Lowell George, Little Feat/Mothers of Invention, heart failure, June 1979.

THE MELLOW SOUND

The counterculture's counterrevolution—an intensely personal, intimate form of music performed by singer/songwriters—became popular at the turn of the decade as young people began looking inward, away from the noise and protest of the previous four years. Songs by such artists as James Taylor, Carole King, and Joni Mitchell would provide the perfect self-absorbed music for what would be soon known as the Me Decade.

The best of the singer/songwriters' material was like psychoanalysis set to an acoustic guitar, with the water bed substituting for the couch. It was the preferred form of music for sensitive collegiates (whose favorite course might be comparative studies in third world underdevelopment, on a pass/fail basis only) and their younger like-minded high school colleagues. To appreciate the music best, flannel shirts, overalls, and work boots should be worn. And if these fashions have gone out of style, the music hasn't. For many who grew up listening to James and Joni, the music would remain the only type of "rock" music they'd still be listening to fifteen-to-twenty years later.

Here's a run down of some of the top troubadors, the monarchs of mellow:

Carole King's ode to soulful introspection, Tapestry, *became the best-selling album to date in 1971.*

15: Syrian troops enter Beirut as peacekeepers.

19: Patty Hearst freed on $1.5 million bail, pending appeal.

28: Carter announces he will send daughter Amy to predominantly black public school in D.C.

#1 Singles:
Steve Miller Band—"Rock 'n Me"
Rod Stewart—"Tonight's the Night (Gonna Be Alright)"

20: Joni Mitchell and John Sebastian perform at Jerry Brown's "California Celebrates The Whales" Concert.

21: Debut of Glass/Wilson opera, *Einstein on the Beach.*

Selected Gold Record Albums:
Led Zeppelin—*The Song Remains the Same*
Firefall—*Firefall*
Fleetwood Mac—*Mystery to Me*

Boston—*Boston*
Ted Nugent—*Free For All*
Donna Summer—*Four Seasons of Love*

Mellow Ground Zero: James Taylor, Jackson Browne, Bonnie Raitt, and Carly Simon harmonize for the No Nukes rally and film.

● **James Taylor:** The son of a medical school dean, this ex-prep school student was hailed as "the first superstar of the 1970s." and was *Time's* cover subject in March 1971. Indeed, in the space of just a couple of years, the rawboned Taylor had gone from playing coffeehouses to playing Carnegie Hall on the strength of his intensely personal songs, many of which chronicled his experiences as a former heroin addict and a former mental patient. His ground-breaking second album *Sweet Baby James* (1970) set the standards for singer/songwriters. "If my tunes have any message, I guess it's to look deeply into your own self for answers," he said in 1971.

● **Carole King:** In an earlier incarnation, with her ex-husband Gerry Goffin, the Brooklyn native authored several early Sixties' pop classics, including "The Locomotion" and "Will You Love Me Tomorrow." Reborn in the early Seventies as a singer/songwriter, she hit paydirt with the LP *Tapestry*, which sold 15 million copies. Part of an informal mellow mafia with Taylor, she played piano on his LP, and he in turn made a hit out of her group-therapy paean "You've Got a Friend." That song hit number one on July 31, 1971; two weeks earlier King's single, "It's Too Late," had finished its fifth week as the nation's top tune.

● **Joni Mitchell:** A waiflike Canadian whose real name was Roberta Joan Anderson, she became a favorite of college coeds everywhere for her sensitive, depressing accounts of busted romances, especially her breakthrough LPs *Ladies of the Canyon* and *Blue*.

● **Carly Simon:** This long-legged publishing heiress likewise plumbed the depths of human misery. A favorite parlor game of 1973 was to guess the identity of the subject of "You're So Vain." Mick Jagger and Warren Beatty had the inside track, but not James Taylor, who by then had become Mr. Carly Simon (a few years after his much-publicized romance with Joni Mitchell ended).

● **Cat Stevens:** The Donovan of the Seventies, this Englishman produced crypto-sensitive LPs with such titles as *Tea for the Tillerman* and *Teaser and the Firecat*. By the Eighties, he decided that this was indeed a wild world and he chucked it all, changing his name and becoming a Muslim. Little was heard from him until 1989, when he shot his mouth off in defense of Ayatollah Khomeini's call to murder *Satanic Verses* author Salman Rushdie. One Los Angeles radio station responded by bulldozing a pile of Cat's LPs.

DECEMBER 1976

16: Swine flu program officially ends.

20: Chicago Mayor Richard Daley dies at 74.

21: "Hurricane" Carter found guilty for second time.

15-23: Tanker Argo Merchant spills five million gallons of oil off Nantucket.

1: Sex Pistol's obscene behavior results in England media ban.

3: Assassination attempt on Bob Marley.

12: Jack Cassidy dies in Boston fire.

22: N.Y. premiere of play *Your Arm's Too Short to Box with God*.

● **Don McLean:** During the winter of 1971–72, a popular guessing game among the would-be hip was just what Don McLean was singing about in his enigmatic hit, "American Pie." Was it about Buddy Holly? John Kennedy? A metaphor for the sixties and the crumbling counterculture? Whatever, the eight-minute-plus song made an overnight star of McLean, a Pete Seeger disciple who was named the 1968 "Hudson River Troubador" by the New York State Council of the Arts. McLean's own answer was just as enigmatic: "I can't necessarily interpret 'American Pie' any better than you can." Eighteen years later, we're just as mystified as what exactly happened the day the music died.

By 1974-75, the original singer/songwriters were beginning to lose their appeal. Perhaps they had worked through their transferences. Nonetheless, they were being replaced by increasingly more synthetic and less soul-plumbing versions. Most notable was John Denver, a former member of the Chad Mitchell Trio who had written Peter, Paul, and Mary's lovely hit "Leaving on a Jet Plane." By the Seventies, he had positioned himself as the sunny apostle of the granola life-style, singing about country roads, sunshine on his shoulder, and rocky mountain highs. He projected a Ewell Gibbons-goes-to-Esalen outlook: "I love to share my life with you," he told his fans. "I am trying to communicate what is in my life, the joy of living."

The second wave of singer/songwriters included America (who produced imitation Neil Young–sounding music and once released five consecutive albums that began with the letter H), Firefall, Seals and Crofts, Dan Fogelberg, and the Souther-Hillman-Furay Band. You could hear all these guys on the so-called mellow sound radio stations that began sprouting in the middle of the decade. These stations fine-tuned rock's hard edges in favor of a programming mix that was so unobtrusive that it would never upset your macramé weaving or your "rap" about your feelings. And of course the mellow sound didn't go away. The concept is just as strong today under the dreaded guise of "light rock" or "soft rock."

The L.A. ID Back Sound

Out in Los Angeles, the mellow sound had its own distinct style: a blend of country and bluegrass, mixed with harmonies that were reminiscent of the

John Denver's echo-chamber-enhanced ballads were a hit among the down-vest-and-hiking-boot set.

The Eagles's "tight" harmonies and laid-back guitar licks remain the most quintessential Seventies sound.

Beach Boys. It was best personified by Jackson Browne, Linda Ronstadt, and the Eagles.

The Eagles began as a country-rock band, but by the mid-Seventies were turning into hard-rocking chroniclers of the decadent, fast-line life-style of Southern California. An enormously successful band (five number-one records from 1975 to 1979), they were also a favorite target of rock critics.

Two of the Eagles, Don Henley and Glenn Frey, had played with Linda Ronstadt on her third solo LP before she really hit it big. Ronstadt was called by *Newsweek* the "high priestess of heartache." She was phenomenally successful (with an assist from producer Peter Asher) with her covers of songs by Martha and the Vandellas ("Heat Wave"), the Everly Brothers ("When Will I Be Loved"), Buddy Holly ("That'll Be the Day"), and Chuck Berry ("Back in the USA"). But she was no mere oldies' recycler. "I don't want just to retread old songs. But I will continue to go backwards to go forwards," she insisted. And her subsequent career has encompassed everything from pop standards to light opera (*Pirates of Penzance*) to mariachi.

Jackson Browne was a critical favorite, perhaps because he never had a number-one record. But he was an introspective who nonetheless cultivated a large following with his LPs *The Pretender* and *Running on Empty*. He also become a well-known spokesman for the "no nukes" movement.

FM CULTURE

The Seventies began just as FM radio was reaching its commercial maturity. Long consigned to classical music, the less commercial FM band lent itself to the long, uninterrupted cuts and album sides that characterized "progressive" rock. Seven-minute singles such as "Hey Jude" and "MacArthur Park" had already tested the outer limits of the talk-intensive AM hit format. On FM, DJs played whole albums without commercial interruption. Pioneered by "freeform" college radio stations, FM radio quickly became as much a self-contained culture as a commerical format. While AM crammed a steady stream of diverse singles between a constant stream of often abrasive commercials, the classic FM progressive station strove to present a scrupulously countercultural image. DJs were more likely to read poetry

20: Carter inaugurated; Jimmy and Rosalynn walk hand in hand from Capitol to White House.

27: U.S. State Department blasts Soviets on human rights.

#1 Singles:
Marilyn McCoo and Billy Davis, Jr.—"You Don't Have to Be a Star"
Leo Sayer—"You Make Me Feel Like Dancing"
Stevie Wonder—"I Wish"
Rose Royce—"Car Wash"

Selected Gold Record Albums:
Barry Manilow—*This One's for You*
Al Stewart—*Year of the Cat*
Norman Connors—*You Are My Starship*
ZZ Top—*Tejas*

and quote Nostradomus than deliver snappy patter. Steeped in marijuana culture, Eastern religions, and a smattering of left-wing politics, the FM announcer (never DJ) was after a particular ambiance, a space for your head, a place to crash while you waited for the revolution to happen.

Yet while AM radio was loud, crass, and deliberately commerical, its rapid-fire delivery of eclectic hits guaranteed a dynamic integration of musical forms. After all, on any good day on Sixties' AM radio you could hear the Stones, followed by the Supremes, Tom Jones, and Creedence Clearwater Revival. This sheer diversity provided an incentive for experimentation that saw music change dramatically from album to album. By the Seventies, FM radio's tendency to deify certain bands as "classics" caused a certain stagnancy to become institutionalized in the musical scene. In addition, FM's penchant for "progressive" rock effectively segregated its audiences from black artists. With the possible exception of Stevie Wonder, most of the early funk giants of the Seventies dwelled on singles-playing formats, most often on the AM dial. By the latter half of the decade, the rock versus disco clash revealed the not-so-subtle racism implicit in FM's segrated dial, as well as the inability of most white listeners to accept any new sounds. Only the advent of punk and new wave forced some (few) FM listeners to accept the general stagnancy of the progressive scene. Up until the Seventies, rock and roll had been a pivotal mirror of the general culture's movement toward racial accommodation. During the Me Decade, most FM stations reflected the tastes and mentality of their all white audiences.

No band dominated the air waves like the **Rolling Stones.** Most FM stations and *Rolling Stone* magazine covered the Stones the way *The Wall Street Journal* covered U.S. Steel. Between tours, the Stones spent most of the decade settling into the roles of decadent superstars and turning out a largely disappointing string of albums. Mick Jagger's marriage to Bianca and Keith Richard's off-and-on romance with heroin dominated the headlines during the early Seventies as the group turned out the classic *Sticky Fingers* and *Exile*

By the mid-Seventies, the Stones could afford to make light of their usual "bad boy" image.

FEBRUARY 1977

7: Stansfield Turner named CIA chief.

8: Hustler publisher Larry Flynt found guilty of obscenity.

17: President Carter sends Soviet dissident Sakharov personal letter of support.

18: *Washington Post* reveals twenty years of CIA payoffs to foreign leaders.

12: Jesse Jackson urges record execs to curb rock's pro-sex and drug lyrics.

15: Sex Pistols sign new bassist, Sid Vicious.

*Grace Slick embraced the Seventies
with stylish aplomb.*

on Main Street LPs. Both albums have moments of brilliance punctuated by druggy tedium. During this period, the Stones were welcomed with open arms by the cultural and political gliterati. Dick Cavett fawned all over them during their '72 tour as they traveled from groupie orgies and coke binges to Upper East Side dinner parties. Keith's heroin habit got him exiled from France in 1974, but such notoriety only increased the Stones' attraction to those in the most elite circles. The group spent most of the middecade churning out such forgettable tunes as "Dancing With Mr. D" and dismal albums like *It's Only Rock and Roll* and *Goat's Head Soup* and the infamously misogynist *Black and Blue*. Megatours seemed to be taking their toll on the boys' creative ability when they surprised everyone with the superlative *Some Girls* in '78. Mired in controversy, the "Some Girls" single incited a backlash with its blatantly racist comments about black girls. Nevertheless, the album proved that the Stones could still produce great rock and roll. Such songs as "Beast Of Burden," "Shattered," and "When the Whip Comes Down" proved that they could rise to the musical challenge offered by a upcoming generation of punk rockers—many of whom held them in contempt for becoming a stale and predictable band.

Having invented rock opera, **The Who** might have spent the Seventies basking in the critical afterglow of *Tommy*. Instead, they kicked off the decade with the raucous *Live at Leeds* and *Who's Next*. Including "Bargain," "This Song is Over," "My Wife," and the overplayed "Won't Get Fooled Again," *Who's Next* is arguably the ultimate Who album as well as the quintessence of Seventies FM rock. Filled with fun, rebellious, and largely undanceable tunes, it provided, particularly with "Behind Blue Eyes," a perfect soundtrack for millions of teenage white boys brooding in their bedrooms.

Long associated with the "acid rock" San Francisco scene, the **Jefferson Airplane** provided one of the most interesting (or depressing) transformations from the Sixties to Seventies while still maintaining their "classic" status on the FM band. By '71, the Airplane was already presenting a spacey, sci-fi image as a "starship," a giant hijacked intergalactic airliner searching for life in outer space. Paul Kanter's "Starship" scenario on *Blows Against the Empire* was the first rock album to win a sci-fi Hugo award. The Starship had to drop some ballast from the Sixties in order to take off. Marty Balin

25: Idi Amin challenges Carter, threatens lives of Americans in Uganda.

20: *Roots* tops best-seller lists.

#1 Singles:
Mary MacGregor—"Torn Between Two Lovers"
Manfred Mann's Earth Band—"Blinded by the Light"
Eagles—"New Kid in Town"

Selected Gold Record Albums:
Foghat—*Night Shift*
Quincy Jones—*Roots*
Kiss—*Dressed to Kill*

MARCH 1977

5: Carter conducts nationwide radio talk call-in show.

6: *The Hite Report* tops best-seller list.

quit in '71, and Jack Cassady and Jorma Kaukonen left in '73 to form **Hot Tuna.** By middecade, **Starship** presented a slick brand of homogenized rock that was light-years away from its flower-power origins. Ravaged by constant touring and a battle with the bottle, Grace Slick had degenerated from a sexy ex-model to a throat-damaged diva whom one critic characterized as "the Elizabeth Taylor of rock and roll." Nevertheless, their '75 album *Red Octopus* knocked Elton John out of the number-one slot to score as one of the biggest records of the year. Their single "Miracles" demonstrated that sappy romanticism could outsell revolution any day. Besides, in the sex-crazed mid-Seventies it became the first top-forty song to blatantly celebrate cunnilingus. In fact, during her live performances, Grace changed the lyrics of "White Rabbit" from "feed your head" to "give good head." Yet for all of these changes, the Starship, and Grace in particular, continued to garner popular and critical acclaim as the last refuge of countercultural rock. Their free live concerts in New York's Central Park attracted huge crowds looking for Woodstock Nation. Yet by the late Seventies, even Slick and Balin had left the group, leaving The Starship to reach even farther orbits without any traces of its original parts.

Rockin' Rod (Stewart) at his spandex best.

Blessed with what many critics consider the best male voice in rock and roll, **Rod Stewart** dominated the seventies with a string of hits from the sublime "Maggie May" ('71) to the ridiculous "Do Ya Think I'm Sexy" ('79). As success carried Rod from his roots with Jeff Beck and the Small Faces, he seemed to revel in his role as Cockney good ol' boy turned celebrity. Squiring a series of stunning blondes from Britt Eckland to Alana Hamilton, Stewart maintained that "my passions are soccer. drinking, and women, in that order." His elaborate Woody Woodpecker hairdo and dandified outfits lent an air of effeminate glitz to his macho image and guaranteed him the widest possible audience. For all of his womanizing and the macho caterwauling in "Tonight's the Night," Stewart could also sing of his friendship for a murdered gay friend in "The Killing of Georgie." By decade's end, Rod had been all but abandoned by serious rock fans and had become, with his spandex leopard jumpsuits and elaborate shows, a kind of male Cher, asking an embarrassed world the synthesized question: "Do Ya Think I'm Sexy"?

For a brief moment during the bicentennial summer of '76, pretty **Peter**

16: Carter makes first "Meet the People" trip, holds town meeting.

21: Indira Gandhi defeated in Indian elections; Morarji R. Desai elected.

21: Brezhnev blasts U.S. "human rights" campaign.

30: U.S.-Soviet arms control talks collapse.

#1 Singles:
Barbra Streisand—"Love Theme from *A Star Is Born* (Evergreen)"
Daryl Hall and John Oates—"Rich Girl"

26: Elvis Costello releases first single, "Less Than Zero."

26: China legalizes Beethoven.

28: *Rocky* and *Network* dominate Oscars.

Selected Gold Record Albums:
Fleetwood Mac—*Rumours*
Bob Seger and the Silver Bullet Band—*Night Moves*
Queen—*Queen*
Waylon Jennings—*Dreaming My Dreams*

Frampton was the hottest thing that rock and roll had ever seen. His long apprenticeship with Humble Pie and as a studio musician on *All Things Must Pass* and *Son of Schmillsson* barely prepared him for the huge success of *Frampton* and the monster *Frampton Comes Alive*. The latter, a two-record set, sold over 8 million copies (a million in its first week), easily shattering *Tapestry*'s mark as the best-selling album of all time. Combining a genial brand of funky guitar with a genuine "niceness" that made the Carpenters look like bikers, Frampton's "Show Me the Way," "Baby I Love Your Way," and "Do You Feel Like We Do" dominated the airwaves for much of

Pretty-boy Peter Frampton sold millions of albums during America's bicentennial binge of niceness.

'76. For all his success, critics savaged Frampton for his relentless blandness. For many Frampton epitomized the process by which rock had gained a world of mass popularity at the expense of its subversive edge. Appealing to teenyboppers and their moms, the flaxen-haired Frampton performed "Jumping Jack Flash" and made it sound, well, nice. Critics attacked his next album *I'm in You* as "preposterously lame." Using his patented synthesizer to sing through his guitar, Frampton performed with robot R2D2 at a '77 concert. Such cute posing did little to win him a wide audience as punk, and new wave gave fans the desire for a little edge in their music. By decade's end Frampton had returned to relative obscurity.

Hot on the heels of the Frampton phenomenon, the souped-up incarnation of **Fleetwood Mac** released their eponymous album and megahit "Rhiannon." The wispy Stevie Nicks played the Rhiannon role as Welsh witch to the hilt, wearing black chiffon, lace, and diaphonous scarves. Capitalizing on Nicks's role as New Age siren, the group released *Rumours* in '77 to unprecedented success, selling 15 million copies. The album had been cut under less than ideal circumstances, with both of the couples in the band, John and Christine McVie and Nicks and Lindsay Buckingham, breaking up. Critics called *Rumours* the "hottest soap opera in the industry." For all of the bad blood, *Rumours* produced a string of huge singles, "Go Your Own Way," "Dreams," "You Make Loving Fun," and "Think About Tomorow." Fleetwood Mac never reproduced the popularity of *Rumours*. Nicks's voice gave out during the tour following the album's release, and the

APRIL 1977

8: Israeli Prime Minister Rabin quits in finance scandal.

10: U.S. Coast Guard seizes Soviet fishing trawlers.

11: California court "frees" five minor Moonies after being "kidnapped" by their parents.

15: UN Ambassador Andrew Young calls British "world's leading racists"; backs Cuban role in Angola; calls South African regime "illegitimate."

18: Citing energy crisis, Carter asks for "moral equivalent of war," (M.E.O.W.).

6: *Airport '77* is week's top grosser.

21: *Annie*'s Broadway debut.

22: *Roots* author Alex Haley charged with plagiarism.

26: Studio 54 disco opens.

group's subsequent *Tusk* disappointed fans and critics alike. Nicks's willowy posing wore fairly thin with audiences as time wore on. One band cut a single called "Sit On My Face Stevie Nicks" in '79.

GRAND FUNK

Grand Funk Railroad was the first band to show the disparity in taste between rock critics and the rock public. The hard-rock power trio (playing an early form of heavy metal) was despised by critics but adored by a legion of fans who were decidedly different from the hip, middle-class kids who had provided the backbone for rock in the late Sixties.

It was unlikely you'd hear "I'm Your Captain" or "Mean Mistreater" coming out of the dorms of most of our great universities during 1970 and 1971. No, Grand Funk's audience wasn't the sensitive crowd, it was the guy who just dropped three downs, swigged a bottle of Boone's Farm, and did a lot of hanging out when he wasn't working at some minimum-wage job.

Grand Funk—guitarist Mark Farner, bassist Mel Schacher, and drummer Don Brewer—were the creation of Terry Knight, one of rock's great hypemeisters. Knight formed the trio—named the Grand Funk Railroad—out of the remains of his own semi-legendary Michigan punk band, Terry Knight and the Pack.

After an auspicious debut at the Atlanta Pop Festival in 1969, they were signed to Capitol Records. Knight masterminded a publicity campaign that he believed could circumvent the acceptable vehicles, radio play and good ink. Knight spent $100,000 on a billboard in Times Square to promote the band's mega-LP *Closer to Home*. He also had the band touring constantly, taking their music to the "people"—that is, the people who were ignored by the elitist rock press. Their music was turgid and overly amplified, and Farner's vocals had the resonance of a hyena, yet with their shoulder-length hair and sweaty, barechested stage presence, they were able to tap into a kind of teenage ennui/frustration that hit the suburbs in '71, the summer that downs replaced grass as the drug of choice. For kids who were growing their hair long for the first time, Farner provided the perfect spokesman. "I protest against people who are down on me because of my hair," he told *Rolling Stone* in 1971. "I really got beat up bad by some straight people at this

Mark Farner: a long-haired role model for hard-assed working class "freaks" who still hated hippies.

motorcycle race. I was the only one there with long hair. I mean no one else even had sideburns, and they pulled out handfuls of hair, kicked me in the ribs. That inspired me to write certain songs."

The critics responded in kind. In May 1971 only six writers showed up at a New York press conference to which Knight had invited several dozen. "Grand Funk is the greatest case of nonrecognition in rock history," he groused.

Knight got his revenge two months later when Grand Funk sold out Shea Stadium in twenty-four hours, a feat that had taken the Beatles three weeks in 1965. By the end of 1971, Capitol was claiming (maybe with some hyperbole) that it sold a Grand Funk record every four seconds.

Shortly after that high point, Knight and the band became embroiled in a public feud, which kept the group involved in litigation through most of 1972. After freeing themselves of Knight, the band added keyboardist Craig Frost, hired Todd Rundgren as its producer, and came back with a more "pop" sound that resulted in two number-one songs, "We're an American Band" (1973) and the remake of Little Eva's "The Loco-Motion" (1974). They had a few more top-twenty hits, but by the late Seventies, they faded and broke up as newer and heavier bands surfaced. Still, for a band that the critics hated, the Funk filed an impressive legacy: 20 million records sold, including ten consecutive platinum LPs.

THE RISE OF HEAVY METAL

Heavy metal—the term was taken from the William S. Burroughs novel *The Soft Machine*—was the first form of post-Sixties' rock that was clearly not intended to appeal to the sensitive, articulate segment that had been rock's primary audience. The music was characterized by thick and chunky power chords cranked up to max volume: nasty and brutish, but not necessarily short. The form originated in late-Sixties experiments in feedback by the Who, the Kinks, the Yardbirds and Jimi Hendrix; flourished sporadically during the Seventies (often under the guise of "hard rock"); and had a stunning rebirth in the Eighties. Mutant teenage boys will always need role models.

The most prominent of the Me Decade headbangers was **Black Sab-**

Deep Purple's Ian Paice (second from left) won fame as the voice of Judas on Jesus Christ Superstar.

9: California judge places Patty Hearst on five years probation.

27: Elvis Presley walks off concert stage for first time in career.

13: Five hundred protesters arrested at Seabrook, New Hampshire, nuclear reactor.

17: Likud coalition's leader Menachem Begin elected Prime Minister in Israeli elections.

#1 Singles:
Eagles—"Hotel California"
Leo Sayer—"When I Need You"
Stevie Wonder—"Sir Duke"

Selected Gold Record Albums:
Foreigner—*Foreigner*
Teddy Pendergrass—*Teddy Pendergrass*
Engelbert Humperdinck—*After the Lovin'*

bath, the Birmingham, England–based band whose dark view of the world inspired mass-murderer David Berkowitz. Ozzy Osbourne, Geezer and the boys were the flip side of the early-Seventies counterculture, which was still struggling to hold on to the sunny optimism of the Sixties. But Sabbath (as well as Grand Funk) became popular at the same time as barbituates; its music might be called the Seconal serenade.

As one critic noted, "Black Sabbath is worthless unless you're planning to o.d. this weekend." On the other hand, one fan had a much more poignant appraisal of the band's music: "It's freaky. It makes you feel like you're in a graveyard. It makes you feel more alive."

Whatever you think of them, any group that could produce songs with such titles as "Paranoid," "War Pigs," "Fairies Wear Boots," "Children of the Grave," and "Am I Going Insane?" will never be confused with John Denver.

Other groups worth noting in the Seventies' heavy-metal pantheon:

Deep Purple transformed themselves from psychedelic interpreters of Neil Diamond songs into a proto-metal band (some say the model for the band in the film *Spinal Tap*). Their "Smoke on the Water" has one of the greatest riffs ever. **Blue Oyster Cult** were nice Jewish boys from Long Island who used heavy metal as a put-on, except its fans didn't understand. **Aerosmith** had a lead singer who looked like Mick Jagger. **Ted Nugent,** "the Motor City Madman," liked to hunt animals and often wore a loincloth to his performances.

LED
ZEPPELIN

As sure as Robert Plant has flaxen, curly hair, as you read this, some disc jockey at some radio station somewhere in the United States is playing Led Zeppelin's "Stairway to Heaven." And as sure as Jimmy Page is bowing his guitar, somewhere some kid has slipped on a pair of headphones and is letting the orgasmic *whoosh* of "Whole Lotta Love" play pong inside his cerebellum.

It doesn't matter if that record is 20 years old or that the kid was born in 1975. Zeppelin has endured, to become the most influential rock band of the Seventies.

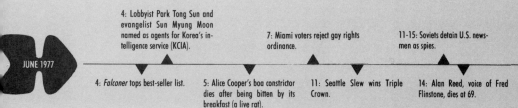

JUNE 1977

4: Lobbyist Park Tong Sun and evangelist Sun Myung Moon named as agents for Korea's intelligence service (KCIA).

7: Miami voters reject gay rights ordinance.

11-15: Soviets detain U.S. newsmen as spies.

21-22: Haldeman and Erlichman begin their prison terms.

4: *Falconer* tops best-seller list.

5: Alice Cooper's boa constrictor dies after being bitten by its breakfast (a live rat).

11: Seattle Slew wins Triple Crown.

14: Alan Reed, voice of Fred Flinstone, dies at 69.

That's a distinction the band didn't earn easily. In 1968, when they first burst on the scene—out of the ashes of the Yardbirds—most "serious" rock listeners and critics dismissed Zeppelin as little more than a pile of noise. And for most of their career, they battled the hostility of the British and American rock press. Part of Zeppelin's popularity may be attributable to the machinations of its Colonel Parker–like manager Peter Grant, who helped orchestrate the band's initial conquest of America. But the band's appeal transcended mere media manipulation. Zep's basic sound was simple: Robert Plant's on-the-verge-of-hysteria singing (often of lyrics that were sexist to the max), backed up by Jimmy Page's manic, blues-based riffs (aided by his mastery of feedback, distortion, and reverb), and a pumping/thumping rhythm section (bassist John Paul Jones and mad drummer John "Bonzo" Bonham). But unlike other heavy metal thudders, Zeppelin leavened its sound with acoustic guitars and hippie/quasi-mystical lyrics (often a product of Page's obsession with the British mystic Aleister Crowley) that inflamed the imaginations of its teenage male audience.

The music was calculated to sound outrageous while listening (1)stoned, (2)through headphones, (3)stoned through headphones, or (4)stoned at a concert in a venue with a seating capacity exceeding 25,000.

Zeppelin was the harbinger of the first serious split in the rock audience between those who came of age with the Beatles and their younger siblings. This became apparent on September 16, 1970, when an opinion poll in the British rock publication *Melody Maker* voted them England's most popular group, beating out the Beatles for the first time in eight years. Not coincidentally, the Beatles had officially broken up less than six months earlier. And three years later, their U.S. tour smashed the Beatles' attendance records. For some of those who came of age in the seventies, they were as close an experience to the Beatles as we could have gotten. Yet Zeppelin received about as one-twentieth the respect the Beatles did.

The band members popularity was buttressed by their reputation as party animals who lived to the fullest the prototypical Seventies rock star lifestyle: They flew to concerts in a private jet on which drugs and sex flowed, and groupies came acalling wherever the boys stayed. Ironically, when the foursome returned to England for periodic rests, they all reverted to the gentlemanly, happy married men they actually were.

Led Zeppelin: How many hotel rooms did they destroy?

30: Carter cancels B-1 bomber program.

#1 Singles:
KC and the Sunshine Band—"I'm Your Boogie Man"
Fleetwood Mac—"Fleetwood Mac"
Marvin Gaye—"Got to Give It Up Pt. 1"

JULY 1977

5: Gen. Mohammed Zia ul-Haq stages coup in Pakistan.

16: *Beatlemania* opens on Broadway.

18: Yankees' manager Billy Martin and batter Reggie Jackson exchange obscenities on national television.

Selected Gold Record Albums:
Peter Frampton—*I'm in You*
Soundtrack—*Rocky*
Bee Gees—*Bee Gees Live*

26: Led Zeppelin cancels tour after death of Robert Plant's son.

Despite their reputation for excess, the band was plagued by its share of tragedy, which some critics suggested was due in part to Page's infatuation with black magic or to his "pact with the devil." Plant was seriously injured in a car crash in 1975; two years later his young son Karac would die of a viral infection. Bonham would check out permanently in 1980, choking on his own vomit after drinking forty shots of vodka on the day tickets were to go on sale for the band's first concert in three years.

After Bonzo's death, the group decided to disband rather to continue without him. While Plant and Page pursued moderately successful solo careers, Zeppelin reformed briefly for much-anticipated appearances at the Live Aid concert in 1985 (with Phil Collins on drums) and in 1988 at the Atlantic Records 40th Anniversary Concert (with Jason Bonham, Bonzo's son, on drums). But the band's absence only enhanced their reputation. Their music lives on, not only on classic rock stations, but in such heavy-metal groups as Whitesnake, Def Leppard, and Kingdom Come, who have made successful careers out of recycling those same riffs that Page, Plant, Jonesy, and Bonzo first conjured up more than twenty years ago.

ZEPPELIN FACTOIDS

• The band's first choices for a name were the Mad Dogs and Whoopie Cushion. Instead, they recalled a suggestion by Who drummer Keith Moon. He had often used the expression "going down like a lead zeppelin" to describe horrendous gigs. Page suggested changing "lead" to "led" so that Americans wouldn't pronounce the name as "leed."

• They played a 1970 concert in Copenhagen under the name the Nobs, because a German woman named Eva von Zeppelin objected to the band's use of her family's name. The term *nobs*, incidentally, is Cockney for the male sexual organ.

• The group reached its absolute height of popularity in March 1975. Powered by the release of *Physical Graffiti*, all six Zeppelin LPs placed on the Billboard charts. In January three Madison Square Garden concerts sold out in only four hours.

• The group was mentioned positively by the two U.S. presidential candi-

Jimmy Page, John Bonham, Robert Plant, and John Paul Jones.

12: Carter commutes G. Gordon Liddy's Watergate sentence.

13: Blackout in New York City results in chaos, rioting, and looting.

22: Chinese Communist party announces rehabilitation of Teng Hsiao-ping and renounces Mao's wife and her "Gang of Four."

#1 Singles:
Bill Conti—"Gonna Fly Now" (Rocky Theme)
Alan O'Day—"Undercover Angel"
Shaun Cassidy—"Da Doo Ron Ron"
Barry Manilow—"Looks Like We Made It"
Andy Gibb—"I Just Want to Be Your Everything"

Women's Wear Daily reports se of "Punk" style.

Selected Gold Record Albums:
Movie Soundtrack—*Star Wars*
Supertramp—*Even in the Quietest Moments*
Donna Summer—*I Remember Yesterday*

dates in the 1976 election. Gerald Ford's daughter Susan stated on The *Dick Cavett Show* that Zeppelin was her favorite band. Jimmy Carter, while addressing the National Association of Record Manufacturers, recalled listening to Zeppelin records during all-night sessions at the Georgia governor's mansion.

● Two of their most popular LPs, *Led Zeppelin IV* (the Runes LP) and *Houses of the Holy*, had neither the title nor the group's name printed on their album jackets. Both went to the top three.

The Commodore's Lionel Richie's hair-style during a peculiar stage of development.

PRE-DISCO FUNK

Brash, self-assertive, and vaguely threatening, black music came of age in the early Seventies—before the all-consuming maw of disco swallowed, homogenized, and chewed it up.

Leading the charge were such artists as Sly and the Family Stone, Marvin Gaye, and Stevie Wonder, who had been steady AM hitmakers throughout the Sixties. But as they gained more control over their own music, their recordings changed, becoming more musically adventurous and lyrically sophisticated. Most of the new black music, though, had interracial appeal and was played on top-forty stations as well as black-oriented radio, the last time such a crossover would occur.

Here's a look at some of the key players and sounds:

Funk: Building on the rhythms of James Brown and Sly and Family Stone, self-contained groups like P-Funk ("Tear the Roof Off the Sucker"), Kool & the Gang ("Hollywood Swinging," "Jungle Boogie"), and the Ohio Players ("Fire," "Love Rollercoaster") made tough-edged music to party hearty to, providing the soundtrack in the earliest discos. White music critics loved funk, especially George Clinton and his band of wackos, but white radio stations didn't—the music

AUGUST 1977

1: *New York Times* reveals CIA "mind control" program.

10: U.S. signs Panama Canal treaty.

13: Bachman Turner Overdrive disbands.

10: N.Y.'s "Son of Sam" is arrested after two summers of tabloid terror.

16: Elvis Presley dies at Graceland.

21: Chinese Premier Hua Kuo-feng declares "cultural revolution" is over with arrest of Mao's wife and the rest of the "Gang of Four."

17: FTD: Elvis' death creates greatest demand for flowers ever.

20: Bookstores order record two million copies of *Elvis: What Happened?*

wasn't as polished as Motown, Philly, or disco—and many of the best funk records never crossed over. Worth checking out: Ohio Players LPs, whose covers featured bald, scantily clad models in various forms of bondage.

Marvin Gaye: The Prince of Motown broke out of his top-forty mold, taking control of his career with his socially conscious LP, *What's Going On* (1971), which showcased a more mature, aware singer willing to take artistic risks. The title song, "Mercy Mercy Me," and "Inner City Blues" were million-selling singles. Gaye reached a sensual peak in 1973 with his LP and single *Let's Get It On*, one of the most erotic statements ever put on vinyl.

Al Green: Some say this velvet-voiced singer out of Memphis was the last of the great soul men. From 1971 to 1976, before leaving the business to become a full-time minister, he had a consistent string of hits ("Let's Stay Together," "You Ought to Be With Me," and "I'm Still in Love With You," among them). Some reports claimed Green saw the light after a girlfriend dumped a boiling pot of grits on him as he was taking a shower (she then shot herself), and he suffered severe burns. Today you may call him the Reverend Al Green.

Isaac Hayes: The one-time Stax producer/songwriter called himself the Black Moses, but the shaven-headed stud looked more like the Black Kojak. His specialty was what he called "hot-buttered soul": long, drawn-out versions of such middle-of-the-road songs as "By the Time I Get to Phoenix," laced with heavy sexual innuendos that became the prototype for cum-a-rama king Barry White. Haye's breakthrough, though, was his memorable version of the theme from *Shaft*.

Sly and the Family Stone: The man who had bridged both black and white audiences in the late Sixties with songs of hope and optimism ("Everyday People," "Stand") turned bleak as he entered the Seventies. Sly's landmark LP *There's a Riot Goin' On* marked a creative departure for him and expressed a lot of the bitterness that had engulfed him.

The Sound of Philadelphia: In 1971 veteran producers Kenny Gamble and Leon Huff ("Expressway to Your Heart") formed a new label, Philadelphia International. It went on to become the most influential black label of the early seventies. Out of their headquarters at 309 South Broad Street, Gamble and Huff supervised a stable of hitmakers, including the

Sly Stone gave a hell of a concert when he showed up.

23: Korean lobbyist Park Tong Sun indicted for bribery of U.S. congressmen.

23: Sebastian "Mr. French" Cabot dies.

26: Ian Drury releases "Sex and Drugs and Rock and Roll."

31: Religious leaders blast ABC TV's *Soap*.

#1 Singles:
The Emotions—"Best of My Love"

Selected Gold Record Albums:
REO Speedwagen—*You Get What You Play For*
Yes—*Going for the One*
Natalie Cole—*Unpredictable*

Stevie Wonder shares an inner vision or two with TV's Barbara Walters.

O'Jays ("Love Train," "Backstabbers"), Billy Paul ("Me and Mrs. Jones"), Harold Melvin and the Blue Notes ("Bad Luck"), The Trammps ("Disco Inferno"), and TSOP (the house band at Gamble and Huff's Sigma Sound Studios whose "MFSB" became the theme song for the incredibly influential dance show *Soul Train*). Their glossy but funky sound would help define the type of music that would come to be known as disco. By 1975 Philly International Records had become the second largest black-owned record company in the United States (behind Motown), but a payola scandal involving Gamble and Huff slowed much of the company's momentum, and they never regained the touch that had propelled them during the earlier part of the decade.

🎵 **Stevie Wonder:** As he grew into his twenties, this Motown artist dropped the "Little" from his name, grabbed control of his material, and released a string of sophisticated and personal LPs, including *Talking Book*, *Innervisions* (in which he wrote all the songs and played nearly every instrument on each track) *Fulfillingness' First Finale*, and *Songs in the Key of Life* (which debuted at number one in 1976). Wonder pioneered the use of synthesizers and electronic keyboards that would become a staple of pop music in the Eighties.

ALICE COOPER

Alice Cooper was not Eddie Haskell. He was not a woman. He was not the devil. He was one of the curious musical phenomenona of the early Seventies, an indicator that the decade was indeed going to be a lot different from the Sixties.

Alice was actually named Vince Furnier, a Phoenix minister's son. He moved to Los Angeles, where the band became a pet project of Frank Zappa and his minions. "Alice Cooper" originally referred to the entire band, but Vince soon appropriated the name for himself, claiming that a Ouija board told him that he was the reincarnation of a seventeenth-century witch.

Despite taking a woman's name, Alice was vehemently heterosexual, unlike some other glam rockers. Alice and his crafty manager, Shep Gordon, were among the first to conceive of rock and roll as theater. As the Sixties moved into the Seventies, they realized that image could be more important

The Jacksons: Then there were five.

SEPTEMBER 1977

11: *Washington Post* reporter Carl Bernstein reveals CIA connection and influence at major newpapers and TV networks.

4: *The Book of Lists* tops bestseller lists.

12: S. African activist Stephen Biko dies in police custody.

4: *Godspell* closes after 2,118 performances.

14: Sixties radical Mark Rudd surrenders after years underground.

18: Ted Turner's *Courageous* defends America's Cup.

19: Ed Koch wins N.Y.'s Democratic primary, assuring mayoral election.

#1 Singles: Emotions—"Best of My Love"

Selected Gold Record Albums:
James Taylor—*JT*
Daryl Hall and John Oates—*Beauty on a Back Stre*
Shaun Cassidy—*Shaun Cassidy*
Carole King—*Simple Things*

than music—a key change in attitude. They also realized that rock works best, as it did in the Fifties, as a vehicle to shock adults. Music wasn't enough (musically, the band was just mediocre, playing your basic clunky proto-metal riffs behind Alice's irritating voice). Because long hair, wiggling hips, and tight-fitting clothes had lost most of their shock value, something else was needed.

So Alice applied some mascara to his eyes and let artificial blood pour out of his mouth and nose. He also created a bizarre stage act in which he would dismember a baby doll, guillotine himself, and writhe with a live boa constrictor draped around his neck. And he would get reams of publicity, all the more to shock Middle America and titillate adolescents. He did both handily, while making it clear to most fans that it was all an elaborate put-on.

You see, off-stage Alice Cooper was about as harmful as Alice Kramden. He played golf with John Lennon, Harry Nilsson, and Neil Diamond. He eschewed drugs, although he did have a fondness for Budweiser and Seagram's V.O. He would later show up as a panelist on *Hollywood Squares*. Alice loved to play the wronged innocent: "They've got me all wrong," he moaned. "Just because I cut the heads off dolls, they say I must hate babies. But it's not true. I just hate dolls."

"I sit and watch sex and violence all day—that's all you get on TV," he related. "It's what America is all about. I actually hate violence. But it's something that's all around us. And anyway, Shakespeare was much more violent than Alice Cooper ever was. In fact, I think if Shakesperare was around today, he'd be one of my biggest fans. I think Walt Disney would be, too, but I don't think I'd let Pat Boone's daughter into one of my shows."

Nonetheless, Alice managed to light up several millions of other people's lives before he went totally Vegas in the late Seventies. He eventually cleaned up his boozing and made a comeback in the late Eighties, positioning himself as the godfather of heavy metal.

Meanwhile, a band that made its debut on January 30, 1973, at a Queens, New York, club called Coventry took very serious note of what Alice Cooper had wrought and thought, Hey, wait a minute, why don't we just take the makeup and the theatrics one step farther? And **Kiss** was born.

The band was conceived by Gene Simmons and Paul Stanley, two ex-

Schlock Rock: One man's decadence was just good clean fun for Alice Cooper.

OCTOBER 1977

3: Indira Gandhi arrested.

4: Senate deregulates natural gas.

6: Florida jury rejects murder defense based on TV "intoxication."

13: Carter attacks oil industry as "biggest ripoff in history."

17: Supreme Court lifts Concorde ban at JFK airport.

14: Linda Ronstadt sings national anthem at Dodger stadium.

20: Two members of the group Lynyrd Skynyrd perish in a plane crash.

30: Consumer Product safety commission predicts 375,000 skateboard accidents in 1977.

Alice and snake sidekick take the stage.

tremely driven New York musicians who had played together in bar bands since 1970. They got drummer Peter Criss from his ad in *Rolling Stone* and then placed an ad in the *Village Voice* that was answered by guitarist Ace Frehley. As Kiss began their ascent out of the glitter dives of Manhattan's outer boroughs, the timing couldn't have been better. Grand Funk and Alice Cooper were fading, and something else was needed to entertain the increasingly younger rock audience. From both these masters, Kiss learned some good rock-and-roll lessons.

Like Grand Funk, Kiss built their reputation by constant touring and word-of-mouth and not with radio play. Like Alice Cooper, they compensated for what they lacked in musical ability with an incredible live show that dwarfed even Alice's most garish excesses.

All members obscured their faces with Kabuki-like makeup, but most of the attention went to bassist Gene Simmons, a former grade-school teacher who once told a teen magazine that "I'm not content to be normal." Tottering on seven-inch, knee-high platform boots, encased in a skin-tight batlike body suit, Simmons vomited blood, spat fire, and wagged his elongated tongue. And as the audiences were driven into a frenzy by this sight, the concerts would end with the equivalent of five sticks of dynamite being detonated.

Also like Alice, Kiss had the perfect pre-video age stage show, which made teenage males delirious and also fulfilled the requirement for any true rock and roll band: They really got adults pissed off. The esses in the band's logo looked like the lightning bolts of Hitler's SS, a comparison that the band's naming of their rabid legion of fans, the "Kiss Army" did nothing to discourage. But when asked about any implications, Paul Stanley would merely shrug. "The deep meaning of Kiss," he said, "is very shallow."

Images of mutant teen fascists and suburban storm troopers aside, Kiss was really more like a comic book come to life. That fact wasn't lost on Marvel Comics. In 1977 they released a comic book chronicling the adventures of the quartet. The hype claimed that the members' actual blood had been mixed in with the red ink. Kissmania cooled in the early Eighties. With two new members, the band began performing without makeup. As heavy-metal elder statesmen, they are still selling out arenas. Here's a scary thought. As today's Kiss makes its way through the rock world, it's not inconceivable

NOVEMBER 1977

#1 Singles:
Meco—"Star Wars Theme/Cantina Band"
Debby Boone—"You Light Up My Life"

Selected Gold Record Albums:
George Benson—*In Flight*
Linda Ronstadt—*Simple Dreams*
Neil Young—*American Stars 'n Bars*

5: Carter vetoes Clinch River Breeder reactor.

6: *All Things Wise and Wonderful* is a best-seller.

19: Egypt's President Sadat goes to Israel in peace bid.

19: *Star Wars* becomes top grossing film to date.

29: House reveals Korean CIA bribery plot in Congress.

that some of the youngest fans may be the children of the original Kiss Army.

DAVID BOWIE

During the Sixties, when long unkempt hair was one's "freak flag" and rallying cry of rebellion, millions of parents groaned that their boys were starting to look like girls. Yet for all the tresses, the ethos of the hippie scene was aggressively hetero. It was not until the early Seventies, when long hair was so passé that every kid from Bayonne, New Jersey, to Dallas, Texas, had hair as long as Meir Baba, that the need to outrage was translated into anything with transvestite overtones.

Like most musical gimmicks, the short-lived glitter rock movement was a British import. With the passing of the Carnaby scene and the hippie look falling into unkempt anemia, glitter injected a bit of glamour into a tired UK rock scene. **Marc Bolan** and **T. Rex** made the most outrageous transition from hippies to glitter rockers. Although touted as the next superstar in Britain, T. Rex had only one big American hit. "Bang-a-Gong (Get It On)" remains one of the great, silly standards of the early Seventies. At the time it was a rude shock, showing would-be eternal hippies that pop music was changing in ways no one could predict. Unfortunately for T. Rex, their hype soon did them in as Marc Bolan was pilloried as a transvestite teenybopper. They figure prominently in Mott the Hoople's stinging anthem "All the Young Dudes" (". . . who needs TV when you've got T. Rex . . .") a song written and produced by David Bowie for Ian Hunter and Mott the Hoople. Mott, another band transforming from folkies to heavy-metal glam, was on the verge of breaking up when Bowie promised to produce them a number one hit. In spite of (or rather because of) a rather blatant gay subtext, "All the Young Dudes" exceeded even Bowie's expectations and gave Mott a hit the group would never equal again.

Glitter was not limited to British imports. The **New York Dolls** used an outrageous drag queen shock-rock look to draw attention to the joyous anarchy of a young David Johanson's pouty Jaggerism and Johnny Thunder's screaming guitar. Though limited to a tiny cult listenership in their time, the Dolls proved precursors to the emerging New York misfit music scene from which punk would spawn. Lou Reed dressed like a biker's

Kiss's Gene Simmons

T. Rex's Marc Bolan was both adored and reviled as the most visible pioneer of Britain's brief fling with glitter.

dream date to promote the *Rock 'n' Roll Animal* album, easily one of the best live rock-and-roll albums ever made. The top-forty success of Reed's anthem to sexual ambivalence, *Walk On The Wild Side*, marks the high-water mark of mainstream glitter decadence before the late Seventies made even this seem passé.

Of all the acts to arrive during the glitter craze, only *David Bowie* outlasted and transcended the genre. This is certainly because both his talent and his genuine freakiness outshined all others. While glitter owed much of its naughty funkiness to its coy bisexuality, Bowie was casually up front about it. In an interview he candidly admitted meeting his wife, Angie, when "they were balling the same bloke." Yet for all of his explicitness, he hardly wanted to be pigeonholed as just a gay entertainer. When asked to perform at U.S. Gay National Anthem in '72, Bowie admitted his wariness of gay liberation and his lack of desire to be caught up in "a group thing."

After the spine-tingling alienation of *Space Oddity*, Bowie's '72 album *Hunky Dory* brought him back to the folkie roots of his days with David Jones and the Lower Third. Although always bordering on the precocious, this album included such classics as "Changes" and "Andy Warhol." Yet no sooner were fans in love with Bowie as the pencil-thin, flaxen-haired waif, than he reinvented himself as Ziggy Stardust, a grotesque and beautiful, bisexual rock-and-roll alien, with white powder makeup, flaming orange woodpecker hair, stacked boots, and glitter derived from Kabuki and Kiss. A consummate actor, Bowie based his Ziggy act on the real-life story of Vince Taylor, an American rock-and-roller driven mad by the business in the Sixties. "I began to wonder what it would be like to be a rock-and-roll star, so basically I wrote the script and played it out as Ziggy Stardust." While other glitter acts, such as Kiss and Alice Cooper, were dismissed as adolescent pap, Bowie's Ziggy incarnation was greeted with critical adulation. The *Village Voice* called him a "stone genius . . . the next Dylan," The New York *Daily News* called him "the Elvis of the 70's," and *After Dark* magazine called him "a hard edged acrylic painting come to life."

Bowie confounded his critics and delighted his fans by constantly changing, shedding roles as fast as they grew on him. From a family steeped in both talent and insanity, Bowie decided early on that he would "have to invent his own world in order to be fulfilled." While idol John Lennon seemed

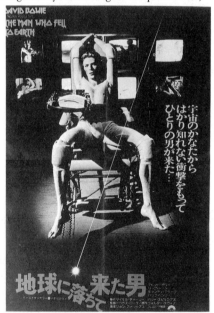

15: Congress raises Social Security tax; called largest "peacetime tax increase" in history.

31: Vietnam and Cambodia clash; break diplomatic relations.

6: Nielson Co. announces serious decline in TV viewership.

14: *Saturday Night Fever* released.

15: Sex Pistols, to appear on *Saturday Night Live*, denied U.S. visas.

to spend the Seventies in an unending identity crisis, inflicting primal scream therapy on his adoring fans, Bowie transcended personality entirely and spent much of the decade behind his Kabuki mask. "I am an actor," he explained. "My whole professional life is an act." From Ziggy, Bowie crashed through the early seventies with bleak difficult works, including *Aladdin Sane* (which depicted a vision of urban hell including "Panic in Detroit") and the Burroughs-influenced *Diamond Dogs*. Bowie followed this up with the "relentless plastic soul" of *Young Americans*, whose title song and "Fame" pandered successfully to the burgeoning disco trend, winning Bowie a whole new world of critics who would never have had time for "Space Oddity." In a few short years, Bowie moved from Ziggy to "retirement" to the Sinatra-like "Thin White Duke" without seeming to bat an eye.

Yet just as Elton-like superstardom beckoned, Bowie bowed out and landed in the movies as the long-suffering alien in *The Man Who Fell to Earth* and moved from Los Angeles's drugs and glitz to Berlin's checkpoint-Charlie-of-the-soul to produce the brooding trilogy of albums, *Low*, *Heroes*, and *Lodger*. During this period Bowie claimed that his act was over and that "he had stopped reinventing himself." Using the minimalist techno-pop Kraftwerk band in his live act, and producing Devo, Bowie kept up with the outer fringes of late Seventies' "new wave" as the music mainstream seemed to be finally catching up with his darker visions.

By '79 it was clear that Bowie was the decade's most influential rocker. His consistent role as actor and artist had paved the way for bands such as the Talking Heads. *Melody Maker* voted *Ziggy Stardust* the most influential album of the decade. Bowie's consistent ability to change, affect, and adopt new musical styles kept him in the forefront while many contemporaries grew stale and earned the contempt of much of the period's angry punk youth. Legend has it that Manhattan's Mudd club once denied Mick Jagger admittance while welcoming Bowie with open arms.

SOUTHERN ROCK

By the early Seventies, in places like Macon, Georgia, or Spartanburg, South Carolina, folks were just getting used to seeing some of their own

Part Kabuki, part Vegas, Bowie's stage performances changed rock and roll forever.

JANUARY 1978

#1 Singles:
Bee Gees—"How Deep Is Your Love"

Selected Gold Record Albums:
Steely Dan—*Aja*
Earth, Wind and Fire—*All 'n' All*
Rod Stewart—*Footloose and Fancy Free*
Aerosmith—*Draw the Line*

3: Vietnamese army siezes 400 square miles of Cambodia.

6: Federal Reserve raises discount rate to support dollar.

young men growing their hair long, sprouting moustaches and beards, acting and looking like those damn northern hippies. Well, at least they could be thankful for some small things: At least their boys weren't wearing high heels and makeup, like some of those strange fellows up in New York City.

No, sir. Their boys didn't play no glam rock. Their guys were getting it on playing nothing but a high-octane blend of blues, country, R&B, and gospel. In short, music to boogie by.

And we don't mean boogie like roller boogie or boogie fever or any of that disco kind of boogie.

We're talking about the kind of boogying that only good ol' white boys—especially if they were under twenty-five—could do as twin guitars howled like cats in heat. It was the backdrop for the perfect mid-Seventies' cruising evening: Hit the road, slam *Live at the Fillmore East* into the tape deck, floor that sucker to 75, and pass the Jack. By the time brother Duane would be into his really outrageous solo on "Whipping Post," you'd be flying high.

Amazing. Just a couple of years after those bozo rednecks blew away the long-haired heroes of *Easy Rider*, it became cool to say you're from the South. And in the unlikeliest of places, such as Long Island, New York, Confederate flags graced bars where bands churned out covers of "Statesboro Blues" as denim-jacketed poseurs clutched long-neck bottles of Budweiser and whooped rebel yells. And this was even before Jimmy Carter got into the White House and had the Marshall Tucker Band play at his Inaugural Ball!

As Charlie Daniels said: "The South's gonna do it again!" And damned if he wasn't on the mark. The best American rock and roll during the early and mid-Seventies was made by guys who hailed from below the Mason-Dixon line.

The Allman Brothers: One of the greatest live rock bands was also the prime movers behind the resurgence of Southern rock. Duane Allman, originally out of Daytona Beach, Florida, had gotten a killer reputation for his session work with black musicians down in Muscle Shoals when he put together the group that would become the Allman Brothers band. His reputation was enhanced by his work with Eric Clapton on the landmark *Derek and the Dominoes* LP, and as the Allmans began touring, their following increased. In concert, they were marvels to behold: the powerful twin gui-

Before the crash: the original Lynyrd Skynyrd.

13: Hubert Humphrey dies at age 66.

24: Soviet nuclear satellite disintegrates over Canada.

26: Evidence links fifteen to eighteen congressmen to Park Tong Sun bribes.

20: Fred Silverman becomes NBC-TV CEO.

tars of Duane Allman and Dicky Betts, the soulful singing of Gregg Allman, plus the thundering dual drummers. The Allmans were like a tight version of the Grateful Dead, without any of that band's mystical self-indulgence.

After Duane's death, the band achieved their biggest commercial success. The Allmans played to an audience af 600,000 at Watkins Glen in July 1973, the premier rock concert of the Seventies. The band dissolved amid rumors that Gregg Allman testified—to save his own hide—against their road manager, who was on trial for drug possession (and would get seventy-five years). Gregg went on to achieve more notoriety when he married Cher and then became one of the first booze burnouts of the Seventies.

Live from Macon: The Allman Brothers Band

Lynyrd Skynyrd: Named after Leonard Skinner, a gym teacher at Jacksonville's Robert E. Lee High School—a crumb who hassled the group about their long hair—this band became the most popular Southern rockers in the wake of the Allmans' dissolution. Their reputation for rowdyism, drinking, and hell-raising, which included throwing bottles at the audience during concerts and a penchant for busting up motel rooms, appealed to their teen audience. Their 1974 hit, "Sweet Home Alabama," a not-so-subtle putdown of Neil Young and veiled praise to Governor George Wallace, was one of the first indications of rock's neo-conservative streak.

Like the Allman Brothers, Skynyrd was a dynamic live band, whose signature tune "Free Bird" (written as a tribute to Duane Allman) is one of the staples of Album Oriented Radio (AOR), ranking next to "Stairway to Heaven" on the all-time play list. And like the Allmans, the band was visited by tragedy: On October 20, 1977, singer Ronnie Van Zant, guitarist Steve Gaines and his sister were killed in a plane crash outside Gillsburg, Mississippi. Ironically, just a few weeks prior to the accident, the band's latest LP, *Street Survivors*, had been released. Its cover depicted the band members standing amid flames and actually included a "Lynyrd Skynyrd survival kit." The cover was pulled from the market, and the surviving members formed a new band, the Rossington-Collins Band.

Marshall Tucker Band: This Spartanburg, South Carolina–based band blended jazz, blues, and country into a melodic mix and had a more pastoral, less rambunctious image than some of its peers. No one named Marshall Tucker was in the band; the group was named for the owner of a rehearsal hall in Spartanburg. Group members were avid supporters of

#1 Singles:
Player—"Baby Come Back"

31: Overdose death for Blood, Sweat and Tears saxophonist Gret Herbert, 30.

Selected Gold Record Albums:
Billy Joel—*The Stranger*
Randy Newman—*Little Criminals*
Bee Gees—*Bee Gees Gold*
Original Soundtrack—*Close Encounters of the Third Kind*

Jimmy Carter, campaigned for him, and were rewarded by playing at his inauguration, one of the first examples of the rock-politics connection. The band suffered its own tragedy as well: Bassist Tom Caldwell was killed in a car crash in 1980.

⬛ And Don't Forget These Good Ol' Boys: The Outlaws, Wet Willie, Molly Hatchet, .38 Special, Grinderswitch, Barefoot Jerry, and the Charlie Daniels Band.

ELTON JOHN

The most popular rock star of the Seventies didn't look like a rock star. Elton John was pudgy, balding, and bespectacled, not exactly the stuff of pinups. In fact, when Elton first burst on the scene in 1970, few expected the former Reg Dwight to become superstar material. He was seen as just another member of the sensitive singer/songwriter school (although most of his lyrics were written by Bernie Taupin), an English analogue of James Taylor. But by early 1973, John had transformed himself into a showman par excellence. He was one of the few Seventies' artists whose appeal cut across the various rock subcultures. "My success was a freak," John told an interviewer in 1979. "I was just the right person in the right place at the right time."

Indeed, Elton John was the perfect entertainer for the mid Seventies. His stage show was highly visual, perfect for the huge baseball stadiums where many rock concerts were now being held. Taupin's lyrics had the veneer of introspection but were decidedly apolitical, offering something you could think about, but not too deeply. John's chameleonlike music—he called it "ultramelodic pop"—aped a number of genres: from soul ("Bennie and the Jets") to disco ("Philadelphia Freedom") to calypso ("Island Girl") to Fifties' rock and roll ("Crocodile Rock") to country ("Country Comfort") to lush pop ballads ("Don't Let the Sun Go Down on Me") to pseudo-Beatles ("Lucy in the Sky with Diamonds").

His songs could be played with equal ease on both AM and FM radio, and he had the stats to prove it: John racked up twenty-three singles in the top forty, fifteen top-ten singles, and five number-one singles; fifteen of sixteen LPs went gold, and two of his 1975 LPs, *Captain Fantastic and the Brown*

A little bit funny. . . . Elton John's penchant for costume changes gave Cher and Liberace a run for their money.

FEBRUARY 1978

1: Accused of having sex with minor, director Roman Polanski flees California.

3: Nicaraguan National Guard bases attacked as civil war spreads.

5: Jim Fixx's *Complete Book of Running* #1 best-seller.

4: Kidnappers hold Calvin Klein's daughter for $100,000 ransom.

15: Leon Spinks dethrones Ali.

23: Debby Boone wins Grammy as top new female vocalist.

14: U.S. announces $14 billion jet sale to Egypt, Israel, and Saudi Arabia.

Dirt Cowboy and *Rock of the Westies*, entered the *Billboard* album charts at number one. When he wasn't scoring solo, John shared his talents with several other performers, including John Lennon on "Whatever Gets You Through the Night" (which would be the former Beatle's only number-one record), Neil Sedaka ("Bad Blood"), and Kiki Dee ("Don't Go Breaking My Heart").

By the middle of the decade, John had become the flashiest solo performer in all rock and roll. His antics at his Steinway keyboard suggested a cross between Jerry Lee Lewis and Liberace. Each set would feature numerous costume changes, and John was liable to be wearing everything from a blue satin Three Musketeers' costume to a spangled drum major's outfit.

As John's hairline receded (after transplants failed), he began covering his head with an increasingly bizarre collection of hats and/or wigs, including one pink hat that was crowned with a light-up model of the Eiffel Tower. John was also an optician's best friend, owning $40,000 worth of glasses, and we're not just talking regular old specs here. One pair had windshield wipers on them, another had frames shaped like grand pianos, a third had his name spelled out across the top in neon lights. He tramped across the stage in foot-high platform shoes and once hired actors who resembled Queen Elizabeth, Frankenstein, and Elvis to join him on stage.

John's career began to tail off in the late Seventies. Many trace that decline to his admission that he was bisexual. John himself claimed that many radio stations stopped playing his records because of that prejudice. The punk/new wave movement, which developed as a response to excessive rock stars like John, also helped contribute. He announced his retirement in 1976, came back in 1978, and undertook another massive tour. Into the mid-Eighties, he was still making hits (one, "Sad Songs," became transformed into a jingle for designer jeans). He announced another retirement in 1984, got married (to a woman), and eventually opted for a simpler lifestyle. In 1988 he auctioned off most of his outfits, art, and antiques, fetching a cool $5 million. And he decided to tour again. But now it was a more conservative Elton who was playing to sell-out crowds. His hair was shorter, he had fewer costume changes, and the stage show was pared down. Elton John had again become a man of his times.

Music for Middle Earth: Rick Wakeman's synthesized escapism reaches absurd heights.

Moog madness: Emerson, Lake & Palmer.

MARCH 1978

#1 Singles:
Bee Gees—"Stayin' Alive"

Selected Gold Record Albums:
Crystal Gayle—*We Must Believe in Magic*
Barry Manilow—*Even Now*
Jackson Browne—*Running on Empty*
Joni Mitchell—*Don Juan's Reckless Daughter*

2: Charlie Chaplin's body stolen from Swiss crypt.

6: *Hustler* publisher Larry Flynt shot.

13: Germany and Japan act to prop up dollar.

14: Coca Cola named official soft drink of Moscow Olympics.

165

ART ROCK

During the first half of the Seventies, rock and roll continued to split itself into a dizzying array of subgenres. For the teens of the period, there seemed to be a sound for every high school clique. Sensitive types could retreat to their rooms and write in their journals to the strains of Joni Mitchell and James Taylor; ass kickers got off on oldies and rebel rock, rock-and-rollers wavered between metal and glam; and the brainy types had a music of their own. For those who needed a little Mussorgsky with their rock, groups like Yes and Emerson, Lake and Palmer laid on a thick layer of pompous arrangements to an undanceable beat.

Inspired by the success of post-Pepper "concept" albums and a growing atmosphere of druggy mysticism, the art rock movement of the early Seventies was spurred by the development of the synthesizer. While the serious electronic music of the Sixties seemed confined to disonant beeps and boops, by decade's end Walter Carlos's *Switched On Bach* was the best-selling classical album of all time. Carlos's stunning work for the soundtrack of *A Clockwork Orange* demonstrated that a synthesizer could be an instrument of subtlety and range.

Subtlety was not to be the hallmark of Seventies' classical rock. **Emerson, Lake and Palmer,** the premier art rockers of the Seventies were a kind of minor-league supergroup, combining Lake from King Crimson and Emerson from the Nice, where he had made a madcap reputation for himself by stabbing synthesizers and zipping through a bastardized combination of *West Side Story*'s "I Want to Live in America" and Dvořák's *New World Symphony* at seventy miles an hour. While ELP's debut album restrained itself to gargantuan organ solos and piano riffs taken from dozens of classics, their later records *Tarkus*, *Trilogy*, and *Brain Salad Surgery* combined Emerson's Liberace-like keyboard work with a staggering penchant for apocalyptic sci-fi scenarios. With songs with such names as "Karnevil 9," "Manticore," "The Endless Enigma," "Aquatarkus," and "The Three Fates," ELP convinced fans that they were absorbing a new age of high culture. In fact, Emerson provided a keyboard variation on the "fast guitar" syndrome of the early Seventies. After all, it wasn't what you played, it's how fast and how "intensely" you laid it down. For all of their classical

The group Yes: Steve Howe, Jon Anderson, Chris Squire, Alan White, Patrick Moraz

14: Israel invades Lebanon; occupies four-to-six-mile security belt.

18: Former Pakistani President Bhutto condemned to death.

#1 Singles:
Andy Gibb—"(Love Is) Thicker Than Water"
Bee Gees—"Night Fever"

22: TV broadcast of *The Ruttles: All You Need Is Cash*.

23: Rumors spread of Beatles reunion.

27: *Dancin'* opens on Broadway.

166

veneer, ELP provided a glitzy concert, complete with smoke, revolving drums, and synthesizer mutilation that was at best a classical variation on Kiss. An early reviewer of an ELP concert says it all: "There must be some relationship between audiences who go to stock car races to see crashes and ones who go to see somebody drop an organ."

Drawing on British folkie roots with an overlay of acid rock, keyboard madness, and a heavy dose of incomprehensible mysticism, **Yes** reigns as the most popular and long-lasting art rock bands of the Seventies. Like ELP, early Yes called on "serious" music to elevate to a higher plane music to get stoned to. With the arrival of Rick Wakeman (from the Strawbs), Yes reached mass popularity in '72 with "Roundabout" from the album *Fragile*. Jon Anderson's icy vocals combined perfectly with Wakeman's keyboard and Steve Howe's crashing guitarwork to obscure the pure meaninglessness of their song's seemingly endless vocals. ("Seasons will pass you by...I get up...I get down") By middecade, after two more sucessful albums (*Close to the Edge* and *Tales from Topographic Oceans*), Wakeman could no longer reconcile his hard-drinking life-style with Anderson's hippy-dippy health food image. On his own, Wakeman produced a handful of concept albums, *The Six Wives of Henry the* VIII, *The Myths and Legends of King Arthur and the Knights of the Round Table*, and *Journey to the Centre of the Earth*, that outdo even Yes for their lame attempt to merge rock with a hokey dungeons-and-dragons imagery using forty-eight-piece orchestras and enormous stage shows. Dismissed as "bourgeoise escapism in its most traditional form" by Robert Palmer, Rick Wakeman's music presented rock at its most grandiose and flaccid, at the farthest reaches from its humble, danceable roots.

SPRINGSTEEN

Deep in the heart of the mid-Seventies' malaise, *Bruce Springsteen's* comet burst on the national scene, buoyed by a fanatical club following and critical acclaim that was just short of ridiculous. By now the Springsteen legend is well enough known. The son of a bus driver from Freehold, New Jersey, a town best known for its racetrack, Springsteen played the Jersey shore bar-and-club scene, carving out a niche for himself in Asbury Park, the tawdry

APRIL 1978

6: Carter signs law raising retirement age from 65 to 70.

7: Carter "defers" production of neutron bomb.

13: Radio City Music Hall saved from wrecker's ball.

Selected Gold Record Albums:
Eric Clapton—*Slowhand*
Chic—*Chic*
Manhattans—*Feels So Good*

3: *Annie Hall* tops Oscars; *Star Wars* wins seven technical awards.

remains of a once-fabled resort. While his first two albums did not exactly bust the charts, his critical adulation paved the way for a blockbuster reception to *Born to Run* (1975). By then Springsteen had expanded his Jersey base to clubs and colleges throughout the country. With his rapid-fire lyrics and myth-making songs, Springsteen quickly caught on as a thinking man's rocker (or a rocking man's thinker). Set against the trendiness of glitter, the fey pretensions of Elton, Springsteen seemed both virile *and* smart—a real working-class hero who sent audiences wild with the slam-bang buildup of songs like "Rosalita" and "Born to Run." Springsteen's sound, built on a blatant imitation of black rhythm sections of Philly sound and Stax Records and personified by his ebullent sax player Clarence Clemens, bridged the white-black sound gap at a time when the gulf between progressive FM rock and top-forty funk made radio seem as segregated as Soweto.

The question remains, was Springsteen for real, or just a creation of Columbia hype and fawning critics? In fact, Springsteen was almost a victim of his own hype. Soon after being signed by Columbia in '72, he was praised to the skies as the "new Dylan." John Hammond, who had uncovered talent for Columbia since Bessie Smith's time, declared Springsteen "better than Dylan." Columbia president Clive Davis made Bruce his pet project and even read the words to "Blinded by the Light" at a board meeting. The problem was, DJs and consumers weren't buying it. Hype alone could not make a star. Bell Records sank $100,000 on Gary Glitter. Atlantic spent twice as much on Barnaby Bye, and M-G-M's promotion of a nonentity named Judie Pulver included a Peanuts ad campaign and the personal endorsement of Apollo astronaut Edgar Mitchell. When Columbia sent out copies of the LP *Greetings from Asbury Park, N.J.* DJs failed to respond. New York DJ Dave Herman (of WNEW-FM) felt that "The Dylan hype was a turn off. I didn't want Columbia to think they got me."

Bruce's '74 *E Street Shuffle* album did even worse. During that year Boston critic Jon Landau caught Springsteen's show and declared, "I have seen the future of rock and roll and its name is Bruce Springsteen." Within a year Landau quit his writing job to work full time as a producer for the future of rock and roll. At the same time, the folks in Columbia's hype department worked overtime to ensure that Bruce's third album paid off their hefty investment in the next Dylan. Throughout the winter of '75, Columbia gave its

How did this brooding, skinny Jersey boy (Bruce Springsteen) get his face on the covers of Time *and* Newsweek *during the same week?*

18: Senate votes to give up Panama Canal in 1999.

24: Economy pushes Carter's approval rating down to 39 percent.

20: Miniseries *Holocaust* watched by 120 million viewers.

23: Sid Vicious records his own version of "My Way."

sales force inspirational cassettes and plied DJs with teasers of a serious new work in progress. On the eve of *Born to Run*'s debut in 1975, Columbia bought out the Manhattan club The Bottom Line for multiple engagements to ensure that an influential crowd of critics and DJs could catch the Boss's phenomenal act. Then in October 1975, in what is still considered one of the greatest publicity coups of all time, Springsteen appeared on the covers of *Time* and *Newsweek* on the same day.

Yet for every skeptic who saw a media cabal, there were dozens of fans happy that *somebody* was making music you could dance to. On an another level, Springsteen was the first musician to fully articulate the darker side of the Seventies. It's not entirely coincidental that he hit it big at the trough of the worst postwar recession. Too young to have experienced the heady Sixties, many of the Boss's fans saw an economy collapsing before they even got their first job. Springsteen's raw energy touched a nerve with this unsettled, undefined breed of latter-day boomers. As one fan explained, "The peace and love thing is over. We've got to take a shot now or settle into the masses."

Could it be hype?

STEELY DAN

Can you believe these two (Becker and Fagen of Steely Dan) once played with Jay and the Americans?

Like their name, a literary reference to William S. Burrough's *Naked Lunch*, Steely Dan was always more and less than it seemed. Not really a group, but an evolving collection of sidemen for nucleus Donald Fagen and Walter Becker, Steely Dan turned out some of the best "progressive" rock of the decade. At a time when irony seemed the only refuge for the active mind, Steely Dan turned out songs biting in wit and wicked in execution. During a decade of pompous lyrics and mindless verbosity from groups like Yes and Jethro Tull, Fagen consistently wrote sardonic little ditties of multi-layered viciousness. During the years when jazz giants Miles Davis and Herbie Hancock were taking their fans on painful and embarrassing excursions into fusion jazz, Steely Dan appropriated licks from Pharaoh Sanders to kick into a sumptuous little song called "Rikki Don't Lose That Number." And what other group could concoct an ecstatic boogie bolero that doubled as a prayer to a Buddhist Bodhisattva? In the decade of the live album, the members of Steely Dan were consummate studio musicians.

24: J. P. Stevens settles suit with unions after year-long boycott.

27: Pro-Soviet coup in Afganistan.

#1 Singles:
Bee Gees—"Stayin Alive"

Selected Gold Record Albums:
Dolly Parton—*Here You Come Again*
Warren Zevon—*Excitable Boy*
Waylon Jennings and Willie Nelson—*Waylon & Willie*

Educated at Bard, an exclusive and decidedly eccentric New York private college, Becker and Fagen marinated themselves in the jazz music of Bird, Coltrane, and Monk. Fagen wanted nothing more than to reproduce the improvisational wildness found on old Prestige jazz albums. At the same time, both leaders were consumed in the music, literary, and drug scene of the late Sixties. Borrowing heavily from both Burroughs and Dylan, most of Steely Dan's lyrics are provocatively obscure and given to any number of interpretations. After all, just what is "Rikki Don't Lose That Number" about? A drug deal? A love affair? A homosexual come-on? Has anyone ever divined the meaning of *Aja*? And what does "Don't Make Me Do It Without My Fez On" bring to mind? Perhaps Fagen said it best when he explained, "Coming out of the Sixties, we were part of the sensibility that had rejected rationality as an operating principle."

Whatever their lyrics implied, Steely Dan remains the smartest, slickest, and most musically sophisticated band of the decade. Although never a mega-success, the group clearly suceeded in bridging the gap between pop music and jazz mastery.

Billy the Kid (Joel) sports one of his more unfortunate haircuts.

MELODY MAKERS

By the early 1970s rock-and-roll counterculture had become the main culture, displacing other forms of music from top-forty and FM play. Through the Sixties, AM play lists could switch from a Supremes' song to Louis Armstrong's "Hello, Dolly" to the Stones' "Time Is on My Side" and back to Shirley Bassey's "Goldfinger" without raising an eyebrow. Rock and roll coexisted with other forms of popular music, such as film themes and Broadway show tunes. By the early Seventies, Broadway songs were no longer getting airplay on rock stations. *Hair* was the last play to send a number of songs into the top-forty, and that was mainly because it co-opted a rock sound. Similarly, movies began to rely on known rock artists to provide popular film themes, such as Paul McCartney's theme from *Live and Let Die* and Carly Simon's "Nobody Does It Better" from *The Spy Who Loved Me.* In the Seventies, such Broadway staples as "Send in the Clowns" and songs from *A Chorus Line* were consigned to easy listening stations if played at all. Oddly enough, "The Candy Man" by Sammy Davis, Jr., was the only

MAY 1978

1: Ethnic Chinese flee Vietnam, join "boat people."

3: Release of film *FM*.

5: Betty Ford ends hospital stay for substance abuse.

8-11: Violent anti-Shah rioting rocks Iran.

9: Former Italian Prime Minister Aldo Moro executed by Red Brigades.

11: China accuses Soviets of border incursion in Manchuria.

crooner hit to cross over onto pop stations, and even this song seemed to have drug overtones.

Yet as rock and roll dominated the airwaves, it also incorporated some of the elements of Broadway song-and-dance numbers. Once loose from John Lennon's rougher edges, Paul McCartney produced a body of music notable for its whimsical tunefulness. While some felt that such "silly love songs" were a step toward insipid pap, for millions of fans McCartney was simply returning to his musical roots in British show music.

Among McCartney's biggest fans and imitators was a brash singer/songwriter from Long Island, New York, named **Billy Joel.** A classically trained child who was a hood for most of his high school years, Joel departed for Los Angeles where he performed as "Bill Martin at the Keyboard" at the Executive Lounge. In L.A., Joel nearly went mad "playing the Buddy Greco role to the hilt." After returning east, Joel used his "Piano Man" experience well. His performance at the '72 Mar Y Sol concert in Puerto Rico caught Columbia's attention. His '73 album *Piano Man* was critically well received, and Joel became a bit of cult figure on the East Coast. But for many, on *Piano Man* he sounded just a little too much like Harry Chapin, and he was typecast as just another sensitive singer/songwriter. This in spite of a debut album that demonstrated Joel's remarkable musical range, from the title ballad to the mock western of "Billy the Kid" to the gritty realism of "Captain Jack," which remains one of the most damning commentaries on suburban white-boy drug culture.

After *Piano Man*, Joel had a few moderately successful albums before breaking out with *The Stranger* in '77, which featured a string of hits including "Movin' Out (Anthony's Song)," "Only the Good Die Young," "She's Only a Woman to Me," and that schmaltz master "Just the Way You Are." The latter song, with its corny refrain and steamy Tom Scott sax solo, established Joel as the premier crooner of the Seventies—a role Joel did not relish in the least and tried to fight with later rock-and-roll numbers like "It's Still Rock 'n' Roll to Me" and "Big Shot." Yet for all of his hard rock posing, Joel was in many ways the Sinatra of his generation. Like Sinatra, he seemed most comfortable in the role of the sentimental hood, a tough guy with a heart of gold crooning the background music to a new generation of suburbanite boomers settling into an adult life of comfort and compromise. Joel's "Scenes from an

The divine Miss M (Bette Midler).

15: Patty Hearst returns to prison.

26: First casinos open in Atlantic City, N.J.

30: Carter condemns Soviet and Cuban roles in Africa.

#1 Singles:
Yvonne Elliman—"If I Can't Have You"
Wings—"With a Little Luck"

15: Bianca Jagger files for divorce.

17: L.A. premiere of *Thank God it's Friday.*

Selected Gold Record Albums:
Soundtrack—*Grease*
Meat Loaf—*Bat Out of Hell*
Steve Martin—*Let's Get Small*
Parliament—*Funkentelechy vs the Placebo Syndrome*

171

The Carpenters: They made the kind of music you could imagine Tricia Nixon actually liked.

Olivia Newton-John, Australia's bland bombshell, took America by storm in the mid-Seventies.

Italian Restaraunt" was "our song" for legions of corny couples. He provides a not-so-wistful look at impending middle age that contrasts severely with Springsteen's last grasp at adolescence and innocence.

Bette Midler's campy brand of performance came directly from a song-and-dance background as bizarre as it was diverse. A Jew from Honolulu, Bette was always different. Arriving in New York in the mid-Sixties, she starved through any number of undignified jobs (which included a stint as a go-go girl in Union City, New Jersey). After landing a three-year stint in *Fiddler on the Roof*, she continued to perform at New York's Improvisation and caught the attention of David Frost's talent scouts. Stints on Frost's show, Merv, and the *Tonight Show* exposed Midler to millions. Yet her most hospitable venue remained the Continental Baths, a gay hang-out where she performed her zany numbers before an audience of hundreds of men clad only in towels.

Backed up by her arranger, the then-unknown Barry Manilow, with her group the Harlettes, Bette carried on like a deranged reincarnation of Garland, Streisand, and Joplin all rolled into one, infusing her numbers with a manic happiness and showmanship that was sadly lacking in most rock performances. Her debut album, *The Divine Miss M*, took the country by storm with her wild and campy takes on songs from the Forties through the Seventies, including the Andrews Sisters's "Boogie Woogie Bugle Boy," the Shangri-la's notorious "Leader of the Pack," and Buzzy Linhart's hippy dippy "Friends." Like Bowie, Midler stood out because she was at heart a dramatic performer. She did not confine herself to the one-dimensional role of rock star or folk singer. Supported by a largely gay audience, Midler popularized an almost transvestite synthesis of pop genres that would set the tone for much of the decade.

Barry Manilow's role as arranger of *The Divine Miss M* launched his seemingly unstoppable career as the premier balladeer of middle America. Rivaled only by the Carpenters, Barry touched the heartstrings of many a Qiana-clad couple with tearjerkers like "Mandy" and "I Can't Live Without You."

Another childhood prodigy, Manilow cut his musical teeth writing and singing advertising jingles. This was not a bad background considering that many of his ad songs are as memorable as any pop hit. They include the Dr.

7: In Annapolis address, Carter blasts Soviet Union.

8-11: NASA scientists fail to reorient Skylab's faltering orbit.

12: Soviets detain U.S. businessman for six days on traffic violation.

15: Supreme Court bans dam project threatening snail darter, a rare species of fish, with extinction.

Pepper theme, Kentucky Fried Chicken's "Get a Bucket of Chicken," and the unforgettable "(And Like a Good Neighbor) State Farm Is There." Although Manilow did sing the McDonald's tune "You Deserve a Break Today," he vehemently denies that he wrote it.

Almost all of Manilow's megahits have all the personality of a slickly packaged commercial. Songs like "Looks Like We Made It," and the infamous "I Write the Songs" all have hugely overproduced orchestrations that push his modest baritone to the point of breaking, creating a synthesized pathos—a kind of polyester passion. Like good pop ballads—or good commercials—Manilow's tunes do not seem to date. They seem to exist in a timeless never-never land of schmaltz that is endlessly recycled on Light-FM. Although undeniably a creature of the Seventies, only his disco-influenced "Cococabana" seems stamped as a particular period piece.

DISCO

It's just after midnight Friday night at Penrod's or some other joint with a phony British-sounding name in a suburban shopping mall. The bar's doing a brisk business in Harvey Wallbangers and tequila sunrises. The dance floor is crammed, although it's hard to tell since it's enveloped in man-made smoke and fog. Over in the corner, a couple of steps from the backgammon tables, some dude in a Qiana shirt is putting the moves on a fox in a spandex halter. Meanwhile, Labelle is cooing away at 1200 decibels:

"Voulez-Vouz Couchez Avec Moi?"

THUMPA THUMPA CHUCKA CHUCKA HUMP ME HUMP ME, the music is saying...

For many Americans of a certain age group, a night at the disco was the quintessential Seventies entertainment experience. Your reaction to the above is a litmus test of your feelings about disco: Either you recalled the scene with fondness that sent you scrounging through your LP collection until you found that scratched twelve-inch record of "Push Push in the Bush," or else you recoiled in horror and scrounged through your closet in search of that "Disco Sucks" T-shirt.

Indeed, disco—the music, the life-style, the attitude—made you define yourself. Do you support it? Do you rail against it? Do you ignore it?

When she (Donna Summer) did MacArthur Park you knew the Sixties were finally over.

#1 Singles:
Johnny Mathis and Deniece Williams—"Too Much, Too Little, Too Late"
John Travolta and Olivia Newton-John—"You're the One I Want"
Andy Gibb—"Shadow Dancing"

24: Briefcase bomb kills presidents of Yemen and S. Yemen.

28: Bakke Case: Supreme Court rules that affirmative action can result in reverse discrimination.

16: *Grease* (the film) released.

15: Jordan's King Hussein takes twenty-six-year-old American bride.

21: *Evita* opens on London stage.

Selected Gold Record Albums:
Rolling Stones—*Some Girls*
Soundtrack—*Thank God It's Friday*
Bruce Springsteen—*Darkness at the Edge of Town*
Gerry Rafferty—*City to City*

Disco was proof positive that the Sixties were over. You had to get dressed up to go out. You actually had to learn dance steps. You probably had to cut your hair to fit in. Spending money on material goods and designer merchandise became desirable ends. Unlike rock music, you weren't expected to experience the music in your head; it was a pure bodily sensation. It was totally apolitical; its only message was to dance, party, and have fun (not such a bad thought for depressing times). If you were a white, heterosexual teenage male who preferred to wear jeans and a T-shirt and sit passively at a stadium-size rock concert, then disco could be an especially threatening experience.

Disco music was the product of three groups that played a small role in the counterculture: gays, blacks, and Hispanics. During the early Seventies, while most white, middle-class student-types were still trying to keep the Sixties alive, others were dancing to a new form of music in "underground" nightclubs, anticipating the future. And when the major forces for keeping the counterculture alive—Vietnam and Watergate—faded, these disco people were ready to come above ground. From these humble beginnings, disco would by the end of the decade become a $4 billion-a-year industry, whose mass-merchandised wares would be suitable for bar mitzvahs and weddings. Quite a cultural assimilation, indeed.

Disco music itself was a blend of several styles: the latest incarnation of rhythm and blues (or rhythm without the blues, as *Newsweek* noted), foremost among them James Brown's make-it-funky beat and Gamble and Huff's sweet and soulful Philadelphia International sound; the icy synthesizer-dominated sound known as Eurodisco, with a hint of the melodies of jazz and swing. The common denominator: a juiced-up beat, usually 125 beats per minute. It was a style that was driven by the producers rather than the artists. In fact, along with the DJs, the producers were the true disco stars. The DJ, through judicious mixing of records, could get the audience to "peak," a sensation that some said often mimicked orgasm.

Anyone could have a hot disco record, and artists as disparate as Frankie Valli, Johnny Taylor, Frankie Avalon, and the Bee Gees all used the ubiquitous disco beat to revive their careers. In fact, most "disco" artists were mere studio creations; only a handful of singers, most notably Gloria Gaynor and Donna Summer, were able to project a distinctive identity. The ear-

JULY 1978

3: China suspends aid to Vietnam after twenty years.

2: Judith Krantz's *Scruples* on bestseller list.

10: U.S. court of appeals legalizes Laetrile, an unproven peach-pit cancer cure.

5: *Some Girls* album cover withdrawn because of celebrity complaints.

19: Anti-Somoza general strike cripples Nicaragua.

20: Carter's drug advisor Peter Bourne resigns after writing improper prescription for quaaludes. Cites marijuana use by members of the White House staff.

liest disco records, like the Hues Corporation's "Rock the Boat" and KC and the Sunshine Band's "Get Down Tonight," had a certain vitality, and they still sound good today.

Merits aside, disco music will be recalled as the soundtrack to what will be seen as "the Seventies life-style," a blend of Sixties hedonism (easy sex, lots of coke, ludes, and poppers) and Seventies fashion-consciousness (platform heels, white suits, spandex) and Me Decade-ism (out on the dance floor, *you* were the star). This life-style was played out primarily at discos, the clubs that were the hyped-up descendants of such mid-Sixties discotheques as Arthur and Cheetah. During the first wave of discomania (1973–1977), most of these clubs basically functioned as singles bars with dance floors. It wasn't until 1977 when Studio 54 opened in Manhattan that the concept of the disco as decadent snob palace took root. That certainly didn't help disco's image with its detractors.

The nightly shenanigans at Studio 54 kept disco on the gossip pages, and the release of *Saturday Night Fever* later in 1977 moved disco to new levels of popularity and acceptance, even as the music became increasingly gimmicky and formulaic.

By '79, disco had become a mainstream phenomenon. Even rock musicians began incorporating the once-despised disco beat into their work. By the turn of the decade, disco had peaked. Finally, the specter of AIDS and the conservatism of the Reagan years drove the music and life-style back underground where it began.

The Brothers Gibb had no trouble co-opting the Disco sound.

25: First "test tube" baby born in England.

25: Yugoslav President Tito charges Cuba with "new colonialism" in Africa.

28: Prices rise at double digit rates in second quarter of 1978.

#1 Singles:
Andy Gibb—"Shadow Dancing"

Selected Gold Record Albums:
Willie Nelson—*Stardust*
Tom Petty and the Heartbreakers—
You're Gonna Get It
Abba—*Greatest Hits*

Great Moments in Disco
Disco Timeline

1971-73: In underground New York clubs, such as Sanctuary and The Loft, disc jockeys begin stitching together r&b, rock, and Latin records and driving their predominantly gay audiences into a frenzy. The scenes are the prototypes of the modern disco.

1973: The lush "Love's Theme" by Barry White and his Love Unlimited Orchestra becomes the first record to emerge from the disco underground and go to number one. White went on to become the equivalent of the black Liberace.

1974: Two more early disco records, the Hues Corporation's "Rock the Boat" and George McCrae's "Rock Your Baby," are early-summer, back-to-back number-one singles.

1975: "The Hustle" by veteran songwriter, producer, and arranger Van McCoy becomes a disco anthem, selling more than 10 million copies and spawning the first major dance craze since the mid-Sixties.

October 1976: No further proof about the ridiculousness of disco: "Disco Duck," a novelty song by Memphis DJ Rick Dees, becomes number one. Alas, his follow-up, a disco tribute to the new *King Kong* movie called "Dis-Gorilla," went nowhere, although Dees went on to become a top DJ in Los Angeles.

March 1977: Studio 54 opens and fascism goes funky. During the next few months through its heavily guarded doors will pass the likes of Jackie Onassis, Truman Capote, Roy Cohn, Liza Minnelli, and "Miss Lillian" Carter.

August 1977: David Berkowitz, the Son of Sam, is arrested, ending his killing spree in which his primary targets were disco-goers. At Studio 54, owner Steve Rubell breaks into the sound system and announces gleefully: "They got him, they got him!"

October 1977: Another disco novelty hits number one: "The Star Wars Theme" as interpreted by studio musician Meco Monardo, who devised the idea for the song in his head after seeing the movie eleven times.

December 1977: *Saturday Night Fever* (a movie based on a 1976 magazine article chronicling events during the winter of 1975) is released theatrically; sales of three-piece white suits multiply and the entire disco movement is revived. The soundtrack LP sells 25 million copies and will become the biggest-selling LP of all time until Michael Jackson's *Thril-*

AUGUST 1978

1: Christina Onassis takes Soviet husband.

2: Phillip Crane enters Repubican 1980 White House race.

4: Unemployment and inflation rise again.

6: Pope Paul VI dies at age 80.

8: White House announces Camp David meeting between Begin, Sadat and Carter.

9: Jimmy Carter invites Muddy Waters to play White House picnic.

ler in 1984.

1977–78: The most creative disco sounds are being made by Chic, a band fronted by former rock musicians Nile Rodgers and Bernard Edwards. The brains behind "Le Freak" and "Dance Dance Dance" were unabashed at their conversion from rock to disco: "We wanted millions of dollars, Ferraris and planes—and disco seemed like the way to get them."

1978: The Bee Gees, three one-time Beatles soundalikes, enjoy a rejuvenated career thanks to their contribution to the *Saturday Night Fever* soundtrack: "Stayin' Alive," "How Deep Is Your Love," and "Night Fever." In March these three songs are in the top ten, making the Bee Gees the first group since the Beatles to score such a triple play.

1978: Disco act A Taste of Honey ("Boogie Oogie Oogie") wins a Grammy for Best New Artist, nosing out such performers as Elvis Costello.

1978: *Thank God It's Friday*, a cheapie exploitation movie about the disco life-style, becomes a hit. Donna Summer plays an aspiring singer crooning "Last Dance."

1978: Disco diva Grace Jones appears on The *Merv Griffin Show* singing "I Need a Man." She's wearing a wedding dress, exposed to reveal a black garter belt as she playfully hits Merv with her leather whip.

April 2, 1979: A smiling Donna Summer graces the cover of *Newsweek*, whose headline proclaims: "Disco Takes Over!" The article begins: "Roll over rock . . . disco is here to stay. . . ." But in just a few months, the lines between the two forms will be blurred as Rod Stewart ("Do Ya Think I'm Sexy?") and Blondie ("Heart of Glass") have disco-tinged hits and Donna Summer cuts a rock song ("Hot Stuff").

July 12, 1979: Chicago DJ Steve Dahl hosts an antidisco rally at Comiskey Park in between games of a White Sox–Tigers doubleheader. He piles hundreds of disco records in a wooden box in center field and sets it afire as the crowd chants "Disco sucks! Disco sucks!"

1980: The Village People, who dress like four gay archetypes and lip-sync to prerecorded music, become a national sensation. No one seems to care that their songs, such as "YMCA," "Macho Man," and "In the Navy," are good-natured paeans to the gay life-style.

May 31, 1980: The last record that could be characterized as a disco record, "Funkytown" by Lipps, Inc., hits number one. Like many disco acts, Lipps, Inc., would never be heard from again.

14-18: House opens investigation into Martin Luther King, Jr., assassination.

15: House extends ERA deadline from 1979 to 1982.

26: Pope John Paul I elected.

30: Prime rate hits 9¼ percent as dollar falls and inflation gains.

#1 Singles:
Rolling Stones—"Miss You"
Commodores—"Three Times a Lady"
Frankie Valli—"Grease"

Selected Gold Record Albums:
Commodores—*Natural High*
Con Funk Shun—*Loveshine*
Rick James—*Come Get it*
Carly Simon—*Boys in the Trees*

PUNK

Mention punk and most people still think of it as a British phenomenon—a short-lived period when kids dyed their hair green, put pins through their noses, and listened to the Sex Pistols before Sid Vicious finally went mad, killed his girlfriend, and stuffed her under a sink. It came and went and left the world safe for such "new wave" bands as the Cars, the Knack, and the Police.

Yet punk was neither British in origin nor short-lived in either duration or effect. The punk attire and attitude can still be seen in every major city or college town. Walk through Berkeley, Ann Arbor, or New York's Village (East or West), and you can see clusters of teenagers dressing like 1977 (not far from other clusters dressing like it were 1968).

If punk has a birthplace at all, it is New York and not London. Such proto-punkers as Lou Reed and the Warhol-inspired **Velvet Underground** and the **New York Dolls** had long gone against the grain of rock's trend toward grand "concept albums," twelve-minute guitar solos, and a pervasive flower-power aesthetic. Yet they remained cult favorites at best, lost in rock's tidal flow toward mellowness.

It took four lads from Queens to get things going. The **Ramones** first played their unique brand of thrashing guitar music at New York's CBGB's in August 1974. Legend has it the audience consisted of five people and one dog. The Ramones played short, fast songs that brought out a primitive urge to dance and laugh at yourself and the music. In the words of Joey Ramone, "We decided to start our own group because we were bored with everything we heard. In 1974 everything was tenth-generation Led Zeppelin, tenth-generation Elton John, or overproduced, or just junk. Everything was long jams, long guitar solos. We missed music like it used to be before it got 'progressive,' we missed hearing songs that were short and exciting and good!" When their attempts to imitate such heroes as the Beach Boys, Eddie Cochran, and Gene Vincent fell flat, they tempered their music to their own style of guitar play and came up with such classics as "I Want to Be Sedated," "Pinhead," and "Blitzkrieg Bop." The Ramones' first album cost $6,000 to produce. Ramonesmania proved contagious as more fans caught on to their deleriously anarchic sound. On July 4, 1976, the boys played a

Patti Smith, the poet laureate of New Jersey.

SEPTEMBER 1978

6: House begins hearings into John F. Kennedy assassination.

4: Best-seller status for *If Life is a Bowl of Cherries, What Am I Doing in the Pits.*

7: Keith Moon overdoses on prescription drug.

16: China hires Pierre Cardin as fashion consultant.

17: Camp David talks result in Egypt-Israel peace accord.

178

Brainy, twitchy, and brilliant: Remember when listening to The Talking Heads was still fun?

bicentennial concert in London before a crowd of ecstatic Brits that included future members of the Sex Pistols, the Clash, and the Damned.

The Ramones did not grow in a vacuum. New York in the early to mid-Seventies was at its nadir. Poised on the brink of bankruptcy, with cars and trucks literally falling through its roads and bridges, New York acquired the gritty low-rent atmosphere conducive to avante-garde experimentation. Living in pregentrified neighborhoods and playing in dives like CBGB's and Max's Kansas City, such groups as the Dictators, Richard Hell and the Voidoids, Blondie, New Jersey's own poet Patti Smith, and the Talking Heads flowered into what would be called punk rock.

If the Ramones personified the slob-punk look, **David Byrne** and **The Talking Heads** dressed like a bunch of squeaky clean college kids in Lacoste shirts and chinos. In 1975 this was not the way to get across as a rock-and-roll band. Like Bowie, Byrne perceived himself as a conceptual artist who inhabited personas of his own creation. Byrne and his band took on an immediate cult following after hitting New York with their snappy songs and his electroshock delivery, which tended to remind listeners of Norman Bates. Richard Goldstein of the *Village Voice* wrote that "Byrne sings in a high somber voice, somewhat like a seagull talking to its shrink." It didn't hurt that their first big song was "Psycho Killer." The Talking Heads were first and foremost a band of baby boomers—white kids from the suburbs.

Never mind the hype: The Sex Pistols during their very brief heyday.

None of their songs relied on the usual clichés of rock and roll. They didn't sing of blues and black suffering they had never experienced. They sang songs about buildings and jobs and had their "Psycho Killer" speak in an obscure French tense. Looking like a mutant fraternity band, the Talking Heads personified the fact that punk was basically white people's music. It was the first subgenre of rock and roll not to rely on black music. For more than twenty years white musicians had used a black art form as a kind of surrogate id—a means of expressing feelings that did not exist in white culture. Punk, warts and all, changed that forever.

Punk would probably have remained a New York cult phenomenon if not for the outrageous debut of Britain's **Sex Pistols**. Like most cultural phenomena, punk was not taken seriously until it was reimported from England. The product of impressario Malcolm McLaren's facile imagination, The Sex Pistols embodied the boredom and existential ennui of Britain's welfare

The Ramones: Did these derelicts re-invent rock and roll?

25: Two planes collide over San Diego killing 150.

29: John Paul I dies in sleep after thirty-four-day tenure.

#1 Singles:
A Taste of Honey—"Boogie Oogie Oogie"
Exile—"Kiss You All Over"

19: Linda Ronstadt's *Living In the USA* ships two million copies.

Selected Gold Record Albums:
Linda Ronstadt—*Living In the USA*
The Who—*Who Are You*
Village People—*Village People*
Atlanta Rhythm Section—*Champagne Jam*

179

state in deep decline. For all of the Ramones' tongue-in-cheek toughness, nothing in American punk quite matched the Pistols for pure nastiness. Then again, even in its deepest malaise, nothing in U.S. culture in the Seventies quite equaled the hopeless, "no-future" atmosphere of mid-Seventies Britain with skinheads, Paki-bashing, and bands of neo-Nazis as part of the rancid milieu. Formed to promote McLaren's punk boutique, the Sex Pistols exceeded his most demented dreams. Banned from television for their riotous behavior and obscene language, the Pistols released their classic "God Save the Queen (She Ain't a Human Being)" only to have it banned by the BBC. This didn't stop it from reaching number two on the charts. Condemned by church, state, and every form of media, the Pistols got press American bands could only dream of. Things didn't get better when they hired a untalented junkie bass player named Sid Vicious who made a name for himself with his own brand of pogo-dancing and for beating a critic with a chain.

For all their bad press, the Pistols' brand of short, brutal songs brought a primal energy back to rock and roll as hundreds of copy-cat bands came out of the woodwork. Bidding a violent good-bye to the boring rock scene of the mid-Seventies, a whole new generation turned on its elders and dismissed them as oppressive farts. For all of the antigovernment rhetoric of the Sex Pistols and later the Clash, it was always clear that the real enemy was the boring musical establishment. "All we're trying to do," said Johnny Rotten, "is destroy everything."

"If it ain't Stiff, it ain't worth a F*&K," was the quaint slogan of the Stiff record label, which introduced such seminal talents as Ian Drury, Wreckless Eric, Elvis Costello, Nick Lowe, and Larry Wallis.

Debbie Harry: How did this peroxide damsel take America by storm?

While the **Clash** emerged from the same anarchistic milieu, the group sought to graft a far more political message onto its raw, exciting music. With such songs as "I'm So Bored with the USA" on its first album, the Clash touched a rebellious chord with listeners bored with the mellow, but not quite ready to give into some of the crypto-nazi regalia of punk. It sold over 100,000 imported copies before being released in the United States. Their double album, *London Calling* (1979) presented a wide assortment of songs and causes with refreshingly hard edged energy and humor. By then many mainstream critics, including *Time* magazine, were ready to call it one of the albums of the decade.

Of all the British talents and demitalents to emerge in this charged atmosphere, **Elvis Costello** is the only one to remain a consistent music opera-

OCTOBER 1978

15: Congress passes Humphrey-Hawkins bill "guaranteeing full employment."

16: Vatican selects Polish Pope John Paul II.

20: Stock market drops sixty points in worst week to date.

10: Soviets announce production of "Orbita" jeans for youth.

13: Sid Vicious arrested for murder of Nancy Spungen.

tor for a firm owned by Elizabeth Arden when he sent some demo tapes to a new record company, Jake Rivera's Stiff Records. His first hit, "Less Than Zero," was a political blast at Britain's fascist National Front. Though Costello's acerbic songs and nasty wit fit in well with the punk atmosphere of the late Seventies, his heart and soul were in American country music. His bittersweet "Alison" remains one of the most touching songs of the period. By the decade's end, the extraordinarily prolific Costello had churned out a spate of albums, each containing more than twenty cuts. Though as musically eclectic as any pop music, bouncing from British show tunes to folk to country and western, Costello's songs centered on the bitter side of relationships and tales of love affairs turning into to power struggles. Resolutely unromantic and rebellious, Costello made a name for himself when he appeared on *Saturday Night Live* to replace the Sex Pistols, who had been denied entry by U.S. customs. Forbidden by NBC to play "Radio Radio" for its antinetwork lyrics, Costello was three seconds into "Watching the Detectives" when he turned around and played the verboten song. He also did little for his public relations in early '79 when he got drunk and brawled in an Ohio Holiday Inn after blasting American rockers as "a bunch of niggers."

By the time Costello played *SNL*, enough Americans had heard of punk to create a demand for a new sound. After years on the fringe, **Blondie** became the first punk or "new wave" band to crash through to the American market in a big way. Centered around the platinum good looks of Debbie Harry, Blondie dished up just the right blend of cheesecake, hard rock, and campy sleaze to win over Middle-American listeners turned off by the rougher edges of punk. Although Harry's sex appeal was clearly a put-on, it was the only sexuality displayed in the otherwise mutant world of punk. Set against the mindless push-push-in-the-bush mentality of the disco craze, such groups as the Ramones, the Pistols, and others had gone out of their way to appear slobbish and repulsive, to desexualize themselves. The Talking Heads, Germany's Kraftwerk, Ohio's Devo, and Gary Neuman, among others, took an asexual nerd aesthetic to its illogical limits. Like Bette Midler, Harry parodied the roll of rock-and-roll siren and, in doing so, reinvented it. It took a dash of disco in the icy, danceable "Heart of Glass" for punk to break into the top forty. By decade's end, Blondie had traveled from CBGB obscurity to appearances on *The Muppet Show*.

The Clash's mix of Marx and rock gave them one of the biggest cult followings of the late Seventies.

25-30: Dollar hits record lows against yen and mark.

27: Begin and Sadat win Nobel peace prize.

31: Anti-Shah strike cripples Iran's oil output.

#1 Singles:
Nick Gilder—"Hot Child in the City"

19: Actor Gig Young murders bride, kills self.

Selected Gold Record Albums:
Billy Joel—*52nd Street*   Alan Parsons Project—*I Robot*
Van Halen—*Van Halen*   Donna Summer—*Live and More*
Journey—*Infinity*

Farrah's cascading hair, the Fonz's leather jacket, Archie's American-flag lapel pin, Kojak's lollypop, and the WJM newsroom: These are the indelible images of Seventies' TV that we will always remember. But more than just these pop icons, many of the institutions of contemporary prime-time TV came of age in the 1970s: the first miniseries, the formalized TV movie (and the first disease-of-the-week movie), *Monday Night Football*, the rise of PBS as a snob/prestige vehicle, and the introduction of the socially "relevant" (that is, the real world) into programming.

In retrospect, the Seventies will also be remembered as the last decade of domination by the three networks, before the VCR became a household item, before the proliferation of cable service. The early part of the decade also saw a renaissance in classic comedies: *All in the Family*, *The Odd Couple*, *The Mary Tyler Moore Show*, and *M*A*S*H*. The limits of conventional comedy/variety show was pushed by the original *Saturday Night Live*.

TV in the Seventies reflected the dual nature of the decade: the first half trying to incorporate the concerns of the Sixties, the second half echoing the escapist, nostalgic bent of the pre-Reagan era.

RELEVANT TV

Does anyone out there remember relevancy? It was one of *the* buzzwords of the late Sixties and early Seventies, like "competitiveness" or "commitment" is today. Relevancy was an early indication of the self-obsessed Me Generation and was a particular favorite of protesting college students. They looked up from their books and wondered just what the hell the Edict

Back when TV really cared. Zalman King and Flora Plumb in The Young Lawyers.

NOVEMBER 1978

2: Soviet cosmonauts return from 139 days in space.

3: Vietnam and USSR sign twenty-five-year pact.

4: Sadat rejects $50 billion Arab offer to reject peace with Israel.

6: *The Womens' Room* tops best-seller list.

19: Nine hundred and eleven Jonestown cultists commit mass suicide at People' Temple, Guyana.

of Nantes has to do with ME?—a hip, aware resident of the counterculture. Precious little, they reasoned.

If college courses could be easily dismissed as irrelevant, then what could one say about television? At the dawn of the Seventies, TV programming was among the most irrelevant aspects of American life. Prime-time programming had little to say anymore to the first generation weaned on TV who now preferred the Grateful Dead to Red Skelton. And this was becoming apparent to the networks. They had made some tentative attempts at developing "hip" shows, such as *The Mod Squad* or *The Music Scene*, but the shows had a pathetic, patronizing appeal. On May 4, 1970, as four students were being killed by Ohio National Guardsmen at Kent State, TV viewers could have seen: Doris Day fouling up a computer company's electric bill on *The Doris Day Show*, the gang from *Mayberry R.F.D.* visiting Palm Springs, and Lucille Ball masquerading as a gum-chewing blond secretary on *Here's Lucy*. Not much to satisfy the youth of America there.

But come fall, the network programmers were smitten with the relevancy bug. They filtered countercultural rhetoric through Madison Avenue and created these slogans for the new season: "We're putting it all together this fall on CBS!" "It's happening on NBC!" and "Let's get together on ABC!" To go along with such avant-garde thinking, the networks came up with three new "relevant" series to prove to a doubting world that these newly groovy executives really meant business: *The Storefront Lawyers*, *The Young Lawyers* and *The Young Rebels*.

At least they tried.

In this era of the yuppie-grubbing barristers of *L.A. Law*, it's hard to believe that a show like *Storefront Lawyers* existed, let alone aired. The series centered around a young lawyer (played by Robert Foxworth, later to be seen as a prime-time heartthrob on *Falcon Crest*) who gave up his position with a prestigious Century City law firm to join two other young attorneys in a nonprofit practice in a poor section of Los Angeles. These lawyers offered their services to poor people who needed legal help but who could not afford an attorney. Idealism aside, the show failed to stir passions, and when it came back in February after a three-week hiatus, it was retitled *Men at Law* and the crew was back, working for the same old prestigious Century City law firm.

Gloria Bunker Stivic shakes her booty.

27: San Francisco Mayor Moscone and City Supervisor Harvey Milk slain by deranged ex-supervisor Dan White.

29: NBC cancels entire prime-time lineup.

#1 Singles:
Anne Murray—"You Needed Me"
Donna Summer—"MacArthur Park"

Selected Gold Record Albums:
Steve Martin—*A Wild and Crazy Guy*
Lynyrd Skynyrd—*Skynyrd's First and . . . Last*
Ted Nugent—*Weekend Warriors*

The Muppets and Robin Gibb—*Sesame Street Fever*
Neil Young—*Comes a Time*

Over on ABC, *The Young Lawyers* featured crusty Lee J. Cobb as the father figure to another group of idealistic young folks who offered free legal advice to indigent clients. Despite such relevant story lines like slumlords and drug busts, the show also vanished.

Those expecting ABC's *The Young Rebels* to depict the life-style of Abbie Hoffman or Mark Rudd were in for a shock. The network didn't have the stones to show those kinds of rebels. Instead, the series was set back in genuinely revolutionary times: 1777. Our heroes were members of the secret Yankee Doodle Society who harassed British troops (read: the establishment), preventing them on one occasion from melting down the Liberty Bell. See, these guys, all metaphors aside, were just a colonial-era version of the Mod Squad: one long hair, his girlfriend, and a freed slave (played by Louis Gossett, Jr., a role he usually doesn't mention). The concept failed; one wonders whether having *The Young Rebels* air in the time slot prior to *The F.B.I.*—ever the bastion of conservative TV—may have been a contributing factor.

So much for the TV revolution in the fall of 1970. If the real world was going to enter our homes, it wouldn't come until January 12, 1971. And it would come from an unlikely source: not from a long-haired, socially conscious L.A. lawyer, but via a beer-swilling, middle-age, loading-dock worker living in the borough of Queens, New York.

ARCHIE

In the early Seventies, the lower-middle class was a group that had been on the media's mind for a couple of years. Country-club Republicans, such as Richard Nixon and Spiro Agnew, had avidly courted them by extolling their virtues as the "Silent Majority"—the tax-paying, God-fearing, hard-working people to whom the excesses and permissiveness of the Sixties were unfathomable. The hard-hat riots against antiwar protestors in the spring of 1970 and the feature film *Joe* further mythologized the group. In the minds of the liberal, upper-class film and TV production communities, the members of the silent majority were curiosities. But from this unlikely source would come a television revolution.

Only a handful of times in the history of television, which is basically a

DECEMBER 1978

1: Shell Oil begins rationing gas to local dealers.

8: Investigators find tape recording of Jonestown mass suicide.

15: U.S. formally recognizes China.

14: *The Deer Hunter* released.

184

reactive medium, can that overabused word *revolutionary* be applied to a series. Rowan and Martin's *Laugh-In* and *Saturday Night Live* revolutionized comedy-variety shows. *Hill Street Blues* and *Miami Vice* revolutionized TV cop shows. And starting on January 12, 1971, *All in the Family* revolutionized that most formulaic staple of TV: the sitcom. It's incredible that the damn thing even got on the air (see timeline).

All in the Family, which was based on a popular British sitcom called *Till Death Do Us Part*, looked like a typical sitcom. It just sounded a whole lot different from what American audiences were used to. Archie Bunker was TV's first authentic blue-collar hero since Ralph Kramden of *The Honeymooners* in the 1950s. Both Ralph and Archie were kings of their castles—or claimed to be—who berated their wives, but usually got their comeuppances at the episode's end. That's where the resemblance ended. Archie spoke what Ralph may or may not have only thought. Out of Archie's BIIG mouth came a barrage of ethnic slurs and half-baked right-wing rhetoric the likes of which had never been heard before on American prime-time TV.

Like *The Honeymooners*, *All in the Family* boasted a fine ensemble cast who became real to us for nearly the entire Seventies: Carroll O'Connor as Archie; Jean Stapleton as his dim-witted but well-meaning wife, Edith; Sally Struthers as their progressive-minded daughter Gloria; and Rob Reiner as her husband, the long-haired liberal sociology student, Mike Stivic.

CBS sensed it was going to air something completely different. The night of the show's premiere, the network hired extra operators for the expected barrage of negative phone calls. As *Hee Haw* ended, the screen was filled by an explanatory word from CBS: "The program you are about to see is *All in the Family*. It seeks to throw a humorous spotlight on our frailties, prejudices and concerns. By making them a source of laughter, we hope to show in a mature fashion, just how absurd they are." An early scene on that debut episode captured the series' new agenda: Mike was seen zipping up his fly as he and Gloria walked downstairs one Sunday morning. It was clear where they had been, and Archie wasn't pleased. "When your mother-in-law and me was going together, it was two years," he chided Mike. "We never. I never. I mean there was nothing. I mean absolutely nothing. Not til the wedding night." Pause and wait for Edith's reply: "And even then . . ."

All in the Family *Timeline*

1966: Movie producer Norman Lear reads about **Till Death Do Us Part,** *a British TV hit that looks at life through the eyes of a bigoted, blue-collar dockworker. He thinks: "If I could only get this kind of thing on American television."*

1968: Lear buys the U.S. rights to **Till Death Do Us Part,** *and in between producing the film* **The Night They Raided Minsky's,** *he and Bud Yorkin develop a pilot based on it called* **Those Were the Days.**

1969: Lear shoots two pilots of **Those Were the Days** *for ABC. The network rejects them.*

1970: CBS expresses interest. Network president Robert Wood is convinced that such a show is what is needed to attract a more sophisticated audience. After getting a halfhearted approval from CBS chairman William Paley, Wood orders the series as a midseason replacement.

1971: The first episode of **Those Were the Days,** *now known as* **All**

in the Family, *debuts. After bat-*
tling network censors, Lear re-
moves one "goddammit" and is
allowed to leave everything else
intact.

1972: **All in the Family** *becomes*
the number-one show. The char-
acter of Edith's big-mouthed
cousin Maude is introduced—she
will get her own popular series
later that year. In the highest

Only 1,000 calls lit up the CBS switchboard; nearly 60 percent ap-proved. Some professional critics weren't as impressed. *Time's* reviewer claimed that "the characters are only gross caricatures who may be different from—but barely more than—inhabitants of any other half-hour American sitcom. The show proves that bigotry can be just as boring and predictable as the upthink fluff of The Brady Bunch. The critic from *The New York Times* called it "tasteless," but a fair number of critics liked the new show and began trumpeting its appeal in print.

By the seventh episode, the show had doubled its viewers. It hit number-one during summer reruns, after winning three Emmys in May. And during the 1971–72 season, as it firmly established itself as the number-one show, *All in the Family* became the subject of frequent debates. It was lambasted by some who said a lovable bigot was a bigot, nonetheless, and that if it really had guts, Archie would say "nigger" instead of the more anachronis-tic "coon." Others said the show didn't go far enough.

All in the Family would go on to become a staple of Pop Americana. Ar-chie's favorite expressions—"Dingbat," "Meathead," and "Stifle yourself"—joined our videocabulary. Archie himself would become a folk hero among some Silent Majoritarians (which confused and amused the lib-eral Democrat O'Connor who played him). Even though a decade has passed since Archie left the air, any narrow-minded person is still conve-niently dismissed as an "Archie Bunker."

Within five years of the show's debut, racial insults and sexual innuendos would be the norm on network TV. But few other shows could deliver the graceful writing or the acting talent of the original. Its legacy is still felt today. Anytime a new barrier is shattered in prime time—if *St. Elsewhere's* Dr. Westphall bares his ass or the couple on *thirtysomething* discuss intercourse—one can draw a direct line from those incidents to *All in the Family's* ground-breaking treatment of rape, menstruation, impotence, and cancer, even all the way back to the first episode, where when Archie came down the stairs for the first time, the sound of a toilet flushing was heard in the background.

Watching *All in the Family* reruns today is like taking a refresher course in the history of the Seventies. Nixon, Watergate, inflation, Vietnam, the energy crisis, the sexual revolution, the women's movement all would be

#1 Singles:
Barbra Streisand & Neil Diamond—"You Don't Bring
Me Flowers"
Chic—"Le Freak"

Selected Gold Record Albums:
Cars—*The Cars*
Chic—*C'Est Chic*
Funkadelic—*One Nation Under a Groove*
Village People—*Macho Man*
Johnny Paycheck—*Take This Job and Shove It*

used as vehicles around which the Bunkers would argue. As the decade wore on, the areas of disagreement grew less black and white. Mike and Gloria became parents and left the show. Edith died and a mellower Archie gamely plodded through as a tavern proprietor on *Archie Bunker's Place*.

And it will be the 1970s where the Bunkers will permanently remain. Today, right-wing bigots are no longer funny, not even the lovable ones.

MARY TYLER MOORE

In the Seventies, Saturday night was no longer the loneliest night of the week. For seven years, even if Watergate, gas lines, or WIN buttons got you down, there were always friends you could turn to: a thirtyish career gal who could "turn the world on with her smile," a chubby, man-hungry Jewish girl from the Bronx; a vain, bubbleheaded anchor; a gruff but good-hearted producer; and a neurotic newswriter.

Thanks, guys, for making the decade that much easier to get through.

And for seven years, we laughed and we fretted and we worried over Mary's quest for romantic and professional fulfillment; Rhoda's weight problems and her problems with her mother; Ted's ego; Lou's marriage breakup; and Murray's frustration at never being a "successful" writer.

The Mary Tyler Moore Show was the product of several creative talents: Mary Tyler Moore (who had already won our hearts as perky Laura Petrie on *The Dick Van Dyke Show*), her then-husband TV executive Grant Tinker (who agreed to do a series with his wife only if the couple could create, control, and cast the series), and the chief writers, Allan Burns (co-creator of *My Mother, the Car*—well; no one's perfect) and James L. Brooks (creator of *Room 222*).

Together they created a masterly sitcom built around Mary Richards, a single career woman who put a busted romance behind her and went to work as an assistant news producer at a Minneapolis TV station. To support Mary, the show's braintrust assembled one of the finest ensembles in TV history: Valerie Harper, Ed Asner, Ted Knight, Gavin MacLeod, Betty White, Georgia Engel, and Cloris Leachman.

CBS rejected the creators' original concept of making Mary a divorcée. In 1970 that was still too risqué for network programmers, even though the

rated episode in the series' history, Sammy Davis, Jr., makes a guest appearance as himself— and kisses Archie.

1973: The characters of feminist neighbor Irene Lorenzo and George Jefferson, the "black Archie Bunker," are introduced.

1974-75: Off-camera, Carroll O'Connor temporarily walks off the show in a salary dispute. On-camera, Mike and Gloria Stivic move into the Jeffersons' vacated house. The black couple has decamped for their own sitcom.

1976: Archie's grandson, Joey Stivic, is born.

1977: The Stivics leave the series, and Archie buys Kelsey's Bar.

1978-79: In the show's final season, Danielle Brisebois joins the cast as Edith's niece Stephanie, further softening the series. We learn that Mike and Gloria have separated.

1980-83: Edith dies; the retooled Archie Bunker's Place airs.

JANUARY 1979

7: Invading Vietnamese overthrow Cambodia's Pol Pot.

16: Shah flees Iran as Ayatollah Khomeini vows return from exile.

19: John Mitchell is last Watergate figure to leave prison.

4: Charles Mingus dies at 56.

13: Soul vocalist Donny Hathaway falls fifteen stories to his death.

national divorce rate was nearing 50 percent. Instead, they reached a compromise: Mary would be a single woman with an active (albeit implied) sex life. She didn't run to her daddy as Marlo Thomas did in *That Girl*. She was truly on her own, providing the first video role model for a generation of women who no longer aspired to be June Cleaver.

MTM was the first sitcom whose characters seemed real. They laughed, they cried, they hollered, and they lived in a world that seemed not appreciably different from our own. As we used to say, we could relate to these people. We rooted for Mary from the very first day (September 19, 1970) that she hesitatingly walked into the WJM newsroom and was told by her boss-to-be Lou Grant: "You have spunk. . . and I hate spunk!" We just knew she'd make it after all.

The show made it okay again to stay home on Saturday nights—especially among those who had given up watching TV. In 1971 a *New York Times Magazine* writer, reporting on the popularity of *MTM* among Upper East Siders, noted: "Mary is so In, actually, that it has become fashionable to drift into the den at a party or even to go home at 9 on Saturday because you simply must not miss this program."

And for seven years, most loyal viewers did not miss the program. When *MTM* aired its final episode on March 19, 1977, it went out while it was still on top with one of the show's most memorable episodes. WJM had been sold and the entire staff (except for Ted, of course!) was fired. As they said their final, teary farewells, the staff locked arms, hugged, and sang, "It's a Long Way from Tipperary."

And Mary says her final good-bye: "I thought about something last night: What is a family. And I think I know. A family is people who make you feel less alone and really loved. Thank you for being my family."

One by one, the newsroom emptied until the last person remaining was Mary. She turned off the lights, closed the door, and as she walked out for the last time, she flashed her smile that could turn on the world.

Most of the gang found gainful employment. Murray went on to *The Love Boat*, Rhoda moved back to New York and her own series, Lou returned to journalism and his own series. But Mary, poor Mary, unsuccessfully tried twice to come back in new series. But there will be, there can be, only one Mare.

Mary Tyler Moore and Phyllis (Cloris Leachman) share a moment.

24: John Connally enters race for Republican nomination.

26: Nelson Rockefeller, age 70, dies of heart attack in company of young female aide.

#1 Singles:
Bee Gees—"Too Much Heaven"

23: Rome court clears Sophia Loren of smuggling charges.

Selected Gold Record Albums:
Blues Brothers—*Briefcase Full of Blues*
Bee Gees—*Spirits Have Flown*
Eddie Money—*Life for the Taking*
Toto—*Toto*

CLASSIC SITCOMS

Here are five other classics from the Seventies, the Golden Age of Sitcoms:

● **M*A*S*H** (1972–83): This was no gung-ho war show like *Combat*, or a wartime sitcom like *McHale's Navy*. One of the few successful shows based on a movie, it centered on a band of Korean War medicos who, inside the tent, cut up the war's maimed and wounded, and outside, cut up with such extracurricular high jinks as skirt chasing. The series played Ping-Pong with our emotions, capturing the pain, camaraderie, and mindlessness of war, but leavening it with dark humor.

M*A*S*H was right for the times. By the early Seventies, Americans were not so keen on war. After all, for more than a decade the Vietnam war has been beamed into our living rooms nightly. And, of course, even though *M*A*S*H* was set in Korea, it was Vietnam that the series was all about. Thus, a multidecade phenomenon: a show about a Fifties war with a Sixties sensibility that aired in the Seventies and Eighties.

The men and women of the 4077th Mobile Army Surgical Hospital were an indelible, unforgettable bunch: Hot Lips Houlihan (Loretta Swit), Frank Burns (Larry Linville), Henry Blake (McLean Stevenson), Trapper John (Wayne Rogers), Radar O'Reilly (Gary Burghoff), and the first cast addition, Maxwell Klinger (Jamie Farr). The series made a star out of Alan Alda, who played the smart-ass but sensitive surgeon "Hawkeye" Pierce. Alda would go on to write and direct several *M*A*S*H* episodes as well as achieve prominence as an outspoken male feminist and prototype for the "sensitive man" of the Seventies.

Thus it was no surprise that the final episode of *M*A*S*H*, aired in 1983, became the most-watched single episode in the history of TV.

● **The Odd Couple** (1970–75): this is the other successful Seventies show based on a hit movie. Each week the voice-over announcer would ask, "Can two divorced men share an apartment without driving each other crazy?" And we knew the answer from the outset: They couldn't. Neato photographer Felix Unger (Tony Randall) and slobby sportswriter Oscar Madison (Jack Klugman) were usually at each other's throats, with often hilarious results. But something must have worked. They lived together for five years.

Felix, Oscar, and the mouth, Howard Cosell.

FEBRUARY 1979

1: Carter grants clemency for Patty Hearst.

2: Heroin overdose for Sid Vicious.

1: Khomeini returns to Tehran, civilian government resigns.

1-5: Chinese Leader Deng visits Washington.

17: Three hundred thousand Chinese troops invade Vietnam.

22: CIA rocked by mass resignations.

189

Klinger, that wacky, gender-bending G.I.

The Bob Newhart Show (1972–78): What a concept! The button-down mind as a shrink! And Bob Newhart as Chicago psychologist Dr. Bob Hartley was the ultimate product of a world gone mad. Like the folks on *MTM*, the people in Bob's world kinda looked like us—but there was always something slightly out of whack. Real-life group therapy can be a laugh riot sometimes—but never as funny as the sessions in Dr. Hartley's office.

Taxi (1978–83): One of TV's finest ensemble comedies took place in the drafty, depressing confines of manhattan's aptly named Sunshine Cab Company. The sitcom boosted the careers of Judd Hirsch, Tony Danza, Andy Kaufman, Danny DeVito, and Christopher Lloyd. Lloyd's "Reverand Jim" Ignatowski, a Sixties burnout, was truly one of TV's more bizarre characters.

Barney Miller (1975–82): This show portrayed the funniest bunch of New York City cops since *Car 54, Where Are You?* but they were more finely drawn. Barney (Hal Linden) presided over a Greenwich Village station house whose denizens included not only his idiosyncratic cops, but a non-stop parade of geeks, freaks, and wackos.

ETHNIC COMEDY

At the dawn of the TV age, we did see ethnic sitcoms like *Amos and Andy*, *Mama*, *The Goldbergs*, and *Life with Luigi*, but they were just translations of "warmhearted" radio programs. But by the mid-Fifties, the long night of white bread began as middle-class WASPy families and their middle-class, WASPy problems, commandeered the sitcom front. In the late Sixties, *Julia*, which centered on a black nurse (played by Diahann Carroll) was hailed as a breakthrough; but in reality Julia lived better than most people—black or white.

By the early Seventies, the swelling of ethnic pride coupled with the ground-breaking of *All in the Family* helped make TV comfortable with a new wave of ethnic sitcoms. Of course, TV is far from being a perfect world: Two of the black protagonists were among the most unlikable characters on TV, and several of the series ran into flak from the very same groups the shows were portraying:

Sanford and Son (1972–77): Redd Foxx starred as the hypochon-

Demond Wilson and Redd Foxx as Fred Sanford and his son Lamont.

driac and irascible Fred Sanford, a Watts junk dealer who was forever pick-
ing on his son and partner Lamont (Demond Wilson)—and just about
anybody else who spoke to him. The sitcom was the second from *All in the
Family*'s Norman Lear. He had bought the rights to the British series *Steptoe
and Son*, and, in fact, had shot a failed pilot starring two white actors before
recasting it as a black-oriented show starring Foxx, the veteran chitlin' circuit comedian known best for his X-rated "party" records. As a tribute to
the star, who was as grouchy as the character he portrayed, Lear renamed
the show *Sanford* since that was Foxx's real name.

Bridget Loves Bernie (1972–73): This was going to be a "hip" update of *Abie's Irish Rose* in which a poor Jewish boy (David Birney) married a
wealthy Catholic girl (Meredith Baxter). CBS had such high hopes for this
show that it gave *B&B* one of the best slots in all TV, airing on Saturday
night between *All in the Family* and *The Mary Tyler Moore Show*. But, oy!
was there a fuss kicked up; CBS never reckoned that Jewish groups wouldn't
be so keen about a sitcom that endorsed and made light of intermarriage.
The series lasted only one season, but it yielded one dividend: Birney and
Baxter fell in love for real and eventually got married (they split in 1988).

Good Times (1974–79): Norman Lear struck again with this spinoff,
which took *Maude*'s maid Florida (Esther Rolle) and returned her to a Chicago housing project with her husband and three children. During the first
season everyone loved the show because it focused on a warm, stable, and
complete working-class black family. But problems developed in 1976
when the father (John Amos) left. His character was written out of the
script, leaving the stereotypical matriarchal black family. *Good Times*
spawned one breakout star: South Bronx–born stand-up comic Jimmie
Walker, who played J.J., the oldest son, an amusing character with plenty
of get-rich-quick schemes. He usually delivered his signature phrase—
"Dy-No-Mite!"—with bulging eyes and a shit-eating grin, which made J.J.
seem to many critics like little more than a slightly hipper version of King-
fish on *Amos and Andy*.

Chico and The Man (1974–78): Twenty-year-old stand-up comic
Freddie Prinze was "Chico," an enterprising young Chicano, who helped
revive the faltering garage run by the crotchety "Man," played by veteran
actor Jack Albertson. Together they generated undeniable chemistry, and

*Freddy Prinze (a Puerto
Rican-Hungarian) gives Sammy
Davis, Jr., (a Jewish Afro-American)
some pointers on ethnic pride.*

26: Computer bank robber
gets eight years in prison.

26: Sadat and Begin sign peace treaty,
ending thirty years of war.

28: British government
loses vote of confidence.

16: *The China Syndrome* released.

this show became an instant hit. Despite the breakthrough of a sitcom focusing on life in El Barrio, some Mexican-American groups objected to Prinze, because he was of Puerto Rican–Hungarian extraction and because they believed his accent was demeaning. Nonetheless, Prinze became an overnight success. But the pressure of instant stardom, combined with a failed marriage and other legal problems, took its toll.

On January 28, 1977, Prinze took nine Quaaludes, picked up a gun, and blew his brains out. The show limped on for the rest of the season and for one season longer with a revised cast. How lame was its limp? Charo came aboard as the voluptuous character known as "Aunt Charo."

The Jeffersons (1975–84): Thanks to his profitable chain of dry-cleaning stores, Archie Bunker's neighbor George Jefferson (Sherman Hemsley) was able to shed the Bunkers forever, moving his family from Queens to a "deluxe apartment in the sky" on Manhattan's Upper East Side. In this second *All in the Family* spinoff, money didn't change George—he remained a swaggering, vain rooster. But George always got his comeuppance, usually from his long-suffering wife, Louise (Isabel Sanford) or from the caustic black maid, Florence (Marla Gibbs). It was Florence who uttered one of the great lines in sitcom history. Checking out her employers' luxurious digs, she rolled her eyes in mock-disbelief and said: "How come we overcame and nobody told me anything about it?"

MINISERIES

Miniseries have become such a normal part of our TV viewing that it's easy to forget that they've been around only since the late Seventies. The British had pioneered the so-called miniseries form, so it's not surprising that the first American ventures into this new genre early in the decade would be BBC imports. It was not until *Rich Man, Poor Man* aired over several weeks in 1976 that American programmers began seeing the potential in long-form television.

But the genre really didn't take off until ABC aired *Roots* from January 23 to 30, 1977. *Roots* went beyond being a new form of TV programming, however; it became a national event. People canceled meetings, movie attendance declined, and even members of Congress asked for early

Roots: *The miniseries that changed television.*

adjournment so they could rush home and watch that evening's installment. In some bars, patrons actually switched off basketball games and put on *Roots* instead.

Such a reaction certainly was not anticipated when Hollywood producer David Wolper had first approached ABC in 1974 about making a TV project out of author Alex Haley's work-in-progress on his search for his family's roots. Black-themed projects were risky, but ABC bit, and by 1975, the network had committed $6 million to the project, which was expanded to twelve hours.

ABC had originally planned to air *Roots* once a week for eight consecutive weeks, but after ABC Executive Fred Silverman screened an advance copy of all twelve hours at home, he proposed what would prove to be bold step. ABC would air the saga over eight consecutive nights in late January 1977 (the idea of airing it during the February sweeps was dismissed, an indication that the network still had reservations about the project).

The drama spanned several generations, beginning with the kidnapping of the rebellious young African Kunta Kinte (played by newcomer LeVar Burton), Haley's great-great-great-great-grandfather who was brought to America in chains as a slave. It proceeded through generations of slavery and finally into freedom after the Civil War. The cast included lots of familiar TV faces, including Ed Asner, O. J. Simpson, Ben Vereen, Chuck Connors, Lorne Greene, and Cicely Tyson.

Admittedly, much of *Roots* was highly melodramatic, not much above the level of the film *Mandingo*. There were shots of bare-breasted women (*Roots* was the first prime-time network show to show frontal nudity, albeit briefly), and each episode contained scenes of flogging and rape.

"*Roots* was one of our most violent shows," admitted ABC executive Brandon Stoddard. "But the violence was done with taste, not to hype or lift up a boring script."

Whatever its dramatic merits were, *Roots* exceeded ABC's

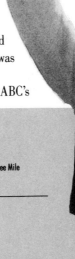

1: Teamsters set nationwide truck strike.

2: Forty percent of population in Three Mile Island area evacuated.

1: Patty Hearst marries ex-body guard Bernard Shaw.

wildest expectations. ABC won in the ratings every night *Roots* aired, and its ratings for the week were the highest any network had ever scored. It was estimated that 130 million people saw some part of the miniseries. (A killer cold spell in the East and Midwest might have helped, said some cynics.) It became a symbol of pride for black Americans.

The miniseries sparked a resurgence of interest in genealogy, as members of other ethnic groups began wondering about their own ancestors. Some pundits claimed *Roots* would usher in a new era of racial harmony, a feeling that was intensified by its airing during the first weeks of the new, feel-good Carter administration. In fact, a poll taken by ABC News immediately after *Roots* showed that whites had become more sympathetic to the plight of blacks because they now understood the roots of our racial problems.

And while that New Utopia hasn't happened, the effect of *Roots* on television was incalculable: The miniseries became a regular small-screen event. But none since have matched the impact of *Roots*.

MARY HARTMAN, MARY HARTMAN

Mary Richards was not the only midwestern Mary we cared about on TV in the Seventies. Several hundred miles south of Minneapolis in the seemingly normal town of Fernwood, Ohio, lived another Mary. She wore her hair in pigtails, covered her skinny body in a little girl's pinafore, and believed that life was just like it was portrayed on television. The idea of a career would have spooked this Mary. Her domain was her home, especially her kitchen, and her biggest concern was the waxy yellow buildup on the floor. Oh, she worried about other things, such as a mass murderer who would kill not just human beings but chickens as well. Yes, this Mary, last name of Hartman,

3: Jane Byrne becomes Chicago's first female mayor.

4: Pakistan's ex-President Bhutto hanged.

6: U.S. withdraws aid to Pakistan.

6: Rod Stewart marries Alana Hamilton.

was, to put it, quite frankly, nuts. And in 1976 we went nuts over her.

The New York Times called *Mary Hartman, Mary Hartman* a "cultural signpost," and *People* magazine called it "a kitchen sink theater of the absurd." And both estimable publications were right. TV had not seen anything like *MH2* before—with its continuing story line and strange plot twists, it resembled a soap opera. But it wasn't a soap opera—it was a parody of soap operas. (But can you parody a parody?) It was funny, outrageously so, but it had no laugh track. And its subject matter went beyond anything seen on the soaps.

It should come as no surprise that the show was the brainchild of Norman Lear, who had already revolutionized the sitcom. But despite Lear's impressive TV track record, his soap-opera spoof had been rejected by all three networks because they thought it was too controversial. Instead, Lear sold the project to fifty-four independent stations on a five-night-a-week syndicated basis (most stations aired it against the network affiliates' 11 P.M. news; others, thinking it was just a kind of off-the-wall soap opera, placed it in the late-afternoon soap-opera ghetto). Lear's gamble was successful: *Mary Hartman, Mary Hartman* became the most talked-about TV sensation of 1976—at least until *Charlie's Angels* debuted later that year.

Louise Lasser, Woody Allen's ex-wife and a brilliant comedian in her own right, played Mary with a blend of innocence, spaciness, and bewilderment. "There's a tremendous anxiety running through her, an angst" Lasser once explained. "The difference is I have a real awareness of mine and she's unconscious of hers." Nonetheless, one often wondered where Lasser ended and Mary began.

Mary's family wasn't too Cleaver-esque, either: Her grandfather (Victor Kilian) was the infamous Fernwood Flasher. Husband Tom (Greg Mullavey), an assembly-line worker, was impotent (which led Mary to have an affair with Fernwood cop Dennis Foley (Bruce Solomon); when Mary wanted to make love to Tom, he'd usually bury his head in a gun magazine. Younger sister Cathy (Debralee Scott) was a nymphomaniac who once had an affair with a deaf-mute. Daughter Heather (Claudia Lamb) was kidnapped by a mass murderer. Like any other TV series, *MH2* had the requisite nutty neighbors: the sex-crazed Haggers—Loretta (Mary Kay Place), an aspiring country/western singer and her bald, bespectacled husband Charlie

(Graham Jarvis), whose nerdy looks belied his studlike abilities in bed (according to Loretta).

The line between TV and real life was crossed frequently. At the end of the show's first season, Mary was chosen the year's "average American housewife" and was invited to appear on *The David Susskind Show*. But being Mary, she couldn't cope with actually appearing on TV and so she suffered a nervous breakdown on the air. And that's how we left Mary until the fall. (When she returned for the second season, she was in a mental hospital, but it was okay because the patients had been selected as a typical "Nielsen" family by the ratings service.

At the height of the show's popularity, Lasser was busted for cocaine possession while shopping for an antique doll house. Actually, she was arrested for overdue parking tickets, and the cops found the coke when they searched her purse. She was sentenced to spend six months in a rehab program and satisfied that requirement by continuing to see her shrink.

The pressure of doing the five-night-a-week show finally got to the high-strung Lasser, and she left in 1977. It continued without her with a new name, *Forever Fernwood*, and a new cast member, Tab Hunter as Mary's father (it was explained that George Shumway had fallen into a vat of chemicals and, after plastic surgery, had emerged looking like Tab). The show never recaptured the following it had during its first season. Nevertheless, the popularity of *MH2* had an emboldening effect on the same networks who had originally rejected it. In the fall of 1977, ABC began airing its soap-opera parody *Soap*, a show that was condemned by religious groups even before they had seen the first episode. Even *MH2* never had that privilege.

Fernwood was also used as the setting for *Fernwood 2-Night*, a bizarre talk-show parody that was the summer replacement for *MH2* in 1977. Its producer, ironically, was Alan Thicke (whose own ballyhooed talk show would flop a few years later), who said the show "would offend the sensitivities of a number of Americans . . . we're offending everybody, regardless of race, creed, color or income level." The show came back in 1978 as *America 2-Night*, with the crew relocating to Alta Coma, California, the unfurnished furniture capital of the world.

SONNY AND CHER

1: George Bush announces bid for Republican nomination.

2: China announces 20,000 killed in four-week Vietnamese war.

3: Margaret Thatcher becomes Britain's first woman Prime Minister.

6: Sixty-five thousand antinuclear power activists descend on Washington, D.C.

Sonny and Cher were the love couple of the Seventies, whose marital ups and downs were chronicled as faithfully as Liz and Dick's a decade earlier. But as the years went by, their marital squabbles became less interesting. What's more compelling to historians is how a shaggy-haired duo, who during the Sixties routinely got themselves thrown out of restaurants, transformed themselves into a glamorous, glitzy Vegas act that became one of the most popular television attractions of the Seventies.

It was Sonny Bono—a canny, crafty character whose shrewd personality was the polar opposite of the dumbo he portrayed on stage—who engineered the transformation. By 1970, Sonny realized the couple's career had hit a dead end. If they wanted to keep living in their twenty-two-room Holmby Hills, California, mansion, they had better do something. Cher wanted to pursue a "funkier, acid-rock" image, but her husband disagreed.

"Cher, go out and buy a dress—a long dress and spend a lot of money," Sonny ordered.

"Go out and get a what?" his incredulous wife responded.

"It's time for you to start looking like a woman, and it's time for us to start appealing to adults," Sonny continued. "That's where the money is."

So the Bonos created a nightclub act and took it on the road. At first they played cow towns, before working their way up to bigger gigs. While appearing at New York's Americana Hotel, the Bonos struck pay dirt. In the audience was Fred Silverman, then a CBS programming honcho, and the "man with the golden gut" definitely had his juices stimulated when he saw the new-and-improved Sonny and Cher. "They could be another George and Gracie," mused Silverman, and he signed the duo to guest-host *The Merv Griffin Show* for a week, which led to a successful summer-replacement show. After the summer, the CBS research report on the duo related that most viewers thought Sonny was "too short" and that Cher "had pimples and couldn't sing." Silverman was undaunted. "Read it and tear it up," he told the show's producers, and then scheduled a permanent prime-time comedy-variety hour for the Bonos. *The Sonny and Cher Comedy Hour* debuted on December 27, 1971, and would eventually become a regular top-ten show.

The Bonos' variety show was the last gasp of that once-dominant TV staple, full of the usual mix of recurring characters, topical skits, musical

Sonny and Cher: A show whose wardrobes have never been equaled.

8: California invokes odd-even gas rationing.

19: Eric Clapton marries Pattie Boyd Harrison (George's ex).

21: San Francisco rocked by gay riots after Milk and Moscone's killer receives light sentence.

24: *Alien* released.

25: Chicago DC-10 crash kills 272.

#1 Singles:
Peaches and Herb—"Reunited"

Selected Gold Record Albums:
Donna Summer—*Bad Girls*
Cheap Trick—*Live at Budokan*
Sister Sledge—*We Are Family*
Cher—*Take Me Home*

Diahann Carroll makes waves during a musical number.

numbers, and guest stars (the latter could be truly amusing: On the debut show of the 1972–73 season, the guests included California Governor Ronald Reagan and the Jackson Five). But on every show, you could always count on Sonny playing the dumb or overly boastful hubby, with Cher zapping him with yet another deadpan putdown. Taking advantage of the freedoms pioneered by *All in the Family*, Cher would routinely zing her husband's Italian ancestry with some choice remark, such as "If you've seen one naked goombah, you've seen them all."

But who really watched for the jokes? Most people watched for a glimpse at Cher's outrageous outfits: slinky, slit, one-shouldered, low-cut Bob Mackie gowns that tested the patience of CBS's censors. Cher's navel became a prime-time attraction, which represented some kind of progress in TV freedom, considering that only a half-decade earlier, NBC had forbade Barbara Eden from baring her navel on *I Dream of Jeannie*.

By '74, however, life was becoming rockier in the Bono manse. Cher's comical jabs seemed more pointed than ever, and you began suspecting that maybe she actually meant some of those nasty remarks. Not unlike the Louds on the PBS documentary *An American Family*, the Bonos's marriage disintegrated in front of the eyes of prime-time viewers. In February 1974 Sonny filed for a legal separation, with Cher filing for divorce two weeks later. The last *Sonny and Cher Comedy Hour* aired in May, even though CBS execs tried mightily to persuade the Bonos to stay together—at least professionally.

Instead, both partners tried solo TV shows, *The Sonny Comedy Revue* and *Cher*, both of which flopped. A few years later they recanted and decided to reunite for the small screen, although by then Cher had married rock star Gregg Allman and given birth to their child, Elijah Blue. The new venture, *The Sonny and Cher Show*, didn't work out and it was gone by the summer of '77.

In the subsequent decade, of course, both Bonos have hardly disappeared from the public eye. Sonny went on to become a restaurateur and mayor of Palm Springs, California. And Cher, after struggling to convince Hollywood that she could be a legitimate actress, won an Oscar for *Moonstruck* in 1988. In 1987 the Bonos held a much-publicized reunion on *Late Night with David Letterman*. By then most of the animosity had cooled.

JUNE 1979

2: Pope John Paul II visits Poland.

3: *The Complete Scarsdale Medical Diet* tops best-seller list.

4: High winds collapse roof of Kansas City Arena.

11: John Wayne dies.

7: Carter approves $30 billion MX-missle program.

18: Carter and Brezhnev sign Salt II treaty; Carter gives Brezhnev symbolic kiss.

Other variety shows:

Tony Orlando and Dawn (1974–76): Fred Silverman also saw the potential in the rainbow-coalition singing group who immortalized "Tie a Yellow Ribbon 'Round the Old Oak Tree." After seeing them perform on the Grammy Awards show, he gave them a summer show (in Sonny and Cher's old time slot), which proved so popular it came back as a regular series.

Donny and Marie (1976–79): The teen siblings hosted this wholesome series on which most of the other Osmonds popped up. Memorable moment: The brothers ganged up on Donny and dumped him into a nine-foot whipped-cream pie.

Flip Wilson Show (1970–74): The black comic cross-dressed for success with his Geraldine Jones character (and many other memorable comic creations) on one of the most popular shows of the early Seventies.

The Captain and Tennille (1976–77): Giving a show to the singers of "Muskrat Love" proved that anyone could have a musical variety show.

THE BRADY BUNCH

The Brady Bunch was a show that was relentlessly middle class during a time when the term became a dirty word. Mom stayed home; Dad was always there. The six kids making up this merged family may not have always gotten along, but by episode's end, all the problems were solved by Mike (Robert Reed) with Jim Anderson/Ward Cleaver-like wisdom.

The series, which aired from 1969 to 1974, typified derivative TV at its best. Created by Sherwood Schwartz (*Gilligan's Island*), the sitcom combined two stock figures of late-Sixties TV, the widow (*Julia*, *The Doris Day Show*) and the widower (*My Three Sons*, *Courtship of Eddie's Father*) into a frothy concoction that resembled *Father Knows Best*.

The only problem was that the show was about fifteen years behind the times. During the early Seventies, the era of relevance, mind you, *The Brady Bunch* was by far the least relevant show on TV. While the real world was falling apart and kids everywhere were screaming at their parents, the Bradys were beset by such problems as what to do with ninety-four books of trading stamps. The Bradys and their kooky housekeeper were walking happy-face buttons.

Alice (Ann B. Davis) in a typically nutty pose.

20: Odd-even rationing spreads as gasoline shortage worsens.

20: Nicaraguan national guardsman kills ABC-TV correspondent.

26: Congress passes $3 billion synthetic fuels bill.

28: OPEC raises oil prices by 24 percent.

29: Little Feat's Lowell George dies of heart attack.

The Brady Bunch provided a better escape from reality than any drug ever ingested by anyone in the Seventies. Even Florence Henderson, who played mom Carol Brady, said so—in so many words: "It was the totally unrealistic and dreamy nature of it that made it special," she said. "I think that lots of kids grow up with problems, whether it's parental divorce or drugs at school. Lots of adults have real struggles in their marriages and their relations with their kids. Life is tough for many people. We gave them life as everybody would want it. We gave them a family with Dad home for the boys every day and a maid to do everything and a big house and nice street and no real sorrows and troubles. That's why everybody liked the show."

Today it's kind of cool to ogle Florence Henderson's miniskirts or Barry Williams's 'fro. You can also get a good sense of just how ugly early-Seventies color schemes were by looking at the tangerine walls and avocado table that was found in the Brady kitchen. For the post-Baby Boomers, the generation that was born in the 1960s, The Brady Bunch has become a cultural icon, having as much impact on them as Leave It to Beaver had on their older siblings.

Ironically, The Brady Bunch never did as well in the ratings as the show that aired after it on Friday nights: The Partridge Family. Shirley Jones and her real-life stepson, David Cassidy, starred in this sitcom about a family that hit it big in the music biz. (It was another typical TV family without a father). They traveled in a psychedelic school bus, a kind of suburban version of the Merry Pranksters, although their musical inspiration was the Cowsills, not the Grateful Dead.

Two months after the Partridges sang "I Think I Love You" on an episode, the song went to number-one. And five-foot-eight, 125-pound David Cassidy became a bona fide teen superstar as a result, his likes and dislikes filling the pages of such mags as Tiger Beat and 16. Cassidy had such a devoted legion of fans that they even crashed his hospital room when he had a gall-bladder operation. But by 1974, he was getting tired of the teen-dream scheme and took a four-year leave of absence from TV. As late as 1976, he was still making LPs, including one whose ad proclaimed: "Only the name remains the same . . . there's a David Cassidy inside David Cassidy you've never heard." Eventually he did come back to series TV, but by

Susan Dey as Laurie Partridge.

#1 Singles:
Donna Summer—"Hot Stuff"
Bee Gees—"Love You Inside Out"
Anita Ward—"Ring My Bell"

JULY 1979

5: Carter cancels TV address; retreats into seclusion.

9: Salt II treaty goes to Senate amid Republican sniping.

Selected Gold Record Albums:
Wings—*Back to the Egg*
Electric Light Orchestra—*Discovery*
Original Cast—*Annie*
Dire Straits—*Communique*

6: "The Hustle" creator Van McCoy dies of heart attack.

that time his younger half-brother Shaun was on his way to becoming a teen superstar in his own right, the David Cassidy of the late Seventies.

POLICE SHOWS

By 1975 those two classic Westerns, *Gunsmoke* and *Bonanza*, had both lumbered off the air. And why not? What could these shoot-'em-ups offer when urban life was increasingly taking on aspects of the wildest frontier town? Not only that, but international terrorists were on the loose, Mike Douglas was on the tube, and Gilbert O'Sullivan was on the charts. A tougher, more violent type of cop was needed on *this* beat. And by mid-decade, we'd have 'em.

However, as the decade opened, two holdovers from the late Sixties—the athletic and hot-tempered Joe Mannix (Mike Connors) of *Mannix* and the by-the-book Steve McGarrett (Jack Lord) of *Hawaii Five-O*—were just reaching their peak. The latter would go on until 1980, but until the end, we would never tire of McGarrett's trademark statement, "Book 'em, Dano," which he'd proclaim to his assistant Danny Williams (James McArthur) during the climactic bust.

The early part of the decade also saw the rise of the loner/gimmick detective. They came in a variety of shapes, sizes, and physical abilities. They were overweight (*Cannon*), blind (*Longstreet*), disabled (*Ironside*) and elderly (*Barnaby Jones*). And in that peculiar logic indigenous to TV, these gimps always managed to outwit their younger, healthier, better-armed adversaries.

 Kojak: An outgrowth of the gimmick/loner was the gumshoe who didn't have matinee-idol looks. And the coolest of them all was Lieutenant Theo Kojak of the NYPD (not to be confused with "Kolchak" the night stalker or "Kodiak," an Alaskan detective). As played by Telly Savalas, the shaven-headed, lollypop-sucking, nattily-dressed Lieutenant Kojak was a tough, cynical, and compassionate cop.

And we're talking about a show with impact here. The police chief of Mooresville, Indiana, changed his name legally to Harold Wayne Kojak. A fifteen-year-old Florida boy cited *Kojak* as his favorite program and inspiration for murdering his elderly neighbor. The man who dubbed Kojak's voice

11: Skylab crashes; debris hits Australia.

12: Mafia chief Carmine Galante slain in Brooklyn cafe.

15: In energy address, Carter reflects on "crisis of confidence."

17: Carter asks entire cabinet to resign.

17: Ted Kennedy hints at White House bid.

12: Minnie Ripperton dies of cancer.

201

Robert Blake and his pet cockatoo, Fred

for Japanese TV—a full-maned man who was never seen—shaved off all his hair.

But of course Lieutenant Kojak left two legacies: his catch phrase, "who loves ya, baby?" and his photo in the window of every Greek coffee shop in Manhattan.

🦜 **Baretta:** Also not much in the good-looks department was Robert Blake, the former child actor who starred as Tony Baretta. He had a pet cockatoo named Fred (with whom he held his most meaningful conversations), and in his scruffy jeans and T-shirt was often indistinguishable from the street scum of L.A. whom he pursued. You may also dig the theme song—"Eye on the Sparrow"—by Sammy Davis, Jr.!

🦜 **Columbo:** Also working the streets of L.A. was another slovenly dressed lawman of Italian extraction. As Lieutenant Columbo, Peter Falk threw on a stained, crumpled raincoat and wandered the streets, spouting cynical remarks. The series used the gimmick of showing the crime being committed at the beginning of the program and then spent the next fifty minutes tracking down the perpetrator. Did you know that Bing Crosby was originally considered for the role of Columbo? But Der Bingle turned it down because he said it would have interfered with his golf game.

By '75, with the war in Vietnam over, the bloodshed came home with *S.W.A.T.* perhaps the most violent series in TV history. These guys were based on L.A.'s real-life Special Weapons And Tactics Squad, which, earlier in the year, had gained fame for its role in the Symbionese Liberation Army shootout. An elite group (they were all Vietnam vets who dressed in paramilitary garb), they handled any job that was too tough for Baretta, Columbo, Joe Friday, or any other L.A.-based cop. ("When people are in trouble, they call the police. When the police are in trouble, they call S.W.A.T.!" blared ABC's promos for the new show.) Using whatever weapons were necessary—the more heavy-duty, the better—they got the job done, treating the Harbor Freeway as if it were the Ho Chi Minh Trail.

The *S.W.A.T.* team's attitude was summarized by its leader, "Hondo" Harrelson (played by Steve Forrest): "If we are going to have a war on crime, cops had better stop being so damned human and lovable and better start acting like an army." If you were getting in touch with your feelings, chances are you didn't watch *S.W.A.T.*

Also unlikely to win a popularity contest among mellow dudes was *Starsky and Hutch*, which applied the Redford-Newman buddy system to TV cops. Paul Michael Glaser and David Soul starred as blow-dried, vaguely hip plainclothes cops who battled pimps and drug dealers, and felt about the Miranda decision the same way Richard Nixon felt about the Constitution. The show featured one of the few cool cars on Seventies TV: Starsky's '74 red-and-white Ford Torino, what passed for a batmobile in the Age of Disco. It saw plenty of action. One episode had more screeching tires than an entire month of demolition derbies.

But the mellow crowd didn't eschew cop shows entirely. Their favorite was *The Rockford Files*, in which James Garner essentially time-warped his Bret Maverick character into the late Seventies. He was an extremely laid-back character, as smooth as an FM rock DJ. He rarely carried a gun, even though he invariably would be beaten up in each episode.

And then it was the 1980s, and *Hill Street Blues* came along, injecting a dose of reality and grit into the TV cop show.

ABC

Until the mid-Seventies, ABC was the dumpster of networks, a perennial also-ran since it was spun off from NBC in 1945. So poorly regarded was ABC, that during the late Sixties and early Seventies a popular joke making the rounds of TV execs was "Wanna know how to end the Vietnam war? Put it on ABC, and it'll be canceled in thirteen weeks."

The laughing stopped in 1975, however, when ABC stormed back, moving from third place to first. If CBS had pioneered a programming revolution in the early part of the decade, then ABC, under the guidance of ex-CBS exec Fred Silverman, heralded the counterrevolution with a diet of sitcoms (*Happy Days* and its two spinoffs) and action shows (*The Six Million Dollar Man* and its spinoff *The Bionic Woman*) geared to kiddie audiences.

Here's a look at the three kiddie sitcoms that helped ABC become the top network of the mid and late Seventies:

Happy Days: Go figure. The coolest Italian juvenile delinquent on TV in the Seventies was a 5-foot-6-inch Jewish graduate of Yale. Of course, put that same guy in a black leather jacket and make him sound like a cut-rate

Brewery buddies Laverne and Shirley prove that sisterhood has always been powerful.

AUGUST 1979

9: White House opposes $1 billion Chrysler bail-out bid.

15: After secret meeting with PLO, Andrew Young resigns from UN post.

17-24: Carter embarks on "Meet the People" river cruise.

27: IRA terrorists blow up Britain's Lord Mountbatten.

23: Peter Tosh Day declared in Brooklyn, N.Y.

version of Marlon Brando in *The Wild One*, and you have somebody who was just born to be on a lunchbox.

And it was Arthur Fonzarelli a.k.a. Fonzie a.k.a. The Fonz as interpreted by Yalie Henry Winkler who provided the reason half of pre-pubescent America tuned in to *Happy Days* on Tuesday nights and helped push ABC out of the cellar.

For a simple show, *Happy Days* has many complex meanings. It was TV's first revisionist show and the first TV show to take place in an era where TV already was invented. It gave us a version of the Fifties that was gaining currency during the troubled Seventies: a trouble-free era of sock hops and malt shops. Trouble is, that version, as popularized in the actual shows of the Fifties, like *Father Knows Best* or *Leave It to Beaver*, was pretty bogus to begin with. So with *Happy Days* you're dealing with kind of a fun-house mirror version of the Fifties. But that was considered mere quibbling by ABC, since *Happy Days* wasn't aimed at those who grew up in the Fifties. It was aimed at their kids.

And to cement its connection to both the Fifties revival and to an earlier TV era, the lead character of *Happy Days* was played by a grown-up Ron Howard, who came of age on TV as the cute tyke Opie on *The Andy Griffith Show* and had also starred in *American Graffiti*, George Lucas and Francis Ford Coppola's extremely popular film on Fifties-style nostalgia. (And to make the *Happy Days–American Graffiti* relationship even more apparent, both productions used Bill Haley and the Comets's "Rock Around the Clock" as their theme song.)

Graffiti's success no doubt must have helped make producer Garry Marshall's sales pitch about a sitcom set in the Fifties much easier. But the fact is that *Happy Days* had its origins several years earlier in a 1972 *Love, American Style* episode in which Howard appeared in a skit set in the Fifties. It wasn't too surprising that he popped up as clean-cut Milwaukee teen Richie Cunningham when ABC slipped *Happy Days* onto its schedule as a midseason replacement on January 15, 1974.

The trouble is, Richie Cunningham was the kind of goody-goody teen that you expected Opie Taylor to become when he grew up. He lived with his Ozzie-and-Harrietish parents (Tom Bosley and Marion Ross) and a younger sister (Erin Moran) and got involved in silly situations with his klutzy pal

Happy Days: *Fifties revisionism meets Seventies sitcom.*

#1 Singles:
Chic—"Good Times"
The Knack—"My Sharona"

SEPTEMBER 1979

3: Dalai Lama embarks on U.S. tour.

5: Cyrus Vance warns Soviets about Soviet "combat" brigade in Cuba.

20: Secret Service protection ordered for Ted Kennedy as he prepares presidential campaign.

8: Actress Jean Seberg found dead after apparent suicide.

15: Abba's first North American tour.

16: Rap is born: "Rapper's Delight" by Sugar Hill Gang released.

Potsie (Anson Williams). Needless to say, during the first season, the show lacked a certain pep. The only edge was supplied by its fifth-billed character, a comical version of the Fifties J.D. If Archie Bunker could be described by the oxymoronic "lovable bigot," then the Fonz, a high school dropout who worked as a mechanic, was most certainly a "lovable hood." The concept made ABC censors slightly wary—they insisted that Fonzie could wear his leather jacket only when he was shown with his motorcycle!

For the first two seasons, the Fonz was kept on a short leash. That changed—as did the show's fortunes—when the producers increased the sitcom's reliance on Fonzie starting in the fall of 1975. At the same time, many of the Fonz's rough edges were smoothed. That didn't bother his fans, who faithfully tuned in to watch him give his trademark thumbs-up gesture and utter his "aaayyh!" Fonz moved into an apartment above the Cunninghams' garage (becoming in effect a member of the Cunningham family) and was rarely seen on his motorcycle again.

In fact, he started acting like a leather-jacketed Ward Cleaver. Projecting a sense of being an authority figure—yet one who was also cool—the Fonz became an unlikely role model. When he urged kids to do all sorts of proper things, such as not to smoke or to get a library card, they listened. The move paid off, and soon *Happy Days* became the top-rated network show.

As the years moved on, *Happy Days* progressed into the early Sixties. New characters like Chachi, Pinky Tuscadero, and Leather Tuscadero were added. The guys went to college, to the army, to real jobs.

Ron Howard left the show in 1980, and finally in 1983, the Fonz had had enough. Both went on to successful careers on the other side of the camera. We're still obsessed by the same synthetic vision of the Fifties that fueled the early *Happy Days*. Something worked, however: Fonzie's leather jacket now is displayed in the Smithsonian Institution.

Laverne & Shirley: In February 1976 *Happy Days* spun off two of Fonzie's friends, Laverne De Fazio (played by Penny Marshall, Garry's sister) and Shirley Feeney (Cindy Williams, who played Ron Howard's romantic interest in *American Graffiti*), into their own series. They worked in a Milwaukee brewery, shared a basement apartment, and became involved in comical situations that were reminiscent of Lucy and Ethel. Although the sitcom was set in the late Fifties, Laverne and Shirley were more like bouf-

29: Pope John Paul II begins ten-day U.S. tour.

21: *New York Post* reports: "Beatles Are Back."

Selected Gold Record Albums:
The Outlaws—*Bring it Back Alive*
Joe Jackson—*Look Sharp*

OCTOBER 1979

6: Interest rates soar as Federal Reserve tries to control inflation.

9: Dow plunges in reaction to high interest rates.

10: City of Los Angeles declares "Fleetwood Mac Day."

fanted versions of Seventies feminists: They were supportive, independent, and feisty working women. Airing a half-hour after *Happy Days*, it became the biggest hit of the second season and was a major factor in ABC's number-one finish in 1976. And eventually it nosed out its progenitor to become the number-one show during both the 1977–78 and 1978–79 seasons.

Mork & Mindy: The second *Happy Days* spinoff made an instant star out of comedian Robin Williams (who until then had been best known for being a cast member of the 1978 version of *Laugh-In*. Mork (from the planet Ork) first appeared in a February 1978 *Happy Days* episode (in which Richie Cunningham dreamt that Mork was sent to Milwaukee of the Fifties to kidnap him). Williams's character proved so popular that he was given his own series that September, and it finished as the number-three series of that season. Mork was an off-the-wall Orkan who was sent to Earth by his superiors to study the odd habits of Earthlings. He landed in a giant egg near Boulder, Colorado, and was befriended by Mindy McConnell (Pam Dawber), who provided the perfect foil for Mork's bizarre behavior. She basically did nothing and let Williams run wild, which was a smart move. Few people, Earthlings or Orkans, could keep up with the manic Williams, a gifted physical comedian, mime, and mimic. As Mork, he also created his own warped Orkan gibberish, culminating each week with his report to Orson, his leader on Ork, with his trademark: "Na nu, na nu." That meant "goodbye" in Orkan, and it soon replaced the Fonz's "aayyh" as the buzz word of choice among elementary-school students. *Mork & Mindy* launched Williams's career, and he has gone on to play memorably comic roles in such movies as *Moscow on the Hudson* and *Good Morning, Vietnam*.

CHARLIE'S ANGELS

Nearly fifteen years after *Charlie's Angels* debuted, none of the Angels likes to talk about the show. Not Farrah Fawcett-Majors, the toothy, well-maned ex-model who became the poster girl of the Seventies. Not cerebral Jaclyn Smith nor spunky Kate Jackson. Not even the replacement Angels, Cheryl Ladd, Shelly Hack, and the forgettable Tanya Roberts want to deal with it. They'd rather talk about their subsequent and current acting achievements.

13: Carter and Kennedy forces clash in early Florida caucus for 1980 delegates.

17: Mother Teresa wins Nobel peace prize.

26: South Korean CIA assassinates President Park Chung Hee.

#1 Singles:
Robert John—"Sad Eyes"
Michael Jackson—"Don't Stop 'Till You Get Enough"
Herb Albert—"Rise"

23: New York City begins announcing names of prostitution clients over radio.

Selected Gold Record Albums:
G.Q.—*Disco Nights*
Ronnie Milsap—*Ronnie Milsap Live*

206

It's as if *Charlie's Angels* were a blot on their permanent record card or something.

Well, lighten up, ladies. Don't you realize you're part of history? Besides ushering in the era of T-and-A TV, *Charlie's Angels* was the first TV show to be revolutionary and reactionary at the same time: a male fantasy coated with the veneer of women's liberation. The Angels were career women—but no dress-for-success outfits for these babes! They were swinging singles, but they were always under the guidance of the never-seen Hef/Howard Hughes figure known as Charlie.

Not that such plotting was uncalculated, of course. When veteran Hollywood producers Leonard Goldberg and Aaron Spelling chewed over the idea of creating a new series about female cops, ABC had warned them about excessive violence. No problem, they responded. We'll just play up a virtue not regularly emphasized on TV cop shows: sex.

So they cooked up a clever little story about three employees of the Charles Townsend Detective Agency: Sabrina Duncan (a former showgirl) Kelly Garrett (the college grad), and Jill Munroe (the athletic one). They were all ex-policewomen, who had been relegated to desk jobs when Charlie offered them a way out: crime solving at higher pay, and all you had to do was go braless and get involved in cases where you had to wear as little as possible.

The formula found instant success during the series' first season (1976–77). Who could resist such episodes as "Angels in Chains"? That was the little adventure in which the Angels were captured while investigating a southern prison farm, chained together, stripped, forced into a shower, and sprayed with disinfectants. Twenty thousand letters poured into ABC after that episode, asking for more of the same. Which viewers got. But despite the predictable howls from feminists, the majority of viewers who tuned in Tuesday nights were women.

As *Charlie's Angels* became America's most popular show, Goldberg and Spelling crowed that the series was actually a force for social progress. "It proves that women can carry a show," they said.

On the other hand, Farrah cut through all the rhetoric when she analyzed the incredible appeal of the Angels: "When the show was No. 3, I figured it was due to our acting," she said. "When we got to No. 1, I decided it could

NOVEMBER 1979

7: Ted Kennedy announces bid for presidency.

4: Iranian students seize U.S. embassy in Tehran; take diplomats hostage.

14: U.S. freezes all Iranian assets in U.S. banks.

1: Born-again Dylan booed by concert crowd in San Francisco.

17: *The Rose* released.

only be because none of us wears a bra."

And no one went braless with bigger an impact than Farrah. Originally the show was going to be built around Kate Jackson, who was the best known of the trio because of her stints on *The Rookies* and *Dark Shadows*. In fact, Jackson and Smith received $10,000 a show at the beginning of its run, while Fawcett copped a measly $5,000. During the middle of the first season, Fawcett became the show's breakout character, and later a megastar, thanks in no small measure to some shrewd media manipulation by her manager/agent Jay Bernstein.

Farrah's face and trademark grin became licensed to kill; the most prominent item was a provocative poster in which she posed in a skin-tight bathing suit. Quite a switch for the thirty-year-old actress who had knocked around Hollywood doing commercials (for Ultra-Brite toothpaste and Wella Balsam shampoo, surprised?) and small roles in TV movies (*The Girl Who Came Gift-Wrapped*) and series. In fact, she was probably best known as the companion and then wife of actor Lee Majors—until the *Angels* came along. Farrah became a national icon: In 1976 *Scholastic* magazine's poll of 14,000 junior high and high school students ranked her as their number-one personal hero.

By the end of the first season, though, Farrah quit the show to pursue other ventures. She had to wait more than five years, enduring such bad movies as *Sunburn* and *Saturn Three*, before finally convincing Hollywood and the world that she could really act. And even though she has done admirable work in the play *Extremities* and the TV movie *The Burning Bed*, when people say the word "Farrah," it's always the image of the toothy gal hanging on the walls of thousands of suburban bedrooms that comes to mind. Now, if only Farrah will acknowledge that.

SATURDAY NIGHT LIVE

Comedy, like every other aspect of popular culture in the late Sixties and early Seventies, reflected a culture divided by politics, age, and dope. While Bob Hope entertained the troops in Vietnam and partied with Agnew and Sinatra, freaky funny guy George Carlin bolted the *Tonight Show* circuit to regale the kids with tales of dope and the seven dirty words you couldn't

Saturday Night Live's *perennial guest host Elliott Gould makes a point with Beldar and the Cone Heads.*

say on the air. It's interesting to look back and consider a time when just cursing and swearing were considered "revolutionary" statements.

Like *Don Kirschner's Rock Concert*, *Saturday Night Live* grew out of the networks' desire to reach "the kids," as latter-day boomers grew in numbers and purchasing power. Premiering in the dark days of 1975, *SNL* went along way toward bridging the gap between "underground" and mainstream humor during Ford's healing interregnum. While Nixon in his prime would have had only contempt for "permissive punks" like John Belushi, Dan Aykroyd, and Chevy Chase, President Gerald Ford made a good-natured visit to the show in spite of Chase's often savage parody of his fumbling manner.

While maintaining an arch, antiestablishment tone, *SNL*'s consistent sarcasm left little room for the righteous posturing of the revolutionary Sixties. In fact, many of the orignal cast, including Chase and Belushi, were veterans of National Lampoon's *Lemmings* stage show, which savagely blasted the sappier side of flower-power culture. A steady stream of guest stars added variety to the ensemble format and allowed some of the strangest cultural combinations in TV history. Ford's patter with Ford imitator Chase, civil rights activist Julian Bond's appearance on Garrett Morris's parody "Black Perspectives," and Paul Simon's attempts to sing "Still Crazy After All These Years" dressed as a turkey showed the extent to which everyone embraced *SNL*'s anarchy. By 1978 New York Mayor Ed Koch could introduce the Rolling Stones (to perform "Shattered") without blinking an eye.

For all of its hipness, *SNL* was largely derivative in its humor, leaning heavily on parody of television's past. That it was live gave a spontaneous edge to the variety show format that had grown dependent on laugh tracks and packaging, while at the same time paying tribute to TV's earliest comedy shows, which were all done live. Appealing largely to latter-day boomers, who had grown up entirely within the TV age, *SNL* flourished in the Seventies' rerun culture and became perhaps *the* seminal show for a second generation of TV viewers.

Buck Henry mediates a Ford-Carter debate between Dan Aykroyd and Chevy Chase.

PBS

Founded in 1969 and subsequently funded and unfunded by an angry

#1 Singles:
M—"Pop Muzik"
Eagles—"Heartache Tonight"
Commodores—"Still"
Barbra Streisand and Donna Summer—
"No More Tears (Enough Is Enough)"

Selected Gold Record Albums:
Eddie Money—*Eddie Money*
Abba—*Voulez Vous*

America's favorite Englishman,
Alistair Cooke.

Nixon administration, PBS—the Public Broadcasting System—has remained remarkably consistent in two things: It is largely subsidized by oil companies, and it is the last refuge of TV snobs who will not admit to watching anything else. This video snobbery was best assuaged with PBS's steady diet of British imports. To watch PBS in the Seventies as it broadcast a steady stream of largely excellent programs, including *Elizabeth R*, *The Wives of Henry VIII*, *Upstairs, Downstairs*, and *I, Claudius*, you could assume that American public television was a mere colony of the vaunted BBC. With the genial Yankophile Alistair Cooke at the helm, Masterpiece Theatre broadcast so many tales of blond and blue-eyed drama that some wags rechristened the program "Master Race Theater."

For all of its Anglocentric fare, PBS did churn out one of the strangest bits of Seventies Americana. *An American Family*, featuring the Loud family live on televison for months on end, remains a curious bit of TV history. "Living" with a TV crew, the Louds were supposed to represent a "typical American family." They proved to be about as typical as *The Addams Family*.

Almost everyone has wondered what their home life would look like under the scrutiny of the TV camera. For the most part, the Loud family life unfolded with all of the unhurried banality of "real life." Toilets flushed, kids fought, and the Beatles' *White Album* played too loudly a few rooms down the hall. Yet, during the course of the show, Pat and Bill Loud broke up and filed for divorce while their flamboyant son Lance surprised no one by "coming out of the closet" and moving across country to live in the Chelsea Hotel. For millions, the Louds performed as a perfectly normal, white rich California family on the brink of going utterly insane. While many had said that TV was driving America to divorce and decadence, here the Louds were proving it right before our very eyes.

Living in a huge California home with four cars (including a Jaguar) and a built-in pool, the Louds hardly represented the demographic center of the United States. And long before the cameras were turned on, a fourteen-year-old Lance had dyed his hair silver in honor of his hero, Andy Warhol. The question remains, who ever thought these people could pass as normal?

While *An American Family* has become a television classic, critics re-

2: U.S. Embassy in Libya attacked.

4: Carter announces candidacy for reelection.

3: Eleven die in stampede at Who concert in Cincinnati; Walter Cronkite blames "a drug-crazed crowd of kids."

10: In NBC interview, hostage questions dying for Shah's sake.

11: ABC, CBS, and White House blast NBC hostage interview.

acted with almost universal horror. Shana Alexander bemoaned the Louds' "Faustian pact with the camera's eye" and damned their life-style of "zombie-like affluence." *Newsweek* hailed their performance as "The Divorce of the Year." Stung by criticism of her life-style, divorce, and personality, Pat Loud replied: "When the carnival atmosphere dies down, I think they'll see some pretty decent people on that tube, doing a better than average job of living together—or apart as the case may be."

The entire Loud family went on Dick Cavett to defend themselves, but Lance clearly stole the show by declaring himself "Homo of the Year" and archly dismissing his folks' on-air divorce. "They've been rehearsing the role for seven years!"

THREE'S COMPANY

Three's Company should have been remembered as little more than a slightly racy, extended *Love, American Style* skit, but it ended up being the quintessential Seventies jiggle TV show. Its ascension in 1977 heralded a major shift in TV tastes; the transition between the Learcom of the early Seventies and the leercoms of the latter part of the decade.

Ironically, *Three's Company* was produced by the same company (and several of the same writers) responsible for *All in the Family* and was also based on an English sitcom (*Man Around the House*). In fact, Fred Silverman had ordered the writers to make *Three's Company* "the same kind of breakthrough in sexiness that *All in the Family* was in bigotry." The coincidences end there.

The plot was simple, too simple: Two attractive single women, Chrissy (Suzanne Somers) and Janet (Joyce DeWitt), needed a roommate for their Santa Monica apartment. And they found him—in a bathtub, sleeping it off from the going-away party for their previous roommate. But a man! What will our landlord think? No sweat, replied the prospective roomie. Tell him I'm gay.

Well, that setup might have conned the landlord, but it presented lots of problems for our hero, Jack Tripper (played by John Ritter), a guy with an overactive libido and a name that left one pondering either its drug or homicidal implications. At moments of extreme horniness, Jack would be lusting

Three's Company: *jiggle TV at its smarmiest.*

20: Congress approves $1.5 billion for Chrysler bail-out.

19: Elvis' doctor charged with illegally prescribing 12,000 pills.

21: Eagles, Chicago, and Linda Ronstadt play benefit for Jerry Brown's presidential campaign.

after Chrissy or Janet or a date and the landlord would walk in. To quell Mr. Roper's worst fears about a ménage à trois upstairs, Jack would have to resort to the worst gay stereotype imaginable. Of such situations are hit sitcoms made.

Fortunately, Ritter (son of cowboy singer Tex Ritter) is a gifted comedian who lent a certain amount of grace to his character. But he wasn't the reason people tuned in on Tuesday nights; Suzanne Somers (who had appeared as the mysterious blond in the white Thunderbird in *American Graffiti*, as well as in Mr. Clean commercials) was. The busty actress enjoyed her anatomically inspired success: "If you've got it, bump it with a trumpet." Chrissy was a one-woman counterrevolution, single-handedly bringing back that favorite chauvinist archetype, the dumb blond. While her fellow video females like Mary Richards and Maude Findlay were breaking new ground, Chrissy worked as a typist ("But I can't type," she once protested, becoming the TV equivalent of Elizabeth Ray). Her outfits, however, were a boon to the pajama and lingerie businesses.

Somers's career was guided by Jay Bernstein, the same guru who masterminded Farrah Fawcett-Major's rise a couple of years earlier. As *Three's Company*'s popularity increased, so did Somers's visibility. Her cheery image adorned dozens of products, and her personal life (as well as her rocky relationships with her co-stars) became tabloid staples. She even made the cover of *Newsweek* in 1978, in a memorable photo in which it looked as if she were falling out of her negligee, as Jack leered over her shoulder. (Somers left the series in 1981 in a bitter contract dispute, but it continued along without her until 1984, when it metamorphised into *Three's a Crowd*, and then finally disappeared.)

If the gay jokes and the dumb-blond jokes weren't enough, then the writers could always rely on impotence jokes to get a surefire cheap laugh. The victim was the dodo landlord Stanley Roper (Norman Fell), who always had a variety of creative excuses to avoid intimacy with his hot-to-trot wife (Audra Lindley). And she had an arsenal of caustic putdowns that dwarfed any insults Cher ever made about Sonny. For the moments of sheer humor they provided, the Ropers were rewarded with their own spinoff. They were replaced by another forgotten TV staple: the dirty old man. This time, he took the form of the new landlord, Ralph Furley (played, inexplicably, by ol' Barney Fife himself, Don Knotts). In addition to being a cut-rate swinger, Ralph's wardrobe—including tangerine leisure suits and paisley ascots—defined Seventies men's fashions at their tackiest.

Three's Company was the Grand Funk Railroad of sitcoms—a show that was hated, positively hated, by the critics (and a favorite target of some fundamentalist groups), but loved by the public. The show was so popular that it ranked either second or third from 1977–1980.

The biggest joke is, however, that *Three's Company* was an illusion. It took advantage of the liberated Seventies sensibility, but never went all the way. It was tease TV with borderline-lewd jokes and double entendres that fell in between Minsky's Burlesque and the junior high locker room. That's it. Nobody ever really did anything—we'd have to wait for the nighttime soaps of the Eighties for the screen to truly steam up. In fact, in a curious way you might say the all-talk, no-action of *Three's Company* presaged the Eighties: Chrissy, Janet, and Jack were the earliest proponents of safe sex.

TOM SNYDER

Long before Geraldo Rivera interviewed Charles Manson, Tom Snyder had the murderous guru on his talk show. Long before Morton Downey, Jr., spewed invective at his guests, Tom Snyder was shouting his down. And long before David Letterman kept us up past our bedtimes, Tom Snyder was making insomniacs out of us.

Snyder was the host of NBC's *Tomorrow* show, a freewheeling talk show that explored television's final frontier: late late night. In this era of twenty-four-hour TV, it's easy to forget that until the Seventies, most stations signed off at 1:00 A.M. or else filled the void with reruns or old movies. NBC had already scored a modest success by programming *The Midnight Special*, a late-night music show for teens on Fridays (the night they could stay up late). In 1973 NBC decided to break the Monday-to-Thursday-night barrier by introducing *Tomorrow*, which began at the ungodly hour of 1:00 A.M. (back then Johnny Carson was still airing for ninety minutes). *Tomorrow* would be a different kind of talk show: no band, no studio audience, no chatty celebrity guests; its host would be provocative and outrageous.

NBC chose the thirty-seven-year-old Tom Snyder. Glib and outspoken,

Tom Snyder, an insomniac's best friend.

30: Break-up of Emerson, Lake and Palmer.

he was just the type of host NBC was seeking. The late hour meant you could get away with talking about things you couldn't talk about during the daytime—subjects that would presumably be of interest to college students, insomniacs, or swing-shift workers.

The show debuted on October 15, 1973, from Burbank (it would later move to New York, then back to California). Snyder's first guests were a marriage "triad"—three persons in one marriage. One segment that showed Snyder at his angriest was cut by NBC censors prior to the program. In an advance tape made available to reporters, Snyder delivered a monologue lambasting former Vice President Spiro Agnew, who had resigned earlier in the week, and blasted the "pious and sanctimonious bilge coming out of Washington . . . just how dumb do they think we are?" That kind of outrage might be okay fifteen years later for Morton Downey, Jr., but back in '73, it was too hot for NBC.

Nonetheless, Snyder received positive reviews from most critics. John Leonard of *The New York Times* captured the essence of Snyder: "He editorializes with his face. He visibly seethes with opinions and that is preferable to being permanently dumbfounded like Merv, vaguely resentful like Johnny Carson, slightly lobotomized like David Susskind. He suffers fools rudely, which is what they deserve."

Indeed, Snyder was an eminently telegenic character: loose-limbed, his six-foot-four frame casually draped on his couch, with a laugh that often resembled Count Dracula's. He raised eyebrow arching to an art, and his creative use of on-air cigarette smoking had not been seen since the days of Edward R. Murrow.

The formula worked. Viewers tuned in to see Snyder tackle subjects such as encounter groups, suicide, group sex, male prostitution, as well as to talk with such controversial guests as Manson, Jimmy Hoffa, and Marlon Brando. By 1976 an estimated six million viewers were tuning in.

At the same time, Snyder's star was rising at NBC. He anchored the newscast of the New York NBC affiliate, and Sunday newscasts, and hosted a couple of network specials. He saw himself as Johnny Carson's heir or, at the very least, the anchor of NBC's evening news. Neither possibility came to pass. Meanwhile, *Tomorrow* was plagued by other problems. In 1980 Fred Silverman (now head of NBC) had brought in gossip columnist Rona

#1 Singles:
Styx—"Babe"
Rupert Holmes—"Escape (Piña Colada Song)"

Selected Gold Record Albums:
Michael Jackson—*Off the Wall*   R.E.O Speedwagon—*Nine Lives*
Jimmy Buffet—*Volcano*   Chicago—*Chicago XIII*

Barrett to co-anchor with Snyder when the program expanded to ninety minutes. They feuded publicly, with Barrett complaining that Snyder didn't give her the respect she deserved. After two weeks she took a hike. Their feud made lively copy, and when she returned in early 1981, the show had been renamed *Tomorrow Coast to Coast*. Viewers were losing interest and finally, in 1982, NBC replaced *Tomorrow* with a new show hosted by a guy who had been a weatherman in Indianapolis back when Tom Snyder was discussing nudism on national TV for the first time. And by the late Eighties, the airwaves would be crammed with shows featuring the kinds of geeks and freaks that once were thought suitable only for one-thirty in the morning.